THE SANDBOX
INVESTMENT

THE SANDBOX
INVESTMENT

The Preschool Movement
and Kids-First Politics

David L. Kirp

Harvard University Press
Cambridge, Massachusetts
London, England

First Harvard University Press paperback edition, 2009.

Library of Congress Cataloging-in-Publication Data

Kirp, David L.
The sandbox investment : the preschool movement
and kids-first politics / David L. Kirp.
p.   cm.
Includes bibliographical references and index.
ISBN 978-0-674-02641-4 (cloth : alk. paper)
ISBN 978-0-674-03235-4 (pbk.)
1. Education, Preschool—Political aspects—United States.
2. Education, Preschool—United States—Philosophy.   I. Title.
LB1140.23.K57   2007
372.210973—dc22   2007009624

To Ed Zigler

Public servant, scholar, mentor, and mensch

CONTENTS

THE SANDBOX
INVESTMENT

Before School

JACK GRUBMAN was desperate to enroll his twin daughters in the preschool run by the 92nd Street Y. By reputation it is the finest in New York City, and it's considerably harder to get into than Harvard. The year was 1999, and Smith Barney telecom stock analyst Grubman was a major player in the overheated market. He went to Sandy Weill, chief executive of Citigroup, which owned Smith Barney, with a complex proposition. In return for Weill's help in getting his daughters into the 92nd Street Y (help that included a $1 million Citigroup donation as well as Weill's gentle persuasion of key board members of the Y), Grubman promised to upgrade AT&T stock, whose chairman Weill needed as an ally, from "hold" to "strong buy." The deal was struck, and the Grubman *filles* took their first step along a well-marked pathway to success.[1]

This is not just a *Bonfire of the Vanities* story about greedy and powerful New Yorkers. The well-heeled have long appreciated the value of nursery schools that pique the curiosity of their offspring, and as demand for these elite preschools has grown, the market has responded.[2]

From Beverly Hills to Boca Raton, wealthy parents are spending upwards of $15,000 a year on the education of their three- and four-year-olds. The nationwide chain that calls itself the Crème de la Crème Preschool—"Disney meets Harvard," as one reporter aptly described it—exemplifies what they are buying. The Crème de la Crème center in Denver features "a bubbling brook stocked with fish" as well as a "bibliothèque" and a theater. Special rooms are reserved for music, math, and computers—the children switch classes every half hour—as well as a "TV station with its four clocks displaying times around the world," and "tennis courts, a child-sized basketball court and a water park." The curriculum for four-year-olds includes French songs and games, as well as D'Nealian Handwriting, Fernand Nathan French, and IBM's "Writing to Read."[3] Even though tuition is more than what Berkeley charges its undergraduates, for well-off parents that's no deterrent. The Crème de la Crème chain keeps expanding, new companies are entering this select market, and some midlevel child care companies are upgrading in order to remain competitive.

At the other end of the social spectrum, the benefits of early education for poor children have also commanded attention. For these kids, though, it's the federal government and not the market that has stepped in. Over the past forty years, the Head Start program, budgeted at nearly $7 billion, has reached tens of millions of three- and four-year-olds from families with below-poverty-line incomes. While a Head Start center will never be confused with a Crème de la Crème preschool—the teachers are usually less well trained and the offerings are far less fancy—the program delivers everything from know-your-letters academic drills and playground etiquette to hot meals and dental checkups.[4]

What *is* new is that more and more middle-class families, who have had to fend for themselves, are insisting on good pre-kindergartens for their own children. These parents are the Jack Grubmans of Middle America. The age-old parental desire to give one's own kids the best chance to succeed has evolved into a nationwide push for high-quality preschool that, like K–12 public education, is paid for with tax dollars and open to all. Nor is it just parents who are behind this effort. The big-tent coalition of pre-K supporters includes politicians and pedagogues, philanthropists, pediatricians, and police chiefs.[5]

The Pre-K Bandwagon

A third of a century ago, Richard Nixon vetoed legislation that would have underwritten child care for everyone. "No communal approaches to child rearing," Nixon vowed, playing to his constituency. When Arizona governor Bruce Babbitt made kids' issues the centerpiece of his state-of-the-state address in 1988, the press ridiculed him for serving up a "dish of quiche" rather than the "meat and potatoes" of government. How times have changed. Ambitious statesmen from both sides of the political aisle are now borrowing from Babbitt's playbook. They see the issue as a winner—a strategy for doing well by doing good. A recent national survey found that 87 percent of the populace supports public funding to guarantee every three- and four-year-old access to a top-notch preschool.[6]

Americans resonate to the theme of "no second-rate children, no second-rate dreams," focus groups report, which is why George Bush repeatedly used that line in his presidential campaigns.[7] Bush's rhetoric turned out to be just that, however, and universal preschool has not been on the federal agenda. But in the states, democracy's petri dishes, the story is entirely different.

Six states—Florida, Georgia, Oklahoma, West Virginia, New York, and Illinois—have passed legislation guaranteeing prekindergarten for all; forty states subsidize some preschool education.[8] And the pre-K trends are positive. Between 2004 and 2006, state lawmakers boosted annual pre-K funding by $1.25 billion. More than 800,000 three- and four-year-olds attend state pre-K classes (that's nearly as many as Head Start has), and enrollment continues to climb.[9]

This isn't a familiar "red state versus blue state" tale, for the allure of pre-K transcends ideology. The states with the highest percentage of four-year-olds attending preschool aren't the usual suspects, they're Oklahoma and Georgia, which aren't known for their social progressivism.[10] In Louisiana, another unlikely wellspring of innovation, Governor Kathleen Blanco pushed for additional state funding for preschool, even in the aftermath of Hurricane Katrina, because "nothing helps a child achieve long-term success in school and in life more than early preparation. The best time to invest in children is in their first three to four years." And so it goes across the country, from Arizona to Arkansas, Connecticut to Kansas. Phil Bredsen, the governor of Tennessee, turned to the Bible in making the argument that his state should double the number of preschool classes. "Train a child in the way he should go, and when he is old he will not turn from it."

Such a profound transformation doesn't occur by happenstance. To a considerable extent the preschool movement has been fueled by a remarkable confluence of powerful research findings from across the scientific universe, the intellectual equivalent of the perfect storm. All the data point in the same direction—early education matters.

Long-term studies of the impact of a top-notch preschool experience on children's life chances have shown that the ripple effects of what took place when a youngster was three years old were still evident well into middle age. Economists have translated those findings into the coin-of-the-realm language of benefits and costs, and their work has confirmed that early education is a wise investment. When neuroscientists issue reports on the rapid development of the brain during the first years of life, their findings add the imprimatur of hard science. Memorable images of the brain at work have given new credibility to the conclusions of myriad papers on child development.

This impressive body of research has taken the argument for preschool out of the area of moral appeal and into the more politically promising domain of evidence-based policymaking. To have an impact, though, the research has to reach a broad audience, whether through newsmagazine cover stories and TV shows aimed at parents and the general public, briefing papers prepared for the National Governors Association, or studies tailored to the Business Roundtable, a powerful corporate lobby. The case for universal preschool picked up steam in recent years because of a sophisticated campaign—bankrolled by activist-minded foundations and run by some of the most effective advocates in the business—designed to shine a spotlight on the issue.

"I've been in the field my whole adult life," marvels Samuel Meisels, the president of Chicago's Erikson Institute, a graduate school in the field of child development. "Suddenly everyone is talking about universal prekindergarten." Dick Clifford, a senior scientist at the Frank Porter Graham Child Development Institute at the University of North Carolina who has also tracked these developments for decades, sees a profound historical shift in the making. "The impact of what's happening to young children is like the effect of the Industrial Revolution on older children. Then, public schools became the norm. Now it's preschool."

This dramatic change in policy—and the deeper shift in public attitudes that it reflects—is especially noteworthy in an era when the overriding political vision is privatization and not public responsibility, when tax cuts and not new services have dominated the agenda, when the prevailing aspiration is the "ownership society" and not the social compact.[11] The nationwide movement for universal preschool is one of the rare contemporary examples of an expanding public square. It aims at reviving the ideal of the common good by persuading taxpayers to support a venture that reaches beyond narrow self-interest to benefit everyone.[12]

How have the research and advocacy come together to make universal preschool an attainable ambition? Across the country, what has sustained—and sometimes subverted—high-quality, publicly financed pre-K? What does the track record of universal preschool portend, not just for the education of three- and four-year-olds but for kids-as-politics more generally? That's what this book is all about.

No Preschooler Left Behind

"Preschool for all" makes a great slogan. But will it be more than a slogan? Will it be of high quality or run on the cheap? Will it embrace the constricted "no preschooler left behind" view of how to educate four-year-olds? One or two badly run state preschool programs could scuttle the entire movement by reinforcing taxpayers' suspicions about the incompetence of government.

"The question isn't 'Will there be prekindergarten?' We've won that battle," says Libby Doggett, head of Pre-K Now, a national advocacy group. "Now the question is 'What kind of pre-K will there be?'"

"I'm an advocate of universal preschool," says Berkeley psychologist Alison Gopnik, whose account of how infants learn,

The Scientist in the Crib, has shown parents a new side of their newborns. But Gopnik's fraught experiences with badly run prekindergartens and early childhood centers have been a reality check. "My nightmare," she says, "is that when it actually happens it will be terrible."

Quality means good teachers and good schools. That requires money. The research shows that well-educated teachers who know how to use research-based approaches can be the make-or-break factor. Classes have to be small, with a teacher and an aide for no more than twenty youngsters, and parents must be engaged as partners in the process. That demands hard work.[13] But in some quarters, the sentiment persists that preschool is just a fancy term for babysitting.

The amount of money spent for each prekindergarten child varies widely among the states, the National Institute for Early Education Research (NIEER) reports, and "high quality and readily available state-funded preschool programs are the exception rather than the rule."[14] That's a sure prescription for failure. "Research shows beyond question that the quality must be there for preschool programs to deliver on the promise of preparing children for kindergarten," says Steven Barnett, an economist who heads NIEER. "When states put preschool policies on the books, but look the other way upon implementation, it's little wonder that many children still enter kindergarten behind their peers."

The other big question mark is what's actually happening in the classrooms. "Ever since Sputnik went up, decision makers have vacillated between emphasizing cognitive skills and focusing on the whole child," recalls Edward Zigler, the first director of Head Start, who heads the Edward Zigler Center in Child Development and Social Policy at Yale.

The skill-and-drill mentality fostered by the federal No Child

Left Behind Act has reached into preschool, a trend that many in the field lament. "It confines our focus on what's important in this period of the lives of children to a narrow, academic set of outcomes," says NIEER's Barnett. "That's a mistake."

This pressure to emphasize reading readiness means that there's less time to devote to encouraging creativity or motivating self-absorbed four-year-olds to work and play well with others, less time as well for science or social studies. Instead, many preschools are turning to direct instruction, using flash cards and a restricted vocabulary as teaching tools. When the Bush administration tested the reading and math skills of half a million Head Start youngsters—the largest test of young children that has ever been administered—while ignoring their social development, the message was clear.

Critics deride this pedagogical strategy as "drill-and-kill," in which children, much like baby chicks, are just fed morsels of information by their teacher. It's an approach reminiscent to that of Mr. Gradgrind, the schoolmaster in Dickens's *Hard Times:* "Teach these boys and girls nothing but Facts. Facts alone are wanted in life." The Bush administration's point man for preschool, Wade Horn, who ordered up the Head Start tests, is untroubled: "Sometimes teaching to the test is really important. You have to teach the alphabet by teaching the alphabet."

Since 1840, when Friedrich Froebel called his Play and Activity Institute a "kindergarten"—literally, children's garden—educators have generally agreed that, while didactic teaching has its place, young children learn mainly from interacting and not through passively listening, understanding and not memorizing, reading for fun and not simply decoding. Memorizing the alphabet song, says Lawrence Schweinhart, president of the High/Scope Foundation, which for forty years has conducted the renowned Perry Preschool study, has little to do with learning the alphabet. "Deciphering a word doesn't mean that you can use it."[15] "The good news is that children can be taught basic academic skills—the fundamentals of reading, writing, and mathematics—in a way that uses, rather than destroys, their natural desire to learn," says Deborah Stipek, dean of the Stanford University School of Education. "Vocabulary can be taught by conversation, awareness of print developed through reading and talking about books, and mathematics learned with games like a pretend restaurant."[16]

This argument over what ought to be taught can be viewed as a skirmish in the ongoing *kulturkampf* in education, with proxies for Allan Bloom and E. B. Hirsch on one side, those for Jonathan Kozol and Jean Piaget on the other, each group using differences over pedagogy as a way of arguing about the character of childhood. But it's not an "either-or, 'more-beer, less-filling' kind of question," says Sue Bredekamp, research director at the Council for Professional Recognition, which develops standards for preschool teachers. Getting the balance right in the classroom is what's crucial, and a diet heavy in direct instruction doesn't do that. Skill-and-drill isn't how middle-class children got their edge, as Stipek points out: "Why use a strategy to help poor kids catch up that didn't help middle-class kids in the first place?"

After Preschool: "Kids First" as the Next Big Idea?

Should high-quality prekindergarten take root nationwide, it will be a major step toward improving children's lives—but just a step. If the aspiration is to have a marked and sustained effect on children, especially poor children, preschool for all is much too narrow a vision. Its benefits come too late, since so much has already happened to children by the time they are four years old. And they end too early, because primary schools have to improve if their impact is going to last.[17] The poorer the children, as Steven Barnett at NIEER points out, the less chance they have of getting a decent public-school education—and poor children who live in poor communities fare worst of all. What's more, preschool pays relatively little attention to other aspects of children's lives, like their health, and although parents' influence dwarfs that of the school, it is silent on the subject of parenting.[18]

No one among the preschool advocates would dispute this diagnosis. But the historical record shows how hard it is to persuade voters to buy into an ambitious and expensive kids-first agenda. A best-seller published at the beginning of the twentieth century confidently pronounced it to be "the century of the child," and doing something "for the children" has been a recurring theme of White House conferences ever since. Still, the record of accomplishments is modest. Looking back, historian Judith Sealander concluded that the past hundred years represented "the *failed* century of the child."[19] The usual explanation is that, while they provide great photo opportunities, children don't matter, politically speaking, because they "do not vote, lobby, or have money to influence public and private authorities. While older Americans have claimed an increasing share of the nation's resources, children have not."[20]

To make America a great place to grow up will surely cost a bundle—far less than the Bush administration's tax cuts or the Iraq war, as liberals are fond of pointing out, but still a bundle. An estimate prepared for the Brookings Institution puts a price tag of $50 billion on providing partially subsidized year-round child care and preschool for youngsters from birth to age five; if such services were free for everyone, then that cost would nearly triple.[21] There is strong evidence that the potential payoff—the impact on both economic productivity and democracy—is greater than anything else in which the government could invest. Will that argument persuade Americans to spend what's required?

The Roadmap

This account begins with a close-up, crouching-in-classrooms look at what has been happening in Chicago, the pivot point of the preschool movement, and in the political environs of Illinois, the first state to guarantee prekindergarten for three- as well as four-year-olds. Some of the nation's finest preschools are located in Chicago's poor Latino and black neighborhoods. The glimmer of a kids-first politics is detectable—this is the first state to guarantee every child access to health care. But all the familiar policy challenges—building a culture of quality in the preschools and paying the bills—are evident as well.

From the specific to the general: the next several chapters dissect the strands of research that, when pulled together, have given intellectual heft to the preschool movement. Chapter 2, which scrutinizes the accounts of exemplary preschools like Perry Preschool and Chicago's Child-Parent Centers, as well as the numberless evaluations of Head Start and more recent studies of universal pre-K programs, shows that early education can have a big payoff, but only if it's carried out in good schools with good teachers. Chapter 3 details how economists, looking at this evidence in terms of "human capital," have demonstrated that top-notch preschools can generate returns on the public investment that far outpace anything that Wall Street can offer. It also explores why, despite the conventional economic wisdom, it's both good policy and good politics to offer early education to all children, not just those from poor families. Chapter 4 explores what has been learned from the lab scientists, both the much-publicized research in neuroscience and the less familiar but equally important genetics studies. This work, from which the knowledge base is exponentially expanding, confirms the pivotal importance of children's experiences, beginning with the impact of the stresses that their mothers endure during pregnancy. Although the research has been relied upon by preschool advocates, it really underpins a far broader kids-as-politics movement. Chapter 5 tells a cautionary tale about child care policy. Despite the best efforts of the advocates, who have urged that child care be viewed through the same lens as preschool, in this realm quality has taken a backseat to head counts of kids merely kept from harm's way while their mothers are working. The child care saga echoes the persisting tension, evident across the children's policy landscape, between the number of kids who are identified as being "served" and the subtle but crucial variations in the caliber of their experiences.

No clear line connects research and policy. How did it come to pass that preschool seized the day, politically speaking? Chapter 6 looks inside the campaign for universal pre-K, and at the role of innovative foundations in molding that effort. It also considers the strategies that conservative groups have adopted. While the right has largely lost the battle over whether preschool should be financed by government, it has had more success in pushing a model that emphasizes parental choice in which prekindergarten their child will attend, rather than assurances that preschools will meet standards of quality. Meanwhile, within the liberal world of children's advocates, questions about the movement's priorities continue to surface: Should the emphasis be on preschool specifically, as the pragmatists argue, or on promoting kids' needs generally? Should the aim be to help poor kids or to secure early education for all? The research and the strategizing are means to the end of making the lives of children better. The last three chapters delve into how politics and policy translate into success or failure on the ground. Chapter 7 focuses on preschool, drawing on accounts from Florida to California. Despite the efforts of luminaries like actor-director Rob Reiner and *Miami Herald* publisher David Lawrence to mobilize the citizenry, slow and steady wins the race: the politics of the *un*-dramatic carries the day. When it comes to a broader kids-first approach, though, leaders who combine vision and ambition have persuaded the public that the society bears some responsibility for the welfare of children. Once that message is heard, the generic public backing of child-friendly policies like preschool and health care is transformed into votes for candidates who make those issues a priority.

The United States prides itself in its exceptionalism and rarely relies on experiences in other countries. Nonetheless, Britain's recent policy history, the subject of Chapter 8, is directly relevant. In less than a decade, that country went from worst in Western Europe to nearly first in its level of support for children, as the goal of eliminating child poverty in a generation turned out to have surprisingly potent popular appeal. Much closer to home, North Carolina's track record since the early 1990s shows that, with adroit political leadership, the needs of young children can take center stage. And in one of the most conservative congressional districts in the country, President Bush's home district in Texas, voters rejected a highly favored Republican candidate largely because she had engineered the removal of thousands of children from the health care rolls. The Texas story is the converse of the North Carolina account, for it demonstrates that politicians who earn a reputation as "anti-children" can be punished at the polls.

What comes next? Will the preschool movement falter, as has happened so often with earlier children's crusades? Or do the notable successes in the drive to expand and improve prekindergarten mean that the United States is becoming a better place in which to grow up?

While only a futurist would offer a confident prediction, the polling data—and, what's more important, the ballot box—point to the conclusion that raising kids is no longer seen as entirely the family's responsibility. Politicians are picking up that message. By way of example, in the 2006 election the Democratic candidate for governor of Oklahoma, one of the nation's most conservative states, made the education and care of infants and toddlers a major theme of his campaign. He won easily. In 2007, Rick Perry, the Republican governor of Texas who had rested his reputation on cutting taxes, submitted a budget that called for a $100 million increase in the state's preschool budget.

Arguments against nanny-state intrusions into the lives of families are no longer sure winners, for the voters are coming to appreciate that, in today's circumstances, by-the-bootstraps individualism isn't the entire answer. Equalizing opportunities for the young is increasingly regarded as both an obligation of the society and a benefit to the rest of us. In this new order, "kids first" holds the promise of becoming a post-partisan theme.

O · N · E

Small Miracles

David L. Kirp and Donna Rosene Leff

THE PRESCHOOL at the University of Chicago's Lab School, a Gothic pile located across the street from the university campus, is a hothouse for the imagination, a place where children engage with their teachers to construct a universe of knowledge.

The Lab School was founded over a century ago by John Dewey, and its guiding philosophy remains Dewey's belief that "the object and reward of learning is continued capacity for growth." Vivian Paley, revered among preschool teachers and parents for her story-filled books that celebrate fantasy play—child's work, she calls it—taught there for a third of a century. She received a MacArthur Foundation "genius" award, and her influence lingers. The principal, Carla Young, acknowledges that sometimes teachers must take the lead in the classroom, that "there's a need to give kids information," but much is left to the children's imagination. "Families that choose the Lab School like the emphasis on inquiry, social-emotional development, autonomy," she says. "The teaching comes out of the organic life of the classroom."[1]

This is as good as prekindergarten gets. If Jack Grubman, the stock analyst who spent so many chips to get his daughters into Manhattan's 92nd Street Y, lived in Chicago, this is where he would want them to go. But most of these kids at the Lab School are the offspring of professors, and they come from a world where thinking is as instinctive as breathing. What if every three- and four-year-old received a Lab School–quality education?

Chicago might seem like an improbable place to begin an account of the preschool movement. By reputation it is, as Carl Sandburg famously wrote, the city of "big shoulders," not symbolic analysts, a "coarse and cunning" city. English novelist E. M. Forster came away unimpressed. Chicago, he opined, was a "façade of skyscrapers facing a lake and behind the façade, every type of dubiousness."[2] Corruption, violence, hog-butchery, and ethnic parochialism; the cold-shoulder treatment given to Martin Luther King, Jr., and his civil rights crusade, and the infamous 1968 Democratic national convention; Al Capone and Richard M. Daley: this is not the stuff of which enlightened social policy gets made.

But there is also a lively progressive streak in the city's history. This is where Jane Addams opened one of the first settlement houses in the country. It is where the juvenile-justice movement had its start, where Saul Alinsky honed the tools of community organizing, and where John Dewey's ideas about democracy and education took shape. Since the legendary mayor Richard J. Daley died in office in 1976, the politics of the city have changed, and so has the economy. Although Daley's son took the mantle of office, the machine is far weaker. Signs of gentrification are everywhere, most visibly in the swaths of green space where the city's most notorious housing projects used to stand. Even the public schools, so wretched for so many years, have been getting better, as pa-tronage politics has largely been supplanted by an ethos of efficiency imported from the business world.[3] "No American city," writes *New York Times* columnist David Brooks, "has changed as much in the past two decades."[4]

Chicago can lay claim to being the epicenter of the universal preschool movement on several counts. For one thing, the movement has been powered by seminal research in brain science, economics, evaluation, and child development, and some of the leading scholars in the field call Chicago their home. Peter Huttenlocher, a neuroscientist at the University of Chicago, pioneered in the research on early brain development that has given preschool the stamp of hard science.[5] His colleague, Nobel Prize–winning economist James Heckman, has constructed elaborate economic models showing the benefits of early education for emotional as well as cognitive development. His work has persuaded bottom line–oriented businessmen to become preschool supporters.[6] At Northwestern, Greg Duncan is bridging the gap between economics and psychology.[7] Erikson Institute, one of the nation's premiere graduate schools in early education, is located in the city, and its president, Samuel Meisels, is among the nation's leading authorities in child development.

What's more, the city and the state led the political bandwagon for pre-K. Chicago mayor Richard M. Daley is an enthusiast. "He gets it," says Barbara Bowman, a cofounder of Erikson Institute, who directs the city's prekindergarten program. Illinois governor Rod Blagojevich has been dubbed a "hero" by Pre-K Now, an organization that promotes universal prekindergarten nationwide, because he has made this issue a priority. The state is the first in the country to pledge that, within a few years, free prekindergarten will be available to all three- as well as four-year-olds. It's also the only state that guarantees health care for all children, and the only state that links support for preschool to the education of infants and toddlers: eleven cents out of every early-education dollar is committed to children in the age group from birth to three.

For anyone interested in observing some of the finest preschools in the country—not just for the offspring of the chattering classes, as at the Lab School, but also for inner-city youngsters—Chicago is the place to go. Several preschools, each with its distinctive philosophy, have become national models, drawing visitors from around the globe and inspiring emulation.

The Child-Parent Centers have been operating as part of the public school system for forty years; when making their case for universal preschool, advocates have relied heavily on their well-documented long-term impact on the children who have attended them. Chicago Commons, a Jane Addams–era settlement house founded in 1894, has adapted a highly touted pedagogical approach developed in the Italian city of Reggio Emilia to the needs of Latino and African American preschoolers. And Educare, a public-private collaboration, aims at reinventing how children from poor families are educated, not just in preschool but from birth until kindergarten.

Less happily, Chicago is also a microcosm of the challenges that the preschool movement, as well as the long-term campaign for kids-first politics, must confront. These shortcomings are as instructive as the successes, and that's another reason to pay attention to the city. The problem is partly a matter of money—public dollars aren't yet sufficient to make good on the promise of prekindergarten for all. It's also a question of quality—while well-designed programs have been shown to benefit kids, low-quality preschools don't, and many children are badly served by the prekindergartens they attend. The no-preschooler-left-behind mentality, as it has been mechanically applied to the education of three- and four-year-olds, makes matters worse.

Both the vision of a great public prekindergarten system and the challenges that the preschool movement faces are abundantly in evidence in Chicago. This chapter begins by elaborating on the political framework within which the prekindergartens operate. Political acumen can make or break any movement, and later chapters of the book pick up that thread of the story. But in this narrative, the spotlight is on the lives of three- and four-year-olds. Show and tell: a look inside a number of preschools offers a richer sense of what the fuss is all about.

The Politics of the Possible

Rod Blagojevich knows the preschool literature—knows enough, anyway, to appreciate how a good early education can transform the lives of poor children. "It's a civil rights issue," he says. "Low-income kids have the right to a level playing field."

For the governor, this has been a voyage from the personal to the political, from the way he is raising his own daughters to the realization that it is vital to provide all children with a good early education. Invariably, when he talks about this topic he returns to the example of his own family, to how his eldest daughter, Amy, blossomed when she started going to the neighborhood Montessori preschool.

"I wish I could say my philosophy was based on Locke or Kant," he says, "but it's just the Golden Rule, something you learn in Sunday school: try to do for all Illinois families what you do for your own family." Some years ago Harvard professor and pediatrician T. Berry Brazelton, the child-rearing expert whose word is gospel to millions of parents, got a call from Patti Blagojevich, the governor's wife, who had a sticky question about good parenting. He had some advice for her then, and he offered more advice to the newly elected governor when he was developing his preschool legislation. "Illinois," said Brazelton, "is a beacon for the rest of the nation."

While all this may sound a bit too warm and fuzzy, Blagojevich has also had to play political hardball to extract preschool dollars from the state legislature. Every year since taking office in 2003 he has boosted the state's prekindergarten budget. His first year on the job was the critical testing time. In the sweltering Springfield summer, lawmakers were still hammering out a budget after the regular legislative session had expired. The children's lobbyists and their legislative allies had agreed to a compromise, accepting a $25 million increase for early education rather than the $30 million that Blagojevich had sought. The governor was furious. "I said $30 million and I meant $30 million," he fumed. He got it.

Rarely is politics a solo performance. Although Blagojevich's passion was essential in getting the universal preschool law on the books in Illinois, that legislation and the continuing increases in the pre-K budget represent the culmination of nearly thirty years of political activism, inside and outside government. They exemplify the politics of coalition building.

In 1979, when Chicago legislator Barbara Flynn Currie first introduced a bill to underwrite preschool for children who seemed destined to fail in school, she confronted virulent opposition. Phyllis Schlafly, the founder of the ultraconservative Eagle Forum and self-proclaimed leader of the "pro-family" movement, believed that if the government put four-year-olds in school, family sovereignty over child rearing would be in jeopardy. "She came down to Springfield determined to kill it, with her supporters wheeling baby carriages to underscore their point," Currie recalls. "Her position was that children belong on the kitchen floor at their mother's knees." In session after session Currie's pre-K bill failed, but she and her legislative allies persisted. In 1985, with a pro-education governor in office, the measure was finally signed into law, but preschool remained a hot-button topic.

While Currie was pushing from inside, the activists were prodding from the outside. "Until the mid-1980s," says Maria Whelan, president of Illinois Action for Children, "each of us would go to Springfield with our little bill, and we'd get nowhere." The key advocacy groups—Voices for Illinois Children, the Ounce of Prevention Fund, and Illinois Action for Children—have been at this business for years. "Now all the major children's groups have joined forces," Whelan says. "We do our fighting in private. We bash out an agenda. Sometimes it involves screaming fights, swearing or storming out, but we speak with one voice."

"We're not afraid to be tough," she adds. "We'll tell the legislators, 'If something bad happens to these kids, then *you* take responsibility!'"

Every year the coalition brings thousands of people, including many parents, to Springfield to buttonhole their legislators. They're not afraid to be tough. A few years back, one of these citizen-lobbyists confronted her representative about the need to expand preschool. "I don't have anything to say about this," the lawmaker said. "Then why are you here?" the parent shot back. Over the years, senior legislators on both sides of the aisle have become allies. "They're not just 'yes' votes," says Action for Children's lobbyist Sessy Nyman, "but people who understand the nuts and bolts."

Chicago philanthropist Irving Harris played a pivotal role in energizing this coalition. Until his death in 2004, Harris was a national exemplar, the go-to guy when it came to children's welfare issues. He helped to create Erikson Institute and, later, the Ounce of Prevention Fund, which delivers support to young parents and their children, in part through Educare, a model zero-to-five early-education program.

Harris, who made his fortune with Toni home permanents, was a great persuader: when he talked, philanthropists and foundations wrote six-figure checks. Harriet Meyer, president of Ounce of Prevention, remembers him saying, with a dollop of Hebrew, "If only we can build a place where kids from chaotic communities can have a predictable, responsive place for the next five years, then *dayenu*—that would be enough."

Harris met with Blagojevich shortly before he became governor. "Irving starts talking about early childhood and Rod's eyes are getting wide," says Meyer. "He gets it." The philanthropist also convinced the McCormick Tribune Foundation to back the coalition, and since 1993 it has spent $70 million on initiatives for young children. More recently Pre-K Now, the national advocacy group, has underwritten the work of the activists. This rare combination—strong advocates and generous foundation support—makes Illinois a leader in what Erikson Institute's Meisels describes as "a statewide effort to create a true system of early education, not just to open more slots."

In 2003, when Blagojevich was elected, the coalition saw its big opportunity. The new governor had campaigned on the theme of ensuring better lives for children—surely that meant preschool for all. The advocates mobilized, and when Blagojevich appointed an Early Learning Council to hammer out a bill, he named Educare's Harriet Meyer as its cochair. Insiders and outsiders worked in tandem to draft what became the "Preschool for All" legislation.

While state prekindergarten had been political dynamite a generation earlier, in 2006 the governor's measure won easy passage. The dissenters did not emphasize Phyllis Schlafly–style ideological objections to preschool, but instead asked whether there was enough money in the state till to pay for it. "What is this kind of a program going to cost in the long term?" wondered GOP state senator Brad Burzynski. State senator Steven Rauschenberger, a two-time candidate for the Republican gubernatorial nomination, was harsher. "It's 'Preschool Not Quite for All.' The governor has no intention of ever funding this. This is a governor with policy attention deficit disorder."

For his part, Blagojevich insisted that preschool would become open to all during his governorship, pointing to his record. To expand the state's prekindergarten program, he had been willing to expend considerable political capital—eliminating nineteen state agencies and 13,000 government jobs—and he vowed to keep pushing until every child had a place. "If there are mobs of parents lining up, that would be a good problem. I'll go in and ask the legislature for more funding." The advocates also maintained the pressure. As Jerry Stermer, president of Voices for Illinois Children, said: "How could we in good conscience not help a whole group of children who could benefit enormously?"

With such strong backing, "preschool for all" will likely become a reality in Illinois under Blagojevich's watch.[8] Still, the question remains: What do these pledges mean on the ground?

Inside the Preschool Classroom: Education's Wild West

The political maneuvering around universal preschool matters greatly, not only for Illinois but also for the national conversation about the issue. In that respect the state really *is* a beacon. But none of it—the political champions, the model preschools, the resident experts—matters as much to ordinary Chicagoans as what transpires in the thousands of prekindergarten classrooms.

While some prekindergartens do a brilliant job of educating the children of families who have few advantages, skeptics still insist that preschool is just glorified babysitting, a place to park the kids while their parents are at work.[9] These youngsters are too young to learn anything in a classroom, the doubters proclaim, and so any mother-substitute can do an adequate job. Economist James Heckman tells the story of a colleague, someone who plainly hadn't spent much time with his own children while they were growing up, who wondered why Heckman was so keen on investing in the education of very young children. "They're just like lumps of clay at that age," his colleague contended.

"Skill begets skill" is Heckman's one-line rejoinder: what children learn early on prepares them for the next stages of learning. There's a mountain of evidence to rebut the "lump of clay" argument, but spending time in a very good preschool class is the most convincing. There, children are as busily and productively engaged as scientists in figuring out how the world works.[10] Peering into those classrooms makes it easier to appreciate how the impact of preschool might reverberate years later.

Yet there are also some prekindergartens where time passes in frenzy or else silence, with kids glued to the TV, watching *Blue's Clues*. An eleven-state study based on classroom observations concluded that "a surprisingly high percentage of the prekindergarten day is spent eating meals and performing routines like hand washing and standing in line. Additionally, children are not engaged in constructive learning or play a large portion of the day."[11]

Parents who send their children to such places aren't indifferent to their well-being. They lack an advocate, or even a *Consumer Reports*-type guide, to help them assess quality, and that makes them susceptible to a hint of glitter—perhaps Bach tinkling in the background—or a sense of order (read: quiet), or simply the appeal of proximity.

What follows is an impressionistic account, not a survey that codifies quality. All but one of these preschools is extraordinary, each in its own distinctive way; the contrast is with a prekindergarten that looks bad only by comparison, but one that is all too typical. What's clearest, not just from these prekindergartens but from visits to others across the city, is the unevenness of their quality.[12] In this respect Chicago is not a model but rather a place that looks like much of America—"the most typically American place," as James Bryce once described it in *The American Commonwealth*.[13]

Urban public schools have been criticized for embracing the dulling conformity of the "one best system."[14] Preschool is different. In many states it is not really a system but a hodgepodge, education's version of the Wild West. Private and for-profit as well as publicly run preschools are all part of the same nonsystem. Because the Illinois pre-K program isn't yet open to all children, income, residence, language, and any one of myriad disabilities are the bases on which children are selected for the state-funded pre-K classes. The effect can seem to be—indeed, can actually be—arbitrary, with some children unaccountably left out in the cold and the nature of the education depending entirely on the luck of the draw.

Expanding the preschool budget is a demanding political task. The bigger problem is maintaining consistently high quality across the pre-K landscape. How can what's known about the best strategies for educating three- and four-year-olds be converted into common practice? How can the aspiration to offer prekindergarten to any family that wants it for their children be realized in a way that provides places for those youngsters and also makes the experience worthwhile? This question confronts not only Chicago but the entire country. The stakes are high—especially if expanding preschool is regarded not as an end in itself but as the prelude to a shift in public priorities that puts children first.

Teach Your Children Well

At their very best, publicly financed preschools offer an education that belongs in the same league as that provided by the University of Chicago's Lab School.

To walk into Laurence Hadjas's classroom in Ray Elementary School, part of the state's prekindergarten program and located just a few blocks away from the Lab School, is to enter a jampacked world of wonders. The children represent a Noah's ark of racial and ethnic diversity, and their teacher, who has come to Chicago via Algeria and France, is a master at her craft.[15]

For much of the time they are in class, these kids choose what they want to be doing. Hadjas is constantly walking around the room, taking everything in and helping the children solve problems that emerge from their projects. In one corner, four kids are building a bridge with Legos. Seeds are beginning to sprout in a planter box, and in the lie-down nook, a girl leafs through a picture book. Two boys are feeding a bottle to a doll in the doctor's office. A pottery shard sits in a box of sand; one of the children has brought it in, and Hadjas has recruited an archaeologist from the university to talk about what can be learned from such a piece of clay. There's a folder full of menus from neighborhood restaurants, and the prices for take-out pizza help kids learn about numbers. Amid the buzz of activity, the room is a picture of order.

The children have learned to take their turn, to put their things away, not to mix up the pieces from different games.

"I'm going to ask you to sit down here to work on your journals," says Hadjas to the eighteen children in her class, motioning to the rug next to her.

A Korean boy shows Hadjas the drawing in his journal, but she can't understand what it is and he doesn't have the English words to explain. He waves his hands. "Is it stars in the sky?" He shakes his head no. "Tell me in Korean," she says, and he does, but Hadjas, who has been trying to pick up the language, doesn't understand. "I'm trying, but I don't know the word in Korean," she says.

The boy waves his arms again and moves his hand up and down, turning it over and up, over and up. She goes to the bookshelf nearby and grabs a Korean phrase book. "Is it a train?" The little boy breaks into a grin. "Yes!" says Hadjas. "Give me five. We did it!"

These youngsters have been labeled by the school system as "at risk." This terminology, while commonplace, is deeply problematic. The label conjures the world as a dangerous place in which children are constantly at jeopardy. "At risk" can mean something that's personal to a child, including anything labeled a disability, or something for which parents are held accountable, such as being single. The language stresses individual pathologies, not the dynamics of the community in which a child grows up, and its use has been expanded to near meaninglessness. The Census Bureau reports nearly half of all youngsters fit one or another of the at-risk categories, including having a foreign-born parent or coming from a poor family. Lumping together all those attributes to create a conclave of the problematic may be bureaucratically convenient, but it doesn't help the children, their families, or their teachers.[16]

Laurence Hadjas's class is a good illustration. Some of the children are identified as poor because their parents are graduate students. Others don't speak English at home—a sign hanging at the front of Laurence's classroom lists eleven languages spoken by the students, everything from Urdu to Ojibwa. Others are here because they are behind their age group developmentally and so may have a hard time with academic work, or they are emotionally troubled. The reasons for such labels can be obvious—during the course of a class, one child cried for two straight hours—but as a practical matter it means that these youngsters are legally entitled, and fortunate, to be here.

Ideally every three- and four-year-old would get an education as good—as rich and playful, as word-stuffed and idea-filled—as this. It's not an impossible dream. While Hadjas has an instinctive sense of how kids learn, she believes that "everything I do can be taught to other teachers," and she spends several evenings a week doing just that. Not every preschool class will have its own Laurence Hadjas. But it is possible for less masterful teachers to work small miracles, for there are models of good practice that can be widely applied.

For the past forty years Chicago's Child-Parent Centers have been educating thousands of three- to five-year-olds in the poor, mainly black and Hispanic neighborhoods of the city's West Side and South Side. These centers, funded with federal compensatory education dollars and part of the public school system, have become nationally renowned because of a well-known study showing their lifelong impact.

The centers weren't Chicago's first public preschools—the federal Head Start program was launched two years earlier, in the summer of 1965—but their philosophy was notably different. Only children from the least-well-off families are eligible for Head Start, which wasn't designed to prepare three-year-olds for the academic rigors of kindergarten but to meet poor children's array of emotional, social, health, nutritional, and psychological needs. Over time, and with a push from the requirements of No Child Left Behind, cognitive skills have come to play a bigger role in Head Start. Still, the program retains its focus on the whole child—sit-down meals served family style are part of the regime, and so is tooth brushing.

By contrast, the Child-Parent Centers are open to all children living in the neighborhoods where they are located. They emphasize language and reading, words and more words, in an attempt to narrow one of the biggest divides between middle-class and poor children. These kids needs a scaffolding of language: how else are they going to go beyond "sad" or "mad" or "glad" to "I lost my composure," which is how one four-year-old at the Lab School responded when asked why she had gotten into an argument?

Involving the parents, both as learners and as collaborators in their kids' education, is another cornerstone of the centers' approach. Every center has a room where parents can hang out; classes for parents range from basic literacy and sewing to GED preparation; there's a class on how parents talk with their children and another for new fathers. Those who developed this model also believed that a year or two of special treatment wasn't enough; that it was vital to provide these youngsters with smaller classes, teachers' aides in every class, and liaisons to stay in touch with their families through the early years of elementary school.

The research project that put the Child-Parent Centers on the

map began in the late 1980s, when Arthur Reynolds, then a graduate student at the University of Illinois—Chicago and now a
University of Minnesota social welfare professor, realized he was
watching a natural experiment unfold. Reynolds compared the
progress of 989 youngsters who attended a Child-Parent Center
with that of children from similar backgrounds who didn't have
the same experience.[17]

From elementary school on, the youngsters who went to one of
the Child-Parent Centers did significantly and consistently better
than those who didn't; those who stayed in the program for five
years, from the time they were three to the age of eight, did best
of all. When they were twenty years old, the research showed,
they were less likely to have been left back for a grade and more
likely to have graduated from high school.[18] And a 2006 update
concludes that the benefits have persisted into young adulthood.
The Child-Parent Center alumni were considerably more likely
to have gone to college, to have health insurance, and not to have
been clinically depressed. They were also 21 percent less likely to
have seen the inside of a prison.[19]

Look at what's going on at one of these centers, and what
makes them special becomes more apparent. The Von Humboldt
Child-Parent Center, in the West Town neighborhood, was planned
with the needs of children and their parents squarely in mind.
The play patios that adjoin some of the classrooms are a riot of
plants and climbing equipment. Each class has a sink for washing
up and its own bathroom; and the central area, flooded with light
from a skylight, is the perfect place to ride tricycles or hold as-
semblies. The parents' room is designed for hanging out as well as
learning.

"This is my home," says Barbara Tchaou, "and it's the homey
feeling that makes the place so special." Tchaou came to Von

Humboldt in 1969, and she became the center's head teacher in 1987. "Most principals move around as fast as horses can trot," notes Barbara Bowman, who runs Chicago's preschool program, but not Tchaou or the heads of the other Child-Parent Centers. They're not interested in changing jobs. Tchaou remembers how, in the mid-1970s, scores of West Town parents massed at a Board of Education meeting, loudly demanding that their neighborhood get its own Child-Parent Center; and she recalls the day in 1979 when, with the mayor and school superintendent on hand, the center opened.

"The teachers don't leave," says Tchaou. "They stay here until they retire," and some of them are among the city's best. In 2005, when the school district wanted to try out a new preschool curriculum, a teacher at Von Humboldt named Daria Zavacki volunteered for the assignment.

In her classroom Zavacki is everywhere at once; whether scripted or not, anything noteworthy that happens becomes a lesson. When one girl accuses a classmate of bullying her, that teary confrontation turns into an occasion for character education, "a way for a youngster to learn 'I'm not a bad kid, I just did something wrong,'" Zavacki explains.

While there is nothing remarkable about her approach, what makes it noteworthy is how she carries it off. "Criss-cross, apple sauce," she says, a phrase known to countless three-year-olds, and the children sit down cross-legged and look up expectantly. It's circle time, and the lesson is about shape and color. Zavacki tells them, "In my bag I have some things. I need you to use your eyes to say what color it is."

"Eric," she asks, "What color is this ball?"

"Pink?" he says.

"That's right. Is it a circle?"

"No, it's a sphere."

"Antoinette, pick something out of this bag. It's a plate . . ."

"Yellow, a circle."

Next Zavacki pulls out an envelope: "What is this thing?"

"Mail, envelope, white, letter, triangle," the kids shout out. She holds up the envelope and compares it with a triangle, showing them the difference between a triangle and a rectangle. There's a rhythmic quality to this conversation. Zavacki plucks something from the bag, talks to the kids, listens to them, and then pulls out something else.

Earlier that day, eleven parents, several fathers among them, had come for an orientation session. "If you're not working or going to school," Zavacki tells them, "we'd like to have you in the parent room or the classroom." One parent asks if she can come more frequently. "Come every day if you want. The better informed you are, the better off the students are."

"We're here for the community. Anyone can come."

Public preschool support isn't limited to public schools like Ray and the Child-Parent Centers. Through its "community partnership" program, the school district subsidizes preschools run by day-care centers, licensed family child-care homes, faith-based agencies, and private schools—everything from settlement houses to storefront for-profits.

Space constraints in the public schools make these partnerships a logistical necessity, and so every state that subsidizes prekindergarten includes nonpublic schools in the mix.[20] The prevailing let-a-thousand-flowers-bloom philosophy, the desire not to re-create the pathologies of the "one best system," treats this diversity as a blessing. Sometimes, as with Chicago Commons, it is.

Diversity can generate remarkable innovation, as with Chicago Commons and Educare, the next stops on this early-education tour. Whether it's housing or health care or higher education, maintaining consistent quality when exemplary programs are expanded to large-scale initiatives is always a trial. So too with prekindergarten.

Chicago Commons, which operates preschools for three-to-five-year-olds in poor, mainly black and Latino neighborhoods in the city's South Side, has been around even longer than the Lab School. It opened in 1894 and was modeled on Jane Addams's Hull House. Consistent with the settlement-house tradition, it concerns itself not just with children's education but with the gamut of families' needs.

The New City School, one of these prekindergartens, sits in a neighborhood so rough that the playground fence is topped with barbed wire. But inside it's a different world. Windows from the corridor open into the classrooms, creating a feeling of lightness and transparency in what used to be a gloomy parochial school. The hallways are crammed with children's sculptures, a fish tank, and a glass case holding a princess standing in front of her castle. Almost everything in the classrooms is made from natural materials. The tables and chairs are wood, not plastic and metal, the dishes are porcelain, the cupboards are vintage 1930s, and there are plants everywhere.

All good prekindergartens display children's artwork, but at the New City School the art is ubiquitous. Umbrellas with crystal raindrops, painted by the kids, hang from the ceiling. Children's drawings tell stories about what they like most about themselves: "I like my hair; my daddy puts gel in it"; "I like my hands because I can help."

On a day we visit, some children decide to paint butterflies during their free time. One boy turns his butterfly into a black shape with yellow dots; the girl at the next easel, dressed prettily in pink, meticulously fashions hers, adding antennae and hearts. At the clay table, children are pounding away with wooden rolling pins and a potato masher, making clay tacos and tortillas. One girl frets that she doesn't know how to make a clay sculpture. "Try it," says an aide, gently coaxing. "You have to try."

"Through art," says Kimberly Cothran, the school's director, "the kids get engaged—with the art and with each other."

Since 1991 Chicago Commons has followed an educational approach developed in the Italian city of Reggio Emilia after World War II. To simplify a complex pedagogy, respect for the child is the central theme; "authentic learning" has to come from children's own curiosity and collaboration with their classmates. Teachers lend their expertise, provoking and stimulating learning while also documenting what the children are doing. And at every step parents are enlisted as participants.[21]

A three-foot doll, a painting of the princess and her castle: these artworks, made by the children and placed on display, show what the generalizations mean. "The children were interested in dolls," explains Cothran. "Their parents taught them how to sew—how to make patterns, which was mathematics. The learning was collaborative, creative in figuring out what the doll would look like. When they were cutting and sewing, they were learning about fine motor skills. Then we talked about where princesses lived, in castles, and they constructed different kinds of castles. They did the painting, and each kid had a favorite color. It was their interest—we built on it—and the parents helped out."

Ever since a panel of experts commissioned by *Newsweek* hailed the preschools of Reggio Emilia as the finest in the world, educators have rushed to mimic the model.[22] Chicago Commons demonstrates how this pedagogy can take root in a very different environment, and educators from across the United States pay the preschool $300 for the opportunity to come and observe what's going on. "For us," says Cothran, "it's not a curriculum that happens to be trendy but a way of life. We're exploring what Reggio means in the context of the inner city."

Educare represents another model of the state-supported preschool—a full-day, year-round program for children from the crib to age five. Like the Child-Parent Centers and Chicago Commons, it is well known outside Chicago. Philanthropists, among them Oklahoma billionaire George Kaiser and the children of investment wizard Warren Buffett, have developed their own versions of Educare.[23] The structure is also distinctive. It's neither a public school nor a private school but a hybrid—"a true public-private partnership," says Harriet Meyer, president of the Ounce of Prevention Fund, which operates Educare in Chicago. "When we built it we didn't say, 'Everyone should fall in love.' We knitted together everything that's possible."

After an initial grant of $1 million from benefactor Irving Harris, the founder of Ounce of Prevention, local foundations and well-heeled supporters—"the elite grass roots," Meyer calls them—underwrote much of the cost for a state-of-the-art building. It was designed to be not just a fine environment for learning but also a place that any community could afford to build. The Chicago public school system donated the land and chipped in some of the construction funds. The program supports itself, says staffer Ann Kirwan, by leveraging every available dollar from federal child-care funds, Early Head Start, and Head Start, as well as state prekindergarten funding.

"We don't want to be a hothouse," Meyer says. "This is the real thing": a working preschool for kids who live in one of the most distressed areas of the city. Still, Educare is also a special thing.

The fact that it was Irving Harris's pet project has given it advantages beyond the dreams of other publicly financed preschools. Ounce of Prevention imports professionals to work with the kids in music and art. It maintains a research unit—a valuable asset because it links pedagogical theories to daily routines, but also an expensive one—and a lobbyist in the state capital, available to work on the campaign for statewide universal preschool. This is not a model that most early-education programs can hope to emulate.

The heart of Educare, says Harriet Meyer, are the youngest children. At a cost of about $13,000 a child, it is far more expensive to work with infants and toddlers than preschoolers, for classes have to be smaller; so, as in all programs that serve babies as well as four-year-olds, the pre-K funds subsidize classes for the youngest kids. Walking past the enclosed play area where a sign reads "Toddlers on the Move," a teacher cradles a two-month-old infant in her arms. In a nearby room, a three-year-old is tending to a younger toddler. Around the corner, a class of four-year-olds is snaking around their classroom, dancing to a tune ("Plant the seed . . . rain comes in the ground . . . the sun comes up . . .") that's being played by a jazz pro.

"We want the teachers to follow the children's lead," says Ann Kirwan, talking about the classes for three- and four-year-olds. "That's how they learn." And they *are* learning, she adds, which eases the transition to kindergarten. Ounce of Prevention has been charting their progress.

"I'm most startled to see the transformation of the kids," says Meyer, "how they blossom over time because of the regularity and continuity of care. That's what I love best about this setting."

Chicago Commons and Educare reflect publicly supported, privately run prekindergarten at its best. The six Teddy Bear preschools in Chicago reveal another side of this public-private partnership.

The chain of family-run, for-profit Teddy Bear preschools looks excellent on paper. Several of its prekindergartens have been accredited by the National Association for the Education of Young Children (NAEYC), which is supposed to be the pre-K equivalent of the Good Housekeeping Seal. "It's a selling point for parents," says manager Heidi Skokal, and it's also a selling point when the company is pursuing public dollars. Teddy Bear enrolls children who receive state prekindergarten funds as well as Head Start youngsters. Although some parents pay the $150 weekly fee out of their own pockets, public money is what keeps Teddy Bear afloat.

On the list of the best affordable preschools compiled by Illinois Action for Children, Teddy Bear shows up alongside Chicago Commons, and it was the first for-profit to join the city's preschool partnership. While this sounds like a tribute to the capacity of the market to meet consumers' demands, Teddy Bear is not a preschool to which you would likely send your own child. (That's what Skokal herself decided: though she could have had a free ride for her own son, she opted instead to send him elsewhere.) Although the Teddy Bear chain is far from the worst prekindergarten program in Chicago, its shortcomings illustrate the weaknesses of the preschool system.

Teddy Bear 1 occupies a storefront on Chicago's Southwest Side, a neighborhood that, a generation or so back, was mainly Irish but is now almost entirely Latino. This is the flagship preschool in the chain, the first to be accredited by NAEYC. Its one big room is divided by chest-high partitions into separate classroom areas, each about fifteen feet square, for toddlers through kids age five, and elementary school youngsters also come there after school to do their homework. Indoors, noise reverberates off the walls, and the outside play area is a small, uninviting concrete lot.

In a class for four-year-olds, the lesson one day is triangles. Worksheets are passed out, and the children are instructed to color in the triangles.

"Stay in the lines, Felix," says the teacher, Nancy Kelly. "You're not tracing the triangle."

"Teacher, I stay in the lines," one girl says proudly.

"You know how to color beautifully. Don't forget to color inside the triangle too. Look at Victor, he's taking his time and doing a good job."

"Teacher, how you do my last name?" asks Victor.

"V . . . I . . . What else?"

"Go do your name, Ernesto. E-R-N-E-S-T-O," she prompts.

"Color the triangles," Kelly says again, this time in an exasperated tone, "*only* the triangles. You weren't paying attention on the carpet. Only color the triangles." She points out the triangles. "Not the oval or the heart. We should remember the triangle has only three sides."

As each child finishes a worksheet, she checks it and then hands the youngster a second sheet with more triangles to color.

One girl turns to her neighbor. "Leticia, do I color the heart?" she asks anxiously.

Leticia shakes her head. "Only the triangle," she says, and she sounds worried. "Uh-oh, she's coloring the other shapes."

"I like the kids when they stay in the lines and color beautiful," Kelly says, but when yet another child asks if they can color the other shapes, she gives up. "Okay," she says, with a wave of her hands.

This isn't the only occasion when a stay-within-the-lines approach to learning about triangles is the focus of a Teddy Bear lesson. In another class of four-year-olds, the children are dressed, one by one, in red plastic slickers. "*Venga!*" says Maria Sanchez. "Come." One by one, each child is told to paint the bottom section of a pyramid. "Stay within the lines. Just paint the base yellow." After the paint has been applied, the child rejoins the group and another child is summoned: "*Venga!*" It turns out that these kids are painting the food pyramid, though they don't know that's what they are doing.

Teddy Bear's managers say they use a program called Creative Curriculum. It is highly regarded by experts in the field, and, as the name implies, it's meant to get kids thinking for themselves. The connection between thinking creatively and coloring triangles isn't readily apparent.

In early education, as elsewhere, you generally get what you pay for, and compared with most preschools, Teddy Bear is cheap. The fee for ten months, for a twelve-hour day that includes three hours of preschool, is about $6,000. That's more or less what it costs the Chicago public schools for the half-day, state prekindergarten program, and in upmarket prekindergartens like the Crème de la Crème preschools profiled in the Introduction, tuition can run three times higher.

The cost-consciousness at Teddy Bear is visible in the dreary quarters and the paucity of educational materials, but the biggest money saver is the teachers' salaries. For the one hundred twenty-five or so children in a Teddy Bear preschool, there is usually only one certified teacher, who floats from room to room. Several other teachers may have an associate's degree, but most have only a high school diploma and have completed a brief training course. These teachers are paid $8.50 an hour—that's less than $300 a week—and those with an associate's degree earn $12.00 an hour. By contrast, a starting teacher in Chicago's public schools earns a minimum salary of $37,000. Some of Teddy Bear's teachers go on to earn their bachelor's degree, but most of them just move on.

Teddy Bear solves the problem of teacher turnover by hiring people—"eighteen and warm-blooded," as one knowledgeable observer described them—who might otherwise be clerking at a big-box store. Whether preschool teachers need a college degree to do well provokes considerable disagreement among researchers. But when they enter the classroom with so little knowledge about young children, it's easy to understand how creativity can give way to coloring in the triangles.

"Superficial task demands, including giving directions and assigning routine tasks, predominate over children's involvement in appropriate conceptual or skill-based activities." That's not an observation about Teddy Bear but the general conclusion of University of Virginia's Robert Pianta, who has looked at preschools nationwide.[24] Unfortunately, those triangle lessons are far more common than Laurence Hadjas's math lesson or the experience, at Chicago Commons, of creating a princess and designing her castle.

Teddy Bear does fill a market niche. The fact that it is inexpensive makes it especially attractive to a school district concerned about its budget. It is also conveniently located for many parents, and it responds to working families' need for full-day, 6:30 A.M. to 6:00 P.M., care. That is why centers that combine child care and prekindergarten have become such an integral part of Chicago's preschool crazy quilt.

Although some educators object to a school's making money— off the backs of its children, as the plaint goes—there's nothing wrong with the profit motive. Indeed, it's the fear of losing clientele to the competition that makes Teddy Bear so attentive to parents' wishes. The elite Crème de la Crème chain operates three prekindergartens in the leafy suburbs.

Nor should anyone come to Chicago expecting to see a replica of France, whose *écoles maternelles* are beloved by child development experts. There, the boast is that at 11:00 A.M. every four-year-old is reading *Babar*. Diversity rules in Chicago. Such variety has its plusses. The Child-Parent Centers are very different from Chicago Commons, Educare, and the Ray Elementary School state prekindergarten, and each program is exemplary. Nor does every good preschool have to be a "model." Bridgeport Catholic Academy, which is located around the corner from Mayor Daley's old home and run by Nativity of Our Lord Church, doesn't attract many visitors. It has neither wonder-teachers nor a mind-bending curriculum, but it does well by its three- and four-year-olds. While the school's children listen to Bible stories during circle time, they also collaborate on the kinds of science and art projects that could be found at a Child-Parent Center.

What *is* problematic is that the Chicago public school system lacks the capacity to close the gap between the good and the not so good. This isn't what Rod Blagojevich had in mind when he expended his political capital on universal preschool.

Money Matters

In the problems that Chicago struggles with—lack of money, unevenness of quality, getting the balance right between encouraging creativity and acquiring specific skills—its school district is hardly unique. Cities and states across the country are finding themselves in the same boat.

The drive for universal preschool has been fueled by research showing that good teachers and good schools have significant long-term payoffs. "Quality is the bottom line, the critical factor," notes John Love, a senior scholar at Mathematica Policy Research and one of the principal evaluators of the federal Early Head

Start program. "Good programs benefit kids, especially high-risk kids. Weak programs have no effect—maybe even a negative effect."

The Illinois legislation sets aside twenty cents out of every preschool dollar for quality-driven initiatives like increasing the pool of certified teachers and offering professional development classes. That's a good strategy, but it's not enough. Consider the plight of the Child-Parent Centers.[25] This program commands national respect. It's an enterprise for which the school district is justifiably entitled to claim bragging rights. When the Rand Corporation, a highly regarded research firm, was asked to estimate the costs and benefits, for California, of a quality preschool education, the researchers looked to the Child-Parent Centers as their exemplar. "We chose it," says economist Lynn Karoly, who led the Rand team, "because it has the unique advantage of being a large-scale, long-term, public school program." Despite this, the centers are on the verge of being closed.

Money is the reason. Their cost, about $8,000 per child each year for a full-day class, makes the Child-Parent Centers a tempting target. Considering the demonstrated long-term payoff of attending one of the centers, that's a bargain. But the figure is high by Illinois standards (a half-day state prekindergarten class costs $6,000 per child; a preschool like Teddy Bear is less than half as expensive), public dollars are scarce, and the school district has other priorities. "These centers should be a model for the city," says Barbara Bowman, the district's chief early childhood education officer, "but when fewer than half of all eligible low-income kids have any program at all, it's a tough call." In fact the call has really been made. "The focus," as Bowman acknowledges, "is on serving the maximum number of children."

Once there were twenty-five Child-Parent Centers; in 2006

there were thirteen. And much of what made the centers so special has been eliminated. The program, with its smaller classes and teachers' aides, no longer extends beyond preschool to the third grade. Instead, children are expected to navigate, on their own, the elementary schools in their rough neighborhoods, where eighth graders are royalty and police visits are common. The practice of assigning a teacher to work with parents, integral to the centers' philosophy, has been eliminated, and despite a long waiting list all the full-day classes have been shuttered. In 2006 the centers' budget was cut by 20 percent.

"The Chicago program has changed a lot over time," says Rand's Karoly. "We know that a particular model like the Child-Parent Centers, with these features, produces this effect. But what happens if you scale it back?" When Arthur Reynolds, who has tracked this program for his entire career, appraised the stripped-down version of the Child-Parent Centers in 2002, he found fewer positive effects. What else could one expect, when what remains of the centers bears only the vaguest resemblance to this once-great experiment.

"The people downtown who make these decisions don't see what works for kids," says Reynolds. "Everyone talks about early education as a priority, but now they're cutting the one program with proven results, ignoring long-term gains because of short-term costs."

This is the "state prekindergarten dilemma," Reynolds adds. "Making preschool universal is important, but preschool must be good enough to make a difference." More Teddy Bears, fewer Child-Parent Centers: if that is the rubric, then for three- and four-year-olds enrolled in publicly funded prekindergartens, the transformative promise of a place like Von Humboldt will go unrealized.

The Child-Parent Centers represent the most dramatic example of economizing, but certainly not the only one. Across the board, "extras" like field trips—excursions to a museum for children who have never before left their neighborhood—are being cut back, and there is less money to create environments as inviting as Laurence Hadjas's classroom at Ray Elementary School.

Money talks in yet another way: wealthy parents can buy a good public preschool education. Jeff Gillespie teaches across the hall from Laurence Hadjas. His class is the working parents' dream, a full-day program that combines an exceptional preschool experience with child care that fits the schedule of busy parents. But while Hadjas's state pre-K class is free, the parents who send their children to the full-day program in Gillespie's classroom pay $8,500 a year to the public schools.

The Chicago public school system runs these tuition-based classes, chipping in $500 per child, partly to balance the books and partly in the hope that well-off families who send their best-and-brightest youngsters there will keep them in the public schools.[26] For the parents, who would have to pay at least twice as much for a top-notch private preschool, it's a bargain, but families without that kind of money are out of luck. Imagine the outcry if the five-year-olds in the kindergarten classes down the hall were segregated in this way.

Laurence Hadjas, fed up with fighting the system, decided to quit her teaching job in 2006. She was not the only one to jump ship. Barbara Tchaou, the head teacher at the Von Humboldt Child-Parent Center, assailed what was happening to her program as "a massacre": "They are amputating every part until soon the heart will have disappeared and they can get rid of it entirely." Tchaou did not stay on to witness the program's demise. "I couldn't stand to see the center close on my watch," she said, and, like Hadjas, she left in 2006.

The Math Lesson

In Chicago, as elsewhere, money is only a means and quality is the end. The caliber of the teacher and the preschool is the ultimate concern, since that's what shapes children's minds. But in setting nationwide testing requirements for elementary school children, Washington has written a narrowly focused pedagogical script that Chicago, like every community, must follow. The federal No Child Left Behind Act mandates that all third graders be tested in reading and arithmetic. These test results have significant consequences for the public schools—parents can transfer their children out of what the law defines as a "failing" school—so school administrators are understandably tempted to begin prepping children very early.

There is also strong political pressure to do this. "Politicians want outcomes," Harriet Meyer at Ounce of Prevention notes, and when the subject is education, the outcomes that matter to them are test scores. Educare was among the first preschools to receive a grant from Early Reading First, a federal initiative whose sobriquet defines its philosophy. That money comes with a push to be more prescriptive, and while Educare remains committed to a developmental approach, it has added direct instruction to its pedagogical kit bag.

"Officially the Department of Education isn't pushing phonics, but unofficially it is pushing a curriculum that is tightly structured, calendar-driven, rather than taking a more interactive approach," said Karen Freel, Ounce of Prevention's vice president for public affairs. "We believe teachers should follow kids' leads— that is how they learn, by focusing on those teachable moments. The government wants to map a month-long experience, and we can't do that as well."

It's not just school administrators who are concerned—parents, too, have imbibed the message that early mastery of the three R's is crucial to later academic success. At Ray Elementary School, principal Cydney Fields tells parents of preschoolers, "This is a developmental program. If you want heavy-duty academics, this isn't the place." But she adds that "it's the way of the world that kids have to test," and so the school has had to temper its child-centered approach.

Erikson Institute's Meisels dislikes what he calls the "tsunami effect" generated by No Child Left Behind, the desire of some officials to rely only on tests as a way of identifying the potential of very young children. "The models that policymakers carry into the educational arena come from lockstep kindergarten-through-twelfth grade," he says. "There's a real naïveté about testing, a belief that the test will reveal the truth. But these preschool tests have never been shown to predict future academic success."

Until the 1960s, Britain administered a nationwide exam that sorted children academically. Their fates were fixed at the age of twelve. Those who did well on the test went on to grammar school and university, while the rest went to vocational school and later found jobs as factory workers and file clerks. In the 1960s Britain junked that system in favor of comprehensive schools. Maybe America is ready for its own version, the "three-plus" examination.

If this sounds unduly alarmist, consider an episode in Daria Zavacki's classroom at the Von Humboldt Child-Parent Center. Parent-teacher conferences are coming up, and the Chicago school district requires that every child be tested. A young boy we'll call Michael, who had just turned three and had joined the class late, needs to be tested.

The teacher's aide, Norma Cervantes, takes on the task. "I want you to use your finger to point," Cervantes says. "Which one is a square?" Michael points to a circle, but then he gets rectangles, triangles, squares, and cones right. The test becomes harder when Cervantes asks Michael to identify shapes as she points to them. He only knows the triangle and the square, and he calls a circle a triangle. Visibly anxious, he chews on his nails. Finally, Cervantes gives him a pencil and asks him to write his name. He produces a wavy line that doesn't even remotely resemble Michael. "Okay, Michael, find something to do," she says, and the boy is released.

This story horrifies Vivian Paley, the legendary Lab School teacher. Academics have a place in preschool, she acknowledges, "as long as we're assuring this isn't highly pressurized." The trouble is that "children are being judged at the age of three by what they used to know by the time they were six or seven," says Paley. "It's the most unfair rewriting of the rules, an unfair rewriting of a child's experience, yet it is getting written in stone."

There can be no return to a more innocent world in which nursery school celebrated play and reading was something that youngsters were formally introduced to when they were six years old. Nor should there be. There are creative, intellectually challenging ways to teach young children how to decipher letters and numbers, as well as how to use them—ways to develop cognitive skills at an early age without making a child gnaw at his nails. Berkeley psychology professor Alison Gopnik distinguishes between "guided discovery—figuring out how the world works, learning to solve new problems" and "routinized learning," where "something already learned is made to be second nature, so as to perform a skill effortlessly and quickly."[27] The one may be sexier than the other, but both are necessary parts of learning.

Routinized learning is what was taking place in Laurence Hadjas's state pre-K class, but in a very nonroutine way. "Which book would you like me to read?" she asked her kids as they settled on a rug. One after another the children came to the whiteboard and put checkmarks next to the book of their choice. Then they tallied the votes. One child counted eighteen votes for the most popular book, the next came up with nine, and the third got eleven.

"Let's count together when I tap the board," said Hadjas. When the children started counting before she did, she gently rebuked them. "Did I tap?" Then, counting as a group, they arrived at ten, the correct answer. Hadjas never told any of the children that they were wrong. And she was teaching arithmetic not as a subject set apart from life but as something useful in ordinary life.

This arithmetic lesson makes hash of the claim that skill-and-drill is the only way to teach children how to count. It does not demand extraordinary pedagogical skills—it's the kind of lesson that, despite their lack of formal education, the teachers at a Teddy Bear preschool could absorb. No doubt Laurence Hadjas—or Daria Zavacki at the Von Humboldt Child-Parent Center, or Kimberly Cothran at Chicago Commons—would have a similarly engaging way to teach children about triangles. If Chicago were to use its state "quality" dollars to offer that kind of training, then preschool for all might be saved from becoming just a matter of counting the number of three-year-olds who pass through the turnstile.

This is the preschool world up close—a governor's passion, a preschool teacher's lesson, a philanthropist's vision, an urban school district's hard choices. While it is a unique story, because Illinois has been a place of early-education firsts, variations on these themes can be found in many places.

In this telling, the broader intellectual and political currents that have come together (more precisely, that have been brought together) to make universal preschool a national movement have emerged only in passing. That remarkable amalgam includes studies like the evaluations of the Child-Parent Centers, which demonstrate the long-term impact of preschool; economists' rendering of that evidence in the language of costs and benefits; the findings from brain science and behavioral genetics that give scientific credibility to the advocates' claims; the ever-growing desire of working parents to provide their children with a solid opportunity to learn, which leads them to push for more than mere child minding; and the campaign mounted by preschool advocacy groups to command political attention.

The chapters that follow unpack these developments. The preschool research is a logical place to begin, since it's essential to know what works and what doesn't. That means sifting through the voluminous evaluations of Head Start as well as more recent studies of state-financed prekindergartens. The starting point is another narrative, the account of the forty-year-long Perry Preschool experiment, the iconic study of the lifelong reverberations of preschool.

T · W · O

Life Way After Preschool

David L. Kirp and Rachel Best

IN THE FALL of 1961, without any fanfare, thirteen three- and four-year-olds entered a preschool class at Perry Elementary School in the blue-collar town of Ypsilanti, Michigan. All of them, as well as the forty-five other children who enrolled during the next three years, were black. They came from poor families, and their South Side neighborhood, with its rundown public housing and high crime rate, was a dangerous place to grow up.

Based on past experience, it was a near certainty that most of these youngsters would fail in school. During the previous decade, not a single class at Perry Elementary had ever scored above the tenth percentile on a national achievement test, while across town, in the primary school that served the children of well-off professionals, no class ever performed below the ninetieth percentile.

The hope was that a good preschool education could rewrite this script. That is just what happened, and the results were far beyond anyone's expectations.[1] The children's lives were so dramatically affected that David Ellwood, the architect of the

Clinton administration's welfare plan, argues that they have become "the most powerfully influential group in the recent history of social science."

"The Most Powerfully Influential Group"

When David Weikart, the moving force behind Perry, started thinking about opening a preschool for poor kids in the late 1950s, the psychologists with whom he conferred were uniformly discouraging. Even though youngsters from prosperous families had thrived in similar settings for well over a century, three-year-olds from poor backgrounds hadn't had the same chance.[2] "I was working in a context where most people felt that IQ was God-given and, unfortunately, low-IQ people were just born that way," Weikart writes in his memoir. This was the era when IQ meant heredity, and heredity was destiny. An intellectually rigorous regime, argued the experts, could actually harm poor children by asking too much of them.[3]

The psychologists had a theory, Weikart conceded, but no evidence. He was just twenty-six, not long out of the Marines and working on his PhD at the University of Michigan, when he became the director of the Ypsilanti schools' special education program. In designing the new preschool he drew on the miscellany of what he knew from his years of running summer camps, his undergraduate education at Oberlin, even research on how rats negotiated mazes that was being conducted at Ann Arbor, as well as on his passion for racial justice.[4]

Would an intensive program work, or were the skeptics right? Weikart decided to conduct an experiment. From a group of 123 South Side neighborhood children, 58 were randomly assigned to the Perry program, while the rest, identical in virtually all respects, didn't have the same opportunity. Random assignment is the research gold standard because the "treatment"—in this case, preschool—then best explains any later differences between the groups.[5]

Most of those who enrolled at Perry Preschool were there for two years, three hours a day, five days a week. The curriculum emphasized problem solving rather than unstructured play or "repeat after me" drills. The children were viewed as active learners, not sponges; the pedagogy called for them to carry out and review what they were learning. The teachers, one for every five or six youngsters, were well trained—most had a master's degree in child development—and were paid public school salaries. Evelyn Moore, one of the original cadre of teachers, who later became president of the National Black Child Development Institute, recalls, "We had beautiful equipment. Anything you wanted for learning was required. It was an exciting adventure."

The teachers also made weekly home visits, offering parents advice and counsel. "Anyone coming [to the South Side] who said they would help their kids, the parents went along with it," says Moore. "The message was, 'Read to your child,'" remembers Blanche Marshall, whose daughter went to Perry in 1962. "If you read the newspaper, put your child on your lap, read out loud, and ask her, 'What did I just read?' When you take her to the grocery store, have her count the change."[6]

At the outset of the experiment, Weikart intended to follow these children only through elementary school. The early findings were mixed. By fourth grade, the preschoolers had higher achievement scores. But their IQ scores, which had spiked earlier, were no higher than the control group's.[7]

Weikart didn't give up. He received a grant from the Carnegie

Corporation to open a research center, the High/Scope Foundation, where the study could be continued. Researchers collected data on the students every year from the time the children were seven years old until they were eleven, then at ages fourteen, fifteen, nineteen, twenty-seven, and forty—an astonishingly long time in the annals of education research.

Just as remarkably, High/Scope was able to keep track of 97 percent of those who were involved in the study. "I've found people on the streets, gone to crack houses where there were AK-47s," says Van Loggins, a gym teacher with two master's degrees, who coached many of the participants when they were teenagers and has stayed in touch with them. "I'm bilingual," he says, "ghetto and English."

The Perry study is not only noteworthy for longevity. It also asks the truly important question: What is the impact of preschool, not on the IQ scores of seven-year-olds but on their lives, outside as well as inside the schoolhouse? The answer is that a superb preschool experience can make a lifelong difference.

As the Perry children progressed through elementary and high school, the differences began to emerge. They were significantly less likely than the control group to skip school, to be assigned to a special education class, or to repeat a grade.[8] Their attitude toward school was better, and their parents were more enthusiastic about the education that their children were receiving. Their high school grade point average was higher. By age nineteen, two-thirds of them had graduated from high school, compared with just under half (45 percent) of those who hadn't attended Perry Preschool.[9]

What's most extraordinary is that the impact of those early years has persisted into middle age. Pick almost any measure that one might care about—education, income, crime, family stability—and the contrast between the two groups is striking. When they were twenty-seven, the preschool participants scored higher on tests of literacy. When the most recent study was completed, in 2004, they were in their forties, many with children and even grandchildren of their own. Nearly twice as many had earned college degrees (one has a PhD). More of them had jobs: 76 percent versus 62 percent. They were more likely to own their own home, own a car, and have a savings account; less likely to have been on welfare. They earned 25 percent more—$20,800 versus $15,300 a year—and this difference pushed them well above the poverty line.

The crime statistics revealed similarly powerful differences. Compared with the control group, fewer of the Perry youngsters had been arrested for violent crimes, drug-related crimes, or property crimes. Only about half as many—28 percent versus 52 percent—had gone to prison or jail.

Preschool also seems to have affected their decisions about family life. More of the males in the Perry contingent had been married (68 percent versus 51 percent, though they were also more likely to have been married more than once), and almost twice as many had raised their own children (57 percent versus 30 percent). They reported fewer complaints about their health and were less likely to use drugs.

There's no way to know just why Perry Preschool was so successful—was it the caliber of the teachers, the hands-on curriculum, the extremely favorable ratio of children to teachers, or the home visits that made the essential difference? Steven Barnett, the director of the National Institute of Early Education Research (NIEER), started working at High/Scope in the early 1980s. He believes that "the creative ferment" was crucial. "You had great teachers, working with these children half a day, then going to their homes and tutoring them, getting to know them really well." To Lawrence Schweinhart, a onetime divinity student who found his calling in early education and who succeeded David Weikart as president of High/Scope, "what matters aren't the specifics of the curriculum but its purpose, the emphasis on thinking and decision-making versus skill-and-drill."[10]

Schweinhart believes that the children's experience at Perry occurred at a particularly opportune moment in their lives. It gave them the tools they needed to do better in school. When they succeeded academically they became more committed to education, and so they stayed on. Then, because a diploma brought new economic opportunities, crime became a less appealing option.

What actually went on inside the classrooms at Perry Preschool? While that prekindergarten is long gone, High/Scope still runs a preschool in Ypsilanti. It's not the same place, of course—there's more space, a nicer yard, and the computer terminals are very popular. What's more, the class isn't composed entirely of black and poor kids, as it was in the 1960s. Now it's a racial and economic potpourri, with the children of doctors and professors sharing the experience with children whose families live in poverty. But the educational philosophy hasn't changed. Children still plan their own activities with the help of their teacher, carry them out, and review what they have discovered: "plan, do, review."

It's 9:00 A.M., planning time, and the kids sit in a circle. Two girls choose to be babies in the nursery corner of the room, and a boy volunteers to be their teenage brother. A few minutes later a "baby" starts to cry, and a bottle doesn't quiet her down. "What else can you do?" asks Sue Gainsley, one of the two teachers in the room, and the "brother" tries reading her a book.

"They're learning how to help each other," says Chris Baisvert, the other teacher, but just then a crisis breaks out over who gets to use the play phone. One of the babies wants it all the time, and the teenager suggests using a timer to take turns. "No!" screams the baby, not quite ready for appeals to fairness. "I want to keep it until I'm ready," and she starts to cry.

"You're a crybaby," says the older brother.

"That's okay," Gainsley tells him. "Sometimes when people are frustrated, they express it by crying."

Meanwhile a boy who said he wanted to build a car with blocks is having trouble. His car is only half finished when Baisvert sits down next to him. "You've got a problem. What are you going to do to solve that problem?"

The boy thinks for a minute. "I need more blocks," he says, and crosses the room to get them.

While the Perry Preschool study has been Exhibit A for the advocates of universal preschool, the prekindergarten didn't work miracles. Not everyone who went there became a model citizen—the crime figures make that plain—and some of those who didn't attend have done well for themselves. But because their opportunities are so constricted, the odds are stacked against kids who grow up in neighborhoods like Ypsilanti's South Side. Bluntly put, these are the children of whom we expect the least—and overall, the life histories of the control group confirm those expectations.

A great many of those who attended Perry found their way to more stable lives. Most of them still live in Ypsilanti, a town that, as Van Loggins describes it, is composed of "indigents and intelligentsia—blacks, hillbillies, and college professors." Former Perry student Charles Dixon, now a sales manager, has moved back to his old South Side neighborhood, where street pharmacists openly ply their illicit trade. Dixon devotes much of his time to his church group, "giving back" to the community. "I'm still using the discipline of the school," he says. "The harder you work in school or in life, the more you get out of it."

Another Perry alum, Marie Thompson, says that when she was in her midtwenties, living on welfare and "borrowing" from her mother, she "woke up one day to decide that was just wrong. I apologized to my mother and went to work in the factory. When I had the money, I bought Mom all new living room furniture. I stopped dating the wrong kind of guys, and eventually I got married." Marie became a union leader in the auto industry, and when she had children of her own, there was no doubt that they would go to preschool.

The Perry Preschool study is inspiring—but does it have legs? In 1964, when she went to Perry, Marie Thompson's family was dirt poor. Now, together with her husband and her two daughters, she is living the suburban dream in a spacious, smartly furnished home on a cul-de-sac where the neighborhood kids congregate when they're not at soccer practice or ballet class. Marie reads to her daughters every day, talks with them all the time, praises them, and pushes them to succeed. How much of a difference will preschool, even a very good one, make for middle-class children like hers?

In the early 1960s Perry Preschool was a haven for learning at a time when pre-K wasn't an option for poor families. A decade later, in Chapel Hill, North Carolina, another such haven, Abecedarian, opened its doors, and it too has become an icon in the preschool movement. The Abecedarian Early Childhood Intervention Project was much more than a preschool. Soon after they were born, fifty-seven children, all of them poor and nearly all African American, were enrolled in the model project's elaborate full-day, year-round program. Some remained there until they were eight years old, and researchers tracked them until they were twenty-one. Compared with a similar group who did not receive the same high-quality education, the Abecedarian alumni had higher IQs. They were three times more likely to have gone to college, more likely to have a good job, and half as likely to have been teen parents.[11] When Irving Harris, the godfather of early education in Chicago, went looking for a model to emulate in his hometown, he picked Abecedarian.

These early experiments—the Perry and Abecedarian projects as well as Chicago's Child-Parent Centers—show that exceptionally good early education can make a world of difference. Today more than half of all four-year-olds attend some kind of prekindergarten or child care center, but almost none of them has an experience remotely akin to that at Abecedarian or Perry. In 2006 dollars, Perry would cost about $13,000 per child, nearly twice as much as Head Start. "No one has tried to replicate Perry," NIEER's Barnett points out. "It's so far from what we do. Let me run a program where I get to hire two teachers for every twelve kids and pay them public school salaries. I'll bet my retirement plan on the outcome. Instead we pay teachers a pittance, give them eighteen kids and an assistant who is just a high school graduate—and then there are complaints that the results haven't been replicated!"

What Barnett is talking about is the voluminous and frustratingly inconclusive research on Head Start, which since 1965 has enrolled nearly 25 million three- and four-year-olds. Making sense of those studies involves a brief historical detour.

High Hopes

Between the late 1950s, when David Weikart started thinking about a preschool for poor black children, and the mid-1960s, America became very a different place. Those social and political perturbations reshaped the landscape of early education.

The story is a familiar one—how equal opportunity became the national watchword, how leadership and not laissez-faire became the marching order from Washington. Achieving civil rights is not enough, declared Lyndon Johnson in the most memorable speech of his presidency: "We seek not just freedom but opportunity, not just legal equity but human ability—not just equality as a right and a theory, but equality as a fact and as a result."[12] While the construction of the interstate highway system was the crowning domestic-policy achievement of the 1950s, the ambition of the Great Society in the 1960s was nothing less than to wage, and win, the War on Poverty.

Head Start became a major weapon in that war. The goal was audacious—to strike "at the basic cause of poverty"—and Johnson was quick to declare victory. "The program this year," he said in 1965, referring to what was then only an eight-week summer preschool, "means that thirty million man-years—the combined lifespan of these youngsters—will be spent productively and rewardingly, rather than wasted in tax-supported institutions or in welfare-supported lethargy."[13] Such outsized claims created impossible expectations.

Social science theories about poverty and intelligence were also changing, and the new paradigms, with their optimistic view of human potential, led to a new emphasis on the early years. During the first half of the twentieth century, most psychologists believed that intelligence was essentially fixed at birth.[14] If those scholars had it right, then it would be a fool's errand to try reducing poverty by raising IQ. But by 1960 Jean Piaget's theories about the stages of children's learning, which treated intelligence as dynamic, had made it across the Atlantic.[15] Konrad Lorenz's research showed the importance of early imprinting—and what was true of ducks might just be true for human beings as well.[16] Leading psychologists, among them J. McVicker Hunt at the University of Illinois and Benjamin Bloom at the University of Chicago, took up the cry, arguing that nurture, not nature, mattered most in determining the course of children's lives. If intelligence was in fact so malleable—if, as Hunt memorably put it, "trying to predict what the IQ of an individual child will be at age eighteen from results obtained during his first and second year is much like trying to predict how fast a feather might fall in a hurricane"—then preschool could radically revise the life scripts of the poor.[17] Hunt claimed that a child's IQ could be raised by as much as 70 points, and that made a splash.[18] "As a graduate student I picked up that IQ was immutable," recalls Ron Haskins, a developmental psychologist at the Brookings Institution who participated in the Abecedarian study. "That's what Hunt and Bloom refuted."

This heady optimism matched the mood of the times. Books with titles like *Give Your Child a Superior Mind* became best-sellers.[19] Foundations pumped millions of dollars into early-education research. In Harlem and in rural Tennessee, some of David Weikart's intellectual fellow travelers started their own preschools for poor children, and both programs reported sizable IQ gains.[20] In 1964, when Sargent Shriver, the first director of the Office of Economic Opportunity, was developing the Head Start model, he paid a visit to the school in Tennessee.

The era was also the golden age for the social sciences, a moment when research drove policy choices.[21] Robert McNamara's whiz kids had brought a model of rational decision making called PPBS (planning, programming, and budgeting systems) to the Defense Department, and the idea quickly took root that every government initiative should be similarly assessed.

Live by evaluation, die by evaluation—almost from the outset, researchers were scrutinizing Head Start. And even though the program was supposed to accomplish many things, among them giving a boost to children's self-confidence and improving family relationships, a single measure, the IQ score, became the benchmark of success. It's easy to see why. IQ was a familiar concept: measures of intelligence had been available for half a century, while the other attributes, like emotional maturity, that Head Start was supposed to foster were squishier and harder to test. The belief that preschool would boost IQ scores was also consistent with the social scientists' growing confidence that intelligence was malleable. That's what had sold the White House on Head Start. At a kickoff event the first lady, Lady Bird Johnson, engaged in a bit of revisionist history, declaring that the program had been designed to raise the IQs of poor children, "some of [whom] don't even know their own names."[22]

As Head Start was being planned, Edward Zigler, who would become its first director, argued for a long-term study along the lines of the Perry Preschool research. But that course of action demands the kind of patience that politicians rarely possess, and Zigler was turned down. "You academicians are purists," Sargent Shriver told the planning group. "If the nation is ever going to have any program, it has to be done right away." The way to "prove this program is valuable," Shriver insisted, was to show gains in IQ scores.[23]

An in-house look at early versions of Head Start that ran for as little as six weeks did produce positive results. But the first major Head Start study reached a very different conclusion.

No lasting effects: that was the damning conclusion of the 1969 Westinghouse Learning Corporation report on Head Start.[24] While IQ scores did rise in the short run, those gains soon faded. Never mind that the Westinghouse study was a flawed piece of research, subsequently picked to death by other social scientists. Never mind, either, that it mainly focused on the summer program, a hastily mounted and soon abandoned effort, rather than the school-year program for three- and four-year-olds. To the hovering critics, who had been put off by the Texas-size claims, this study proved that Head Start was just a dead end.[25] Ever since, "fadeout" has been the preschool skeptics' favorite word.

The hope during the Great Society years was that science would become the handmaiden of social progress, conclusively showing that government initiatives like Head Start ("my favorite," Sargent Shriver called it) were making real headway against the root causes of poverty.[26] But Lyndon Johnson's dream, that Head Start could wipe out poverty in a generation, was jettisoned almost immediately. In 1968, barely three years after the program was launched, Johnson himself was talking not about how early education could transform America but about its potential impact over the long haul. "The task is great, the work hard, often frustrating, and success is a matter not of days or months, but of years—and sometimes it may even be decades."[27] By the time the Westinghouse study was published, Richard Nixon was in the White House. The Great Society was history, and so were its great expectations. The country had gone to war with poverty, the jibe went, and poverty won.

A few years before the Westinghouse report was issued, University of Chicago sociologist James Coleman undertook a major study for the Department of Health, Education, and Welfare, titled *Equality of Educational Opportunity Survey*, which sounded a deeply pessimistic note about the possibilities of policy. Differences in how much money public schools spent—whether for higher-paid teachers, better-stocked libraries, science labs, anything within the purview of policymakers—had little if any effect on children's performance in school. What mattered most were the youngsters' own backgrounds and those of their classmates.[28] In the media, the Coleman report was mischaracterized as having concluded that, in education, nothing works. Edward Zigler, who at the time was riding the waves at Head Start, recalls that it "started to push the pendulum from over-optimism concerning the effects of compensatory education to a nihilistic view that such programs were a waste of money."[29] That skepticism only grew with the publication of Berkeley psychologist Arthur Jensen's controversial and influential article, "How Much Can We Boost IQ and Scholastic Achievement?"[30] On the basis of a seemingly careful review of the research in quantitative genetics, Jensen offered a bleak answer: "Not much."

Appearing when it did, the Westinghouse report could well have spelled the demise of Head Start. As it was, the study confirmed what was quickly becoming a widespread belief, that preschool for poor children was doomed to fail.[31] While Head Start did survive, in good part because its supporters were adroit political entrepreneurs, its supporters stopped talking about the benefits for children and started emphasizing its instrumental value to working mothers, who needed a safe place where their children would be cared for. Head Start's budget shrank, enrollment was halved, and funds for research in early education dried up. By the outset of the Reagan administration, Head Start, one of the few survivors of the Great Society days, seemed poised on the brink of elimination.

It was the Perry Preschool study that came to the rescue of Head Start. David Weikart's persistence had paid off. The children who attended Perry Preschool and other experimental programs during the 1960s were now teenagers, and the value of their early experiences was becoming ever more apparent. But because each of the new studies involved only a small number of children, the findings hadn't shaken the dominant belief that preschool was a proven failure. In the late 1970s the researchers decided to pool all their data, call themselves the Consortium for Longitudinal Studies, and publish the results. The resulting volume, *As the Twig Is Bent,* proved to be the next best thing to a long-term study of Head Start. Finally there was good news about early education that could grab the attention of the policymakers.[32]

As the Twig Is Bent confirmed that IQ gains did diminish over time, and in this respect the Westinghouse study was probably right, but that was the least memorable change in the children's lives.[33] All the studies showed the same thing—the teens who had attended a good prekindergarten were less likely than their peers to have repeated a grade or been assigned to special education. Over the long haul preschool *did* make a difference.

The national press picked up the story. These studies "refute the notion that the results of 'early intervention' are worthless," the *Washington Post* reported, and the *New York Times* made the same point.[34] The Perry Preschool project got the most attention. It was among the most carefully conducted of the studies, and it had the most impressive results. What's more, unlike any other preschool research of that era, it converted school achievement into a dollars-and-cents payoff, and that gave the reporters a new way to frame the research.

Soon enough, the media started attributing to Head Start the successes of Perry Preschool, even though the two programs were similar only in the fact that they both enrolled three- and four-year-olds. Head Start classes were twice as large as those at Perry, few Head Start teachers had college degrees, they were paid considerably less than public-school teachers, turnover was high, and the pedagogy was haphazard. But this confusion didn't come about entirely by accident. David Weikart and Lawrence Schweinhart at High/Scope wanted to trumpet their findings, and Peggy Pizzo, who worked at what was then the Carter White House, was interested in giving a boost to the beleaguered Head Start program. Pizzo persuaded the Carnegie Corporation, which had financed much of the research, to hold a press conference in November 1979 that planted the idea of an association between Perry Preschool and Head Start. The journalists took it from there.[35]

The linkage wound up benefiting both parties. Favorable press coverage helped win additional foundation support for High/Scope, enabling the researchers to continue tracking the Perry preschoolers, and that longevity has given the study its cachet. Meanwhile Head Start garnered a decade's worth of publicity, all of it flattering and much of it inaccurate. In 1984 the *Washington Post* described Perry as a "long-term study of a Michigan Head Start program" that showed that "well-run government programs can make an important difference," and the reporter's mistake became contagious. Three years later the *New York Times* reported that "Head Start, one of the jewels of the Great Society, has proven that high-quality early childhood education for the disadvantaged produces youngsters much more likely to finish high school, hold a job, and avoid welfare and crime." It was, of course, Perry Preschool, not Head Start, that the journalist had in mind. In 1989 a *Newsweek* article summarizing the latest Perry Preschool findings was headlined "Everybody Likes Head Start."

Research had come to the aid of Head Start, but not in the rational way that the 1960s dreamers had imagined. It was skillful marketing of the findings from a wholly different program that turned the tide.

As Head Start's star rose, so did its budget. By 1992 the program whose fate had been in doubt a decade earlier had become "the motherhood and apple pie of government programs. Everybody, rightly, is crazy about it."[36] Shades of Lyndon Johnson: the first goal specified in the "Goals 2000" legislation, passed in 1994, was that, by the start of the new millennium, all children would start school "ready to learn," with access to "high-quality and developmentally appropriate preschool." And Head Start seemed to be the surest way of getting there.[37] "This was the moment when people stopped focusing on child care [a major concern of the children's lobby during the Reagan and Bush administrations] and started thinking about universal preschool," says John Love, a senior researcher at Mathematica Policy Research.

It was too early, however, to declare victory for Head Start. When Bill Clinton proposed a big increase in its budget so that, finally, every eligible child could be enrolled, the conservatives mobilized. They had caught on to the fact that "the studies of the Perry project actually don't tell us very much about the efficacy of Head Start."[38]

The Half-Full or Half-Empty Glass

"Is early childhood education working?" The National School Boards Association asked this bottom-line question, and it wasn't meant rhetorically. What's remarkable is that the plaintive query was posed not in 1976 or 1986 but in 2006, more than two generations after Perry Preschool opened its doors.[39]

Money makes a difference. When the government commits to the level of support that exemplary programs like Perry Preschool demand, then the answer is plainly yes. But when it comes to pre-K, talk is easy and budgets are tight. Florida is a dispiriting example: in 2004 the voters there amended their constitution to require "high-quality preschool," but the state hasn't delivered the funds necessary to make that happen.[40] There isn't a single state that is spending anything close to the $13,000-per-child cost of Perry Preschool, let alone making the kind of multiyear commitment required by Abecedarian.

The research on Head Start's impact is so voluminous that, by rights, it should answer the question that the School Boards Association and numerous politicians have posed. From the outset, Head Start has been both a research lab and a social intervention. The Rand Corporation, asked by the government to design a comprehensive evaluation of the program, reported that Head Start had already "been exposed to more critical scrutiny than almost any other single federal program"—and that was in 1974.[41] Hundreds of studies have been conducted since then, and scads of articles have sought to summarize them. The research is continuing: one national survey is currently following children and families until the end of kindergarten or first grade, and another is assessing "child care" programs ranging from top-notch preschools to home care by fathers.[42] Wading through this material is like ascending a social science Tower of Babel without an Esperanto dictionary in hand.

"Does early education work?" puts the matter too loosely. The right questions are what kind of early education works best, and for whom? "Should prekindergarten programs serve both three-year-olds and four-year olds?" Edward Zigler asks. "Is a half-day program enough? What level of teacher education is needed? What are the benefits of a prekindergarten system based only in the public schools . . . ? What children benefit most?" Unfortunately, as Zigler notes, these fundamental issues are almost never explored.[43]

Some things *are* clear. Although Head Start kids record higher IQ scores and better achievement-test results at the end of preschool—which means they're learning something—this difference typically vanishes after a year or two in school. The same is usually true for reading and math scores; by third grade, the children who didn't attend Head Start have caught up. This is partly because of the sub-par elementary schools that poor children, and especially poor black children, all too frequently attend.[44] On the positive side of the ledger, Head Start youngsters are less likely to be left back or assigned to special education, and that bodes well. But because policymakers demand quick answers, it's rare to find a study that tracks children as long as into fourth grade, let alone until they're forty years old, as with the Perry preschoolers, and so their futures are fated to remain another great unknown.

Quality really *does* matter. It doesn't take superstar teachers in the Perry Preschool mold to make a difference, just better trained and better paid ones, as well as livelier classrooms and a curriculum, like High/Scope's, that engages kids' minds, not just their talent at parroting.[45] And the better a child's early education, a 2005 national child care survey analysis concludes, the more likely that early gains in reading and math achievement will be maintained. That's important, since third-grade test scores do a good job of predicting academic success down the road.[46]

The most methodologically rigorous evaluation of early education, the congressionally mandated study of Early Head Start, confirms the need to deliver something of real value. The babies who received a good early education, and whose parents got help with child rearing, were better off than those who had just one or the other kind of support. By the time they entered kindergarten, the youngsters from the Early Head Start centers who had gone on to attend Head Start when they were three did the best of all.[47]

The reverse also holds true. Classrooms that are mediocre or worse, with too many children for a teacher to notice, led by untrained instructors who have little sense of how children learn, may actually make things worse. Kids in those preschools sometimes turn out to be more aggressive later.[48] In preschool, as in life, you get what you pay for.

Almost all Head Start studies end when the children are in the third or fourth grade. The one substantial attempt to estimate Head Start's impact over the long term, carried out by Janet Currie and her colleagues at the University of California, Los Angeles, adopted a clever design. Currie compared the life histories of siblings, one of whom did and one who didn't participate in Head Start. Overall, the children who had been in Head Start were more likely to graduate from high school and attend college. But, disturbingly, only white children appeared to have benefited. This study was published in 1995, when the best-seller *The Bell Curve* was getting lots of attention by recycling Arthur Jensen's old claim that intelligence was largely inherited, and Currie touched a nerve when she identified race-specific effects.[49] She was vilified by some of her colleagues; in preschool circles a noisy, nasty argument at a national child-development conference has become the stuff of academic legend. "I was a pariah among early childhood advocates for years," says Currie. Later, she says, "I was dropped from the Head Start evaluation because I might tell the truth." In a 2002 study, Currie and her UCLA colleagues concluded that African Americans who attended Head Start benefited in one respect: they were less likely to have been booked or charged with a crime.[50]

The evidence is "uneven," says John Love at Mathematica, "and for some it's unconvincing." Estimable social scientists read the same studies very differently. NIEER's Steven Barnett identifies "lasting benefits" from Head Start, but Ron Haskins at the Brookings Institution does not. To make matters more confusing, Haskins reads Barnett's analysis of the evaluations differently than Barnett himself does.[51] These thrusts and parries can be dismissed as intramural squabbling, quotidian life in social science Babel.[52] But they are unhelpful to the National School Boards Association, whose members wonder whether it's worth spending money on preschool. Nor are they useful to Congress, which spends nearly $7 billion a year on Head Start.

A 1997 report by the Government Accountability Office concluded that the thirty years' worth of studies were "inadequate for use in drawing conclusions about the impact of the national program in areas such as school readiness," and Congress commissioned the Head Start National Impact Study in the hope of getting better answers. High time, said Haskins, a veteran of the Head Start wars: "Despite the fact that Head Start has been in operation since 1965, there has not been a random-assignment national study of the program that could provide a solid answer to the question of whether the typical Head Start program actually helps poor children increase their school readiness and subsequent achievement."[53]

Yet to hardly anyone's surprise, the first installment of this ongoing inquiry, released in 2005, delivered a mixed message. The children who attended Head Start did slightly better than those who did not attend in identifying letters, and their vocabulary was larger. The three-year-olds (but not the four-year-olds) were less likely to act out. Parents of the Head Start kids read to them more and spanked them less. That's all to the good. But these gains were generally small—two more letters for the four-year-olds, for instance—and on other key measures, including early math learning and motivation to learn, the Head Start experience had no statistically significant impact.

"Right now," Haskins points out, "the lack of longitudinal data, the inconclusive effects, the absence of knowledge of the 'active ingredient' in quality preschool, the lack of a plan to efficiently use all preschool and child care dollars, and the moderate effects of preschool and Head Start make it difficult to use research to move preschool forward at the federal level." While Congress could be pardoned for believing that, in underwriting the National Head Start National Impact Study, it would get answers to its questions, that didn't happen. What's needed, Haskins says, is yet another study, a "$1 billion demonstration with solid research."

Did the 2005 report show a glass that was half full or half empty? The reactions from Head Start's supporters and critics were as predictable as a Noh drama. They called to mind the famous *New Yorker* cartoon of an artist who, having set up his easel amid a bucolic landscape, sets about painting a surrealistic tableau. "I paint what I see," the caption reads.

"I paint what I see": the spokesman for the Bush administration, Wade Horn, saw a glass in need of refilling. It's "evidence that we can do a better job," he told the press. In a widely circulated broadside, Douglas Besharov at the conservative American Enterprise Institute bemoaned Head Start's "broken promise." The few gains that this latest research reported, he said, were "limited, making them unlikely to lead to later increases in school achievement."[54] The full-glass contingent included the National Head Start Association, which asserted that the study showed "very

good progress," and a distinguished group of researchers, among them John Love, who pointed out that the positive achievements were at least as noteworthy as those from other highly touted programs, such as delivering better child care and reducing elementary-school class sizes. To a skeptic, however, such thin praise only pointed to the wisdom of ending all such initiatives.[55] But to complicate matters further, the random-assignment feature of the experiment, intended to give credibility to the research, turned out not to be so random, since some of the children who were turned away from their neighborhood Head Start program found their way to another center. That means children who attended Head Start were actually being compared with one another, and this makes the impact of Head Start seem smaller than is really the case.

Pity the poor policymaker trying to make sense of this. What's more, the findings show the built-in limitations of this line of research: while the study does a decent job of demonstrating the impact of Head Start on standardized achievement tests, it can't answer the real question—Does the experience change children's lives over the longer term?

The Head Start study "reinforces a developing professional consensus about the program's limitations," the American Enterprise Institute's Besharov argued.[56] By "professionals," he had in mind both foundations and politicians who, as he noted approvingly, were moving away from Head Start and toward state prekindergarten. Some less ideological voices were saying much the same thing. Dick Clifford, a senior scientist at the Frank Porter Graham Child Development Institute at the University of North Carolina, had concluded that merging Head Start with state pre-K was worth a try. "If the states are serious, let's figure out whether they can do this."

Out of the Morass?

The model programs like Perry Preschool still offer the most convincing evidence that preschool can change the arc of children's lives. But to use those findings in arguing for *universal* prekindergarten, as the advocates have done, is indulging in a bit of bait and switch.

To be sure, "lots of working- and middle-class kids repeat grades, and lots of them are assigned to special education," as Lynn Karoly at Rand points out. "There's good reason to believe they would benefit from access to good preschools." But until recently there was no proof that preschool helped middle-class youngsters.[57] Two 2005 studies, one by the National Institute for Early Education Research and the other by Georgetown professors William Gormley and Deborah Phillips, begin to fill that research gap. They conclude that prekindergarten can boost academic achievement across the board. The NIEER report focuses on five states, representing a broad cross section of the country, while the Georgetown study takes a closer look at what's happening in a single city, Tulsa, Oklahoma, where preschool has been widely available since the mid-1990s.

These evaluations assess the impact of attending a high-quality preschool, with small classes and well-prepared teachers, on the academic performance of children from kindergarten to second grade. The research design that both studies use approximates the Perry Preschool gold standard of random assignment. Essentially, children who barely made the age cutoff to be eligible for prekindergarten were compared with those, otherwise identical, who just missed being eligible.[58] While some of the children who weren't eligible to attend Tulsa's pre-K doubtless stayed at home or spent their days watching TV at a neighbor's house, many enrolled in programs like Head Start or went to a child care center.

The findings hearten the prekindergarten advocates. Across the five states in the NIEER study, the good preschool experience resulted in gains in vocabulary equivalent to about three extra months of a child's development—and this is a critical difference, since the vocabulary test does a good job of predicting a child's later success in reading. On a test of early math skills like simple addition and subtraction, children who went to a state preschool scored an average of 13 percent higher. The Tulsa project reported even more impressive results, including vocabulary test-score gains equivalent to approximately seven months of development. In both studies, the gains far exceed those identified in the Head Start study, a finding that drives home the familiar point—quality is essential.[59]

What's more, middle-class children benefit from good preschool as well. In the Tulsa study, poor youngsters made the greatest gains—that's to be expected, since they started out further behind—but all the prekindergarteners did better than those who weren't enrolled.[60] This also seems to be the case in the five-state study: the impact was similar in the two states where preschool was open to every child and the three states that enrolled only poor youngsters, suggesting that social class didn't have a big effect. These state prekindergartens weren't extra-special—this isn't Perry Preschool on a mass scale—but evidently they were good enough that children from varied backgrounds learned a lot.

This is the conventional way to talk about the impact of preschool, relying on the metrics of education, such as reading and math scores. But the Perry Preschool study has become the most widely cited research in the field partly because it added another dimension to the findings. Beginning in the early 1980s, the life stories of the Perry children were translated into the language of economics. Those appraisals showed that preschool not only changed the lives of children but also made everyone else better off. Benefits and costs, consumers and investments, externalities and tradeoffs are the terms in which much of the current policy conversation is carried on. That's why economists have become pivotal figures in the preschool movement, as unlikely—and not always reliable—allies.

T·H·R·E·E

The Futures Market

ECONOMISTS have been among the most ardent, and effective, supporters of preschool. Not only have they done major scholarly work on the subject; they also go on the hustings, writing op-eds in the *Wall Street Journal,* giving talks to business leaders and public officials. Because decision makers listen to what they have to say, their support has reframed the discussion. Spending money on preschool is no longer regarded simply as something good for the young or as a way to pique children's curiosity. It is also perceived as the best strategy for maintaining America's competitive position in the world market—an "investment" in "human capital" that promises to generate "exceptional returns."[1]

These arguments have swayed powerful groups like the Business Roundtable, a group of Fortune 500 CEOs who, naturally enough, concentrate on the bottom line.[2] They have also been used to convince politicians, generally skeptical about do-goodery, that it is wise to spend tax dollars on prekindergarten. And they have been instrumental in recruiting unlikely allies like chiefs of police and district attorneys, for whom the evidence that preschool can reduce crime rates is eye-opening, as well as seniors, who are encouraged by the fact that children who go to preschool will be able to shoulder more of the tax burden when they grow up.[3]

The economists themselves are the preschool movement's least likely allies. They can be as gloomy in their appraisal of public initiatives as Eeyore in *Winnie the Pooh*, which is why the field has been called the dismal science. For many years economists believed that the surest way to reduce inequality and generate productivity was to proceed straightforwardly, redistributing wealth rather than investing in people. "The familiar definition of poverty," says Eugene Smolensky, former dean of the Goldman School of Public Policy at Berkeley, "is a lack of money. Give people money and they won't be poor." When University of Chicago economist Theodore Schultz delivered the presidential address to the American Economic Association in 1960, he found it necessary to assure his colleagues that "looking at human beings as capital goods" did not "reduce man once again to a mere material component, something akin to property."[4]

Since then, however, economists have elaborated on the idea that human capital, like physical capital, is what shapes economic growth—a version of the proverb about teaching a man to fish rather than giving him a fish.[5] If inequalities in human capital drive disparities in income, then redistribution won't do the trick; the underlying inequality must be addressed.[6]

This way of thinking gained support in the 1970s, after large-scale experiments showed that distributing dollars to the poor had the perverse effect of increasing unemployment and divorce rates.[7] Yet while investing in people seems a fine idea, the trick is to figure out how best to do it. One seemingly logical answer—

turning laid-off blue-collar workers and high-school dropouts into sought-after knowledge workers by giving them job training—has proven problematic. Highly touted programs like the Job Corps have had meager results, as the training has not typically led to better jobs. Nor have most of the recent innovations in primary and secondary education, such as charter schools, had much of an impact on student achievement.[8]

Economists are the magpies of social science, which is why there is an economics of almost everything for which there are data to be found, from sumo wrestling to abortion.[9] Confronted with the disappointing outcomes of job training and new K–12 initiatives, some of them began to poke around in early education.[10]

Prekindergarten wasn't an obvious terrain for economists to explore. Although there is a seemingly straightforward relationship between job training or high school experience and economic productivity, the link between improving the lives of toddlers and building a more prosperous society is less readily apparent. When economists started writing about kids, they didn't have a theory of child development in their heads, and so, in designing their models, they didn't distinguish between three-year-olds and fifteen-year-olds. But by the 1990s some astute members of the tribe had come to appreciate that high-quality early education was a smart public investment—a far better investment, in cost-benefit terms, than Job Corps or charter schools. The results of the Perry Preschool study, as seen through the prism of economics, propelled this newfound interest.

Cost-Benefit Analysis Gives the Preschool Movement Legs

In the fall of 1980 Steven Barnett, then a graduate student in economics at the University of Michigan, made his way to the High/

Scope Educational Research Foundation in nearby Ypsilanti, the home of the Perry Preschool study. At that time most labor economists reluctantly accepted the proposition, propounded by psychologists such as Arthur Jensen, that intelligence was fixed, but the ongoing Perry research was demonstrating that intelligence was more malleable than the hereditarians supposed. It showed that it was possible, through early education, to give children with a low IQ a better shot at success in school and afterward. That finding had potentially powerful economic consequences.[11]

High/Scope president David Weikart was an educator, not an economist, and his research had revealed the educational effects of Perry Preschool. Now, with Barnett's help, he wanted to demonstrate the economic returns as well. Presciently, he appreciated that the study would make a bigger splash if the findings were converted into the language of costs and benefits.

"The major advantage of cost-benefit analysis," says Arthur Reynolds, a psychologist and policy analyst by training who has been studying Chicago's Child-Parent Centers for a generation, "is that benefits for multiple outcomes can be summarized in dollar terms."[12] Whatever can be tabulated contributes to the bottom line, Steven Barnett adds, since "all program effects and all costs are on an equal footing."[13] What's more, because there is a common metric of dollars and cents, different policies can be pitted against one another. Reduce class size for sixth-graders or educate three-year-olds? The easiest way for policymakers to decide is to compare the cost-benefit ratios.

Cost-benefit analysis, the economists' staple, is not conceptually complicated. Add up the expenses—in this case, that's primarily the cost of the preschool education—and then tote up the benefits and compare the two. But in reality, things aren't so simple. The calculations can be controversial—what is the present value of a benefit like greater tax revenue that won't be realized until 2020? Of necessity a great deal gets omitted from the cost-benefit equation, especially things that can't be easily priced. How, for instance, does one value the special "blue-ness" of Lake Tahoe when calibrating the consequences of pollution? How does one tabulate the impact of Hurricane Katrina on the quirky culture of New Orleans, or the effect on the psyches of those who lived in a West Virginia hamlet, when a flood has wiped out their tight-knit community?[14]

The Perry Preschool cost-benefit analysis takes into account several outcomes, like special-education placements and crime rates, rarely included in prekindergarten studies. Still, there's no way to know the impact on a family of a child's attending Perry, no way to appraise the effect on a three-year-old child who, because there was a prekindergarten to go to, could escape, for a time, from the troubled terrain of Ypsilanti's housing projects.[15] In the Perry study, the gauge of citizenship for those who attended the preschool was not whether they were more likely to vote, or run for political office, or volunteer for charity work. The single measure was their criminal record. Might the fact of having gone to Perry have had an effect on the likelihood that a youngster would later smoke, use drugs, or become pregnant? Perhaps so, but since this information was not collected, it isn't part of the cost-benefit calculation.[16]

Because of the intangible character of many of these items, assigning a dollar value to them is difficult. But since rates of return have become the way of keeping score—and determining what program deserves public dollars—whatever is entered into the equation becomes the benchmark for policymakers. A child entering kindergarten should know ten letters—that is the standard that Congress has established for Head Start, for it's far easier to specify the ABC's and incorporate them into a cost-benefit analysis than to define emotional well-being.

At Perry Preschool an initial cost-benefit analysis was done in the mid-1970s, when the youngsters were fifteen years old. But because they were still in high school, many critical milestones, like graduating and getting a job, lay ahead of them; of necessity, the findings were largely speculative. By the time Steven Barnett undertook his analysis, however, the former preschoolers were nineteen, and their life trajectories had come into sharper focus.

Labor economists treat graduation from high school as critical, so Barnett's finding that preschool boosted graduation rates was of considerable interest to them.[17] The Perry participants were more likely than those who hadn't attended preschool to be working, to be earning more, and to have some savings. There was a payoff, especially to taxpayers and potential crime victims, that could be traced back to a half-day program that these nineteen-year-olds had attended in the early years of their lives. "The conclusion that one year of the Perry program was a good investment for society is nearly unassailable," Barnett wrote. "The conclusion that two years was a good investment is quite strong."[18]

In 1996, when the Perry Preschool participants were twenty-seven, the second installment of Barnett's cost-benefit analysis, *Lives in the Balance*, appeared. At that point, they were making significantly more money, and were more likely to own a home and a second car, than those who had missed out on the opportunity to go to preschool. They were also significantly less likely to have spent time in prison. The return for every dollar that had been spent on preschool, Barnett calculated, was $7.16. That figure was unmatched by any other social program, and the widely reported finding brought the Perry research into the mainstream of economics.[19]

Eight years later, when the most recent installment of this remarkably long-running study was published, the Perry participants were in their forties. The cost-benefit ratio had risen to an astronomical seventeen to one, and the annual return on the preschool investment exceeded 11 percent. Perry Preschool had outperformed the stock market by nearly two to one.[20]

Beyond Perry:
The Endorsement of a Nobel Prize–Winner

Soon enough other economists chimed in, and they came at the issue from complementary angles. Clive Belfield, an economist at Queens College and coauthor of the 2004 Perry Preschool study, found that the public schools would realize big savings by offering high-quality pre-K, since retention rates and special-education placements would be considerably lower. That finding drew the attention of cash-strapped school administrators. Since publishing that paper, Belfield says, "I've gotten calls from many states, asking me if I would take a look at what's going on there."[21]

John Donohue at Yale and Peter Siegelman at Fordham applied the metric of cost-benefit and found that savings in prison time alone would more than pay for the cost of a Perry Preschool–caliber program. "Society should begin the process of trying to see whether such interventions can actually be carried out on a meaningful scale," they concluded, "rather than unthinkingly committing itself to a policy of massive prison construction."[22] That way of framing the question, the dollars-and-cents value of preschools versus prisons, prompted Fight Crime: Invest in Kids, a national advocacy group representing police chiefs and district attorneys, to make preschool a top priority.

"I thought of the problem in economic-development terms," says Art Rolnick, another economist who has become intrigued by early education. As the research director at the Federal Reserve Bank in Minneapolis, during the 1990s Rolnick had tried convincing city officials that subsidizing sports stadiums was a money-losing proposition. The practice of pitting municipalities against one another in bidding wars to lure companies like Mercedes-Benz or Boeing was, at best, a zero-sum game—what one city gained, another lost—that caused legal as well as economic headaches.

The 2001 recession gave Rolnick an opening to inject early education into the conversations. "Confronted with budget deficits," he wrote, "public officials and citizens ask themselves the question: What is the best use of our limited resources?"[23] The answer, he said, was early childhood development. Two years later, when he started talking about prekindergarten, the studies showing the outsized returns from Perry Preschool, Chicago's Child-Parent Centers, and the Abecedarian Project were widely known, as was the research on early brain development, and Rolnick spread the word. His position at the Federal Reserve gave him access to business and community leaders who had never thought about preschool. Soon enough his phone was ringing off the hook. "There's a movement in this country," he says.

Rolnick has also promoted his own early education scheme: a preschool voucher for all poor three- to five-year-olds in Minnesota, and mentoring for their parents, starting when the children are still in their cribs. "I have a strong belief in the market mechanism for delivering results," he says—"where there's competition, there's innovation"—and so his plan relies on high-quality private preschools selected by parents. This choice-driven, family-partnership concept has won him friends among organizations like the Taxpayers League of Minnesota, which is normally allergic to any new public initiative.

"The program won't come cheap," Rolnick adds, "but it doesn't cost more than two or three sports stadiums."

Art Rolnick's mentor in the economics of early childhood was James Heckman at the University of Chicago. Heckman is an economist's economist, legendary among his peers for his brilliance in constructing statistical models of complex phenomena. He won the Nobel Prize in 2000 for his methodological wizardry, and at the ceremonies in Stockholm he delivered a lecture with the forbidding title "Microdata, Heterogeneity, and the Evaluation of Public Policy." Even in its published form this speech is tough going for many economists; for most of the guests on that balmy evening, decked out in their ballroom finery and penguin suits, basking in the afterglow of a wine-and-cigars banquet, it was doubtless impossible to follow.

But Heckman isn't only a numbers geek. "I've never just wanted to sit behind my desk with my equations," he says. He has a reformer's zeal to reduce inequality, a commitment molded by his having grown up in the Jim Crow world of the 1950s South. "Trying to understand the sources of black-white disparity will occupy me throughout my life," he says.[24]

The best way to think about these social problems is to construct economic models, Heckman argues, reciting what he regards as the shortcomings of other disciplines. "Psychologists are narrow in their focus, insistent on an unrealistic standard of proof—if it's not significant at the .01 level [that means there's a 99 percent probability that the results aren't due to chance] it gets discarded," he says with disbelief. "Bench scientists—those who study emotional attachment in chimpanzees, for instance—are doing important work, but while they want to be relevant to policy they are essentially pure researchers." He scoffs that the typical approach in program evaluation is to take the data, look for whatever is statistically significant, and then analyze it. By contrast, economists begin with a theory, he says, "a model that can be tested, and what's important can be isolated. The hope is to come up with the ingredients of an intervention that works. A single good model is worth a thousand empirical studies."

Heckman was one of the economists whose intellectual gaze shifted progressively downward during the 1990s, from job-training programs for adults to K–12 school reform to prekindergarten.[25] He wanted to devise a model for understanding how individuals develop skills—what economists call a production function for human capability. As he read omnivorously—reports on everything from the research on maternal attachment in rats to the long-term effects of Chicago's Child-Parent Centers—and spent endless hours talking with the topflight researchers, everything converged on a single conclusion: that investing in young children generates the biggest economic return.[26]

The smartest move that anyone can make is to pick the right family to be born into, since parents have the biggest influence over how children turn out. Although there is no way to swap families, no kibbutz for America, sending a disadvantaged youngster to a place like Perry Preschool helps to narrow the gap. "Because those children are more highly motivated to succeed, they will do better in school, even though their IQ scores don't improve. Skill begets skill and learning begets learning."[27] Prekindergarten is important, since early investments increase the returns to later investments; but what happens afterward is important as well, because those later investments make the early ones pay off.[28]

Economists who study education usually focus on reading and math test scores, rather than on what Heckman refers to as the soft stuff. "When you start talking about a mother's love or giving people emotional support, well, that sounds like you've been watching *Oprah*."[29] But his own research on high school dropouts led him down the *Oprah* path. "People who take the high school equivalency test are just as smart as high school graduates who don't go on to college," he says, "but they're the wise guys. They don't have the necessary motivation and self-control to succeed." That's why they typically make less money, are more likely to wash out of the military and less likely to go back to school.[30]

When Heckman traced this train of thought back to preschool, the importance of the "soft stuff" became even more apparent. "The data on the expulsion of kids from preschool indicate that there's a problem," he says.[31] "And if you ask kindergarten teachers, they'll tell you that they can easily teach letters and numbers. Their real concern is whether kids can control their emotions, work together, and avoid physical violence." In a 2006 study, Heckman compared the long-term effects of cognitive and non-cognitive ability.[32] Early reading and math scores are as reliable in predicting how much a person will earn later in life as measures of an individual's feeling of self-worth. But when it comes to criminal behavior, smoking, drug use, or becoming a single parent, emotional maturity is often a better indicator.[33]

A good preschool, Heckman argues, shouldn't fixate on either book learning or playground learning. This assertion won't come as news to Vivian Paley, the longtime teacher at the University of

Chicago's Lab School whose books describe in loving detail what life is like in the best of those classrooms.[34] Nor will it impress Robert Sternberg at Yale, who for thirty years has been studying the multiple dimensions of intelligence.[35] But the fact that this point is being advanced by an unlikely ally, a Nobel Prize–winner in a hard-nosed field, who arrived there by a different intellectual route, gives the proposition fresh legs. Since economists are the only social scientists to whom policymakers regularly listen, Heckman is better positioned than anyone else in academe to confront the "no preschooler left behind" mind-set.

Universal Preschool and the Economists' Blind Spot

In a 2006 *Wall Street Journal* opinion piece, "Catch 'Em Young," Heckman makes the economist's case for offering good, state-supported prekindergarten to disadvantaged youngsters. But for him, universal pre-K is another story. "Children from advantaged environments receive substantial early investment" from their parents, he argued, and so "there is little basis for providing universal programs at zero cost, although some advocate such a policy."[36] For "some," read "the Pew Charitable Trusts." You can imagine the "ouch" emanating from the foundation's Philadelphia headquarters, since Pew has made "prekindergarten for *all*," not just for some, its theme. Yet Heckman's stance is consistent with the position taken by most economists, whatever their political stripe. That makes them unreliable allies in the campaign for universal pre-K.

Efficiency—bang for the buck—is the economists' usual starting point, and concentrating public dollars on poor kids, rather than spreading them among all children, seems like an Economics 1 example of efficiency. No one has studied the long-term effects of the 92nd Street Y in Manhattan or the University of Chicago's Lab School. What would be the point, since most of the four-year-olds lucky enough to have been taught by someone like Vivian Paley are children of privilege? Because youngsters from fraught backgrounds begin so far back in the intellectual- and cultural-capital derby, they are likely to gain more from pre-K, in the process narrowing the social-class gap in education. Pre-K for the disadvantaged, Heckman argues, represents one of those rare policies "that promotes fairness and social justice and, at the same time, promotes productivity in the economy and in society at large."[37]

In short, focusing on poor children looks to be both fairer and more efficient. For most economists, that's case closed.

Reopening this issue requires separating the economists' methods from their worldview, which is inattentive to slippery matters like politics and ethics. It also means challenging a way of thinking that gives pride of place to elegant models, with their power to simplify, rather than the complicated and complicating facts on the ground.

"This bias against universalism collides with Planet Reality," says NIEER's Steven Barnett, one of the few dissenters in the trade. While the direct cost of targeted pre-K programs is lower, he argues, in practice targeting has never meant that poor kids get a Perry Preschool–type education. Instead, the teachers usually have weaker credentials, often just a high school degree; even Head Start requires teachers to have only two years of college. The lack of quality is no coincidence, says Barnett: "Programs for the poor are poor programs."[38]

Helping *all of us* and not just *them*—that division makes all the difference in the world. In theory, concentrating state prekindergarten entirely on poor children should help to close the education gap, and that would be a good thing. But a study carried out by two World Bank economists concluded that, when the voters effectively set tax levels, the poor are in fact *worse* off when a program is targeted, because the citizenry is willing to pony up much less money.[39] That apparent paradox suggests that the conventional economic wisdom may be wrong—offering preschool to every child might actually be more efficient.[40]

"What's required is to intervene early, often, and effectively," says Isabel Sawhill, a senior economist at the Brookings Institution who was an associate director at the Office of Management and Budget in the Clinton administration.[41] Sawhill and Georgetown University public policy professor Jens Ludwig have proposed a nationwide initiative, which they label Success by Ten, that would focus on poor children. Until the age of five, the youngsters would go to an Abecedarian-type center; for the next five years, to age ten, they would enroll in Success for All, a program that has had success in improving reading achievement. Sawhill is among the ablest analysts around, and on its merits, the proposal looks reasonable. But Success by Ten would cost $40 billion a year, and despite the contention that the investment would eventually pay off two or three times over, the congressional track record, from Head Start to the present, suggests that it will be a hard sell.

Forty years ago the *Equal Educational Opportunity Survey* concluded that the best thing the public schools could offer to poor children was the chance to attend school with classmates from better-off families.[42] Children learn a lot from one another. Cultural capital rubs off, and so do vocabulary words.

What's true of school-age children is even truer when it comes to three- and four-year-olds, whose implicit rules of etiquette are less race- and class-conscious. The available evidence points in that direction. A nationwide study in Britain found that youngsters from poor families who go to preschool with middle-class kids do better than those who are educated in social and economic isolation.[43] And the same appears to be true for children enrolled in Georgia's universal preschool program: when it comes to reading and math achievement, poor kids do best in socially mixed classes.[44]

Most parents send their children to pre-K in their own, typically homogeneous, neighborhoods. But some do look elsewhere for, say, a Montessori preschool, which can attract a mix of students because of its educational philosophy. To be sure, such natural integration is rare—and no one is talking about putting three-year-olds on buses to desegregate the nurseries—but universal prekindergarten may be the last and best, if remote, hope for bridging social divides. That hope will vanish if only poor and working-class children can enroll in state-sponsored preschools, because economic segregation will have been codified into law.

"I've been troubled from day one that we came up with a system that segregated kids," says Edward Zigler, who, when he ran Head Start, was lambasted for attempting to open the centers to middle-class youngsters. "Does anybody think that that is a moral society?"

Making prekindergarten available to everyone could well boost its political appeal. Despite what some economists think, this isn't a criticism but an apt illustration of what Alexis de Tocqueville, in touting American democracy, described as "self-interest rightly understood."[45] It's why government builds highways and libraries—and it's why, even as the War on Poverty ended so ingloriously, Social Security and Medicare, two federal programs that benefit everyone, have flourished.[46]

A 2006 Brookings Institution policy brief comes to a similar conclusion about the value of universalism via another route. By 2035, the report concludes, a national, high-quality, universal preschool program open to all three- and four-year-olds would start paying for itself; by 2080 it would add an estimated $2 *trillion* (in 2006 dollars) to the annual gross domestic product. That's a 3.5 percent increase in the GNP, and the analysis doesn't incorporate other well-documented benefits, like cutting crime rates.[47] What's more, middle-class as well as poor youngsters gain. No bright line separates poor and not-so-poor children when it comes to the skills they bring to the classroom. As things stand, the families caught in the middle, earning too much to be eligible for Head Start but not enough to afford high-quality pre-K, often wind up in threadbare child care centers like the Teddy Bear preschools in Chicago.[48]

The Limits of Economic Reasoning

"In 2004 I was at a luncheon with some politicians, journalists, and civic leaders," Art Rolnick of the Minneapolis Federal Reserve recalls. "The speaker, who was from a local pre-K group, was talking about why it's so important for children [that we] support early development. I raised my hand. 'You are making a moral argument,' I said, 'but I can make just as good a moral argument for K–12, or higher education. I suspect there's some economic research about preschool.'" Rolnick has the economist's unthinking arrogance about ethics; he presumes that all moral propositions are on the same plane, and so, unlike cost-benefit formulations, don't help in making policy choices.

From the initial study of Perry Preschool in the 1980s to the latest state-by-state cost-benefit analyses, the effects of early education on civic engagement have never found a home in the economists' equations. Yet without an engaged polity to set public priorities, America is no more than an economic engine.

Elsewhere, universalism has been promoted mainly because it contributes to nation building. It goes hand in hand with the idea that, when it comes to basic matters like education and social security, a country is stronger if everyone is in the same boat.[49] "There should be no sense of inferiority, pauperism or stigma in the use of a publicly provided service," wrote Richard Titmuss, the architect of the British Labour Party's post–World War II agenda, "no attribution that one was being or becoming a 'public burden.'"[50] Turn back the clock a generation in the United States, to the 1984 Democratic national convention and New York governor Mario Cuomo's memorable keynote speech that summoned the country to reclaim the vision of itself as the shining city on a hill. While convention speeches are notoriously unmemorable, this one sticks in the minds of many who heard it (Google, our collective memory, registers 11,900 hits). Is there a persuasive way to put out the same call today? If not, then almost by default the language of "investment," "cost-benefit," and "returns"—the language of economics—will continue to dominate the public conversation.

The economists' calculations have provided preschool activists with a potent frame for their position. No longer must they come hat in hand, pleading, like claimants for so many causes, that preschool is morally right. Instead they can appeal directly to pocketbook interests. Talking about prekindergarten in terms of what's good for the economy is a marked improvement over the laissez-faire view that families should be left entirely to their own devices when it comes to preschool education. Still, it is a vocabulary that can tell only part of the early-childhood story, a point of view that can encompass only a fraction of what children, and society, need.

F·O·U·R

The Imprimatur of Science

David L. Kirp and Jeff Wolf

THE IMPRIMATUR of science has been a godsend to the advocates of early childhood education, because claims rooted in science readily trump arguments premised on hunch or hope. And when the advocates point to scientific studies as intellectual backing, it is almost always neuroscience to which they are referring.

This research, coupled with the long-term studies of Perry Preschool and the calculations of economic benefit, has been effectively used by advocates of preschool to argue their case. Yet neuroscience isn't only, or mainly, focused on three- and four-year-olds. Its interest, considerably broader, is in the shaping of a child's potential, from the moment of conception, through intrauterine experiences, through adolescence, and even beyond. As the political focus expands to encompass the concerns of children more generally, neuroscience—and genetics as well—will become even more pertinent.

Neuroscience: Wiring the Brain

The findings from brain science are indeed dramatic: 100 billion neurons at birth; neural synapses created and discarded at astonishing speeds early in life. At no other time in life does the brain evolve as rapidly as during the first years. The brain's early development is crucial—and by extension that makes good preschool crucial as well.

In broad terms, the research supports the advocates' contention. From laboratory experiments on rats and chimpanzees, as well as from Romanian orphanages—horrific natural experiments—emerge findings that occupy a central place in the prekindergarten dialogues. They buttress the results of studies like Perry Preschool, which show that early education can shape life prospects.

But bench science and advocacy are fundamentally different enterprises. Science traffics in provisional findings, not certainties, and today's results are subject to revision tomorrow. To date, the research has more to say about the effects of deprivation than enrichment; it cannot specify that educational regimen "X" is most beneficial for children. Yet when this science is marketed for popular consumption, sound bites often stretch the boundaries of knowledge beyond the breaking point. Advocates understandably want to use whatever comes to hand in making their case, but too often this leads to "campaign journalism," as scientific results are selectively interpreted to conform to the activists' agenda.[1] This frustrates the scientists, whose credibility depends on the accurate reporting of their work. It should also worry the early education movement, since the risk of hype is disillusionment and backlash if the promised payoff fails to materialize.

"The field has gone as far as it can based on advocacy," Jack

Shonkoff told a standing-room-only crowd at the 2004 meeting of the Society for Research in Child Development. Shonkoff, a pediatrician by training, directs the Center on the Developing Child at Harvard. He has situated himself at the intersection of the latest research and the design of smart policy. As coeditor of the highly influential book *From Neurons to Neighborhoods*, published in 2000, he brought together leading scholars from an array of disciplines to craft a state-of-the-art assessment; the Center on the Developing Child, which he founded in 2006, has carried on that work.[2]

"The problem in the field is oversimplification," Shonkoff told the gathering. "What's needed is a real scientific base."

This "real scientific basis" remains largely a promise, not a reality. Despite the claims of the most ardent advocates, no straight line connects the research in neuroscience to the betterment of ordinary children's lives. When parents inquire about the best preschool for their youngster, or teachers want to know whether the Reggio Emilia approach or Direct Instruction is the most effective pedagogical strategy, brain science has nothing to contribute—not yet, at least. But that doesn't mean, as the revisionists contend, that the importance of the first three years to brain development is merely a "myth."

The claims and counterclaims about the relevance of brain studies are confusing to policymakers as well as to parents. What's to be believed? One-liners such as "the myth of the first three years" versus "use it or lose it" don't begin to do justice to the research. Early education, like much in the life history of infants and toddlers, affects the architecture of a child's brain. But that's just part of the story. Neuroscientists are beginning to understand that what happens before birth—the stresses and toxicities that can accompany pregnancy—also has life-shaping repercussions. And they are learning as well about the brain's plasticity, its remarkable capacity to remake itself throughout most of the life cycle. These findings are consistent with what's being discovered across the scientific universe. Until recently neuroscience, quantitative and molecular genetics, cognitive and developmental psychology, and bioecology were distinct and sometimes warring dominions. But in an intellectually momentous paradigm shift, the research in these fields is converging on the proposition that, in comprehending human development, the old dichotomy between heredity and environment can no longer be maintained. The language of developmental influence is changing to reflect this paradigmatic shift. Rather than speaking about nature *versus* nurture, the frames of reference are nature *through* nurture and nurture *through* nature.[3]

That's why early education is meaningful—and it is also why early education isn't the *only* thing that is meaningful. There is no better example of this dynamic than the development of the human brain.

The "Pop Star" Brain

In July 2005, advocates of universal preschool from around the country met in Marina del Rey, California, to plan a state-by-state campaign. They knew how to put together coalitions and get things done. The activists had been handpicked by Libby Doggett, executive director of Pre-K Now, an advocacy organization funded by the Pew Charitable Trusts as part of its multipronged strategy to stump for universal preschool nationwide. Doggett is perhaps the wisest head in the business, and the organizers she selected came from states where universal prekindergarten looked to have the best shot.

There was considerable discussion at that gathering about

which pitches worked best—what belonged in the "message box," in the lingo of social marketing—and the brain (along with the "economic investment" argument) had pride of place. "Ninety percent of the brain's development occurs by age five," said Susanna Cooper, communications director for Preschool California, that state's main pre-K lobbying group. This contention makes people prick up their ears, which is why it had been inserted into the message box.[4] But it makes neuroscientists shudder, for such precision is misleading—the implication that the die has been cast by the time a child enters kindergarten is just plain wrong.

The "90 percent" assertion also troubles those in the early education community who concentrate not on preschool but on the needs of infants and toddlers. With public dollars scarce, the two camps find themselves scrapping for funds, and for the most part the pre-K partisans are winning.[5] Beginning in the mid-1990s, the birth-to-three advocates made much of the supposed fact that 75 percent of the brain's growth occurred by the age of three. Now they watch the parade pass them by. Not only is prekindergarten siphoning money; it is also hijacking their science.

Despite the reservations of the researchers and the anxiety of the babies' champions, neuroscience has been front and center in the long march for universal prekindergarten. "I care about the brain research," says actor and filmmaker Rob Reiner, who has done more than anyone in the country to popularize it, "because it's a way of getting people to pay attention."

On April 17, 1997, eight years before this pre-K advocates' caucus in California, a White House conference titled "What New Research on the Brain Tells Us about Our Youngest Children" marked the culmination of a well-orchestrated publicity campaign organized by Rob Reiner and his wide circle of friends.[6] Developmental neuroscience—a field that only a few years earlier had been the province of the specialists—was everywhere in the news.

Reiner is no more than one degree of separation from any opinion shaper in the country. Beginning in the mid-1990s, when the needs of young children became his consuming passion, he used his Rolodex to great advantage. Over the course of the next two years, he enlisted Hollywood stars, White House staffers, foundation officials, early childhood researchers, and public relations experts—to considerable effect. In the spring of 1996, *Newsweek* ran a cover story titled "Your Child's Brain," and the number of requests for reprints, well over a million, broke the magazine's record.[7] A special *Time* magazine report, "How a Child's Brain Develops," focused on the "breathtaking" discoveries that "underscore the importance of hands-on parenting."[8] *Good Morning America* and the *Today Show* both broadcast week-long series on the new brain science.

Politicians, following the herd instinct of the breed, leapt aboard the bandwagon. Georgia Governor Zell Miller, who in 1995 had launched the nation's first universal preschool program, started sending every new mother home from the hospital with a classical music CD, in the belief that Mozart could stimulate the brain, while Florida lawmakers, similarly impressed by this so-called Mozart effect, required that babies in child care centers receive a daily dose of classical music.[9] ABC aired an hour-long television special in 1997 called *I Am Your Child,* written by Rob Reiner and narrated by Tom Hanks. Anyone who was anyone, from Oprah Winfrey and Billy Crystal to Colin Powell and First Lady Hillary Clinton, made an appearance on the program.

The 1997 White House conference was the crowning event for

Reiner's crusade. The first lady's opening remarks were broadcast to schools and hospitals in thirty-seven states.[10] Some of the country's leading scientists and physicians were in attendance, as was David Hamburg, president of the Carnegie Corporation. A 1994 Carnegie Corporation report titled *Starting Points* had made only fleeting reference to neuroscience, but those few paragraphs, rather than the detailed discussion of the "quiet crisis" in the lives of poor children on which the report focused, had kick-started the drive.[11]

The new brain research, Hillary Clinton declared, marked a scientific revolution of Copernican proportions. "Fifteen years ago we thought a baby's brain structure was virtually complete at birth. Now we understand that everything we do with a child has some kind of potential physical influence on that rapidly forming brain."[12] In his cameo appearance, President Clinton was similarly exuberant. "We have gone across the globe, we have gone into the skies, and now we are going deep into ourselves and into our children. In some ways, this may be the most exciting and important exploration of all."[13] It was like the *Star Trek* script, slightly rewritten—the brain, and not space, had become the final frontier.

The Clintons are politicians, not researchers, and they were delivering a motivational message, not nuanced science. "No neuroscientists ever got up there and said that 'zero to three' was the most important time for learning," recalled Carla Shatz, a developmental neurobiologist at Harvard Medical School who attended the event.[14] The first lady herself sounded a note of caution. "I hope this does not create the impression that, once a child's third birthday rolls around, the important work is over," she said. But for many parents that was the take-away message.

"A break in logic occurred," noted Shatz. What began as an effort to help those kids whose chaotic early experiences put them in the greatest danger of future failure turned into a middle-class parenting frenzy. Building on the momentum generated by the White House conference and the TV special, Reiner launched the I Am Your Child Foundation and began producing star-studded child-rearing videos; the initial video was titled *The First Years Last Forever*. The foundation later changed its name to Parents' Action for Children, signaling an expanded mission: the mobilization of parents nationwide "to demand change and act on behalf of their children." Universal preschool is high on the group's priority list.[15]

Although the scientists embraced the advocates' goals—that's why so many of them came to the showcase event—many of them disliked how their findings were being represented. In September 1998, when a group of distinguished researchers came together to swap notes, those overstatements were a topic of mutual concern. Afterward, meeting organizer Charles Nelson, a developmental neuroscientist now at Harvard Medical School, sent a letter to Rob Reiner that expressed his colleagues' unhappiness. "The jury is still out about the importance of the first few years of life," Nelson wrote. But that kind of nonfinding wasn't something the I Am Your Child Foundation could use.[16]

The brain has bedazzled the early education movement. During the 1990s preschool advocates mined the relevant neuroscience literature, boning up on topics ranging from neural connections to Romanian orphans. Although little of what they unearthed was actually new, when the movement took off the findings looked like nuggets of pure gold.

Use it or lose it—that is how, at least in the early days of the campaign, the scientific findings were interpreted. At the University of Chicago, in studies dating to the 1970s, Peter

Huttenlocher and his research team counted the number of synapses (the microscopic junctures between neurons) in the brain at various stages of life. During a child's first three years those synapses are being created at a superfast rate, Huttenlocher reported. Subsequently the connections that go unused are selectively eliminated, while those that get stimulated are integrated into the architecture of the developing brain. The advocates extrapolated from that finding to the conclusion that if infants don't acquire certain abilities by the age of three, when synaptic pruning begins, then they can never acquire those skills.

A series of experiments conducted by Harvard Medical School researchers David Hubel and Torsten Weisel, started in the 1960s, seemed vividly to illustrate this point. When the researchers stitched shut one eye of a kitten for the first three months of its life, the kitten remained permanently blind in that eye.[17] Their research earned the scientists a Nobel Prize and apparently offered proof that early experience was critical. It was easy enough to imagine that what was true for kittens held true for human babies as well.

Studies of deprived children also underscored the weightiness of early experiences. In the 1990s Sir Michael Rutter and his associates at the University of London began to trace the life stories of children who had been treated inhumanely as infants and toddlers in Romanian orphanages, and were later adopted by British families. Some of the children had a hard time forging emotional connections, and confirming physiological evidence of the enduring effects of their first years was found in chemical analyses and brain studies.[18] Conditions in those orphanages were less like an American ghetto than a gulag. Still, the prospect that children growing up in dicey neighborhoods in the United States might suffer similarly long-lasting damage was treated as giving scientific warrant to intervention—not for removing them from those homes, but for guaranteeing them good care and education. Consistent with the findings on the Romanian orphans, a host of animal studies identified the durable, traumatic effects of taking baby rats and chimpanzees away from their mothers. And at the other end of the enrichment-deprivation spectrum were animal experiments intimating that enhancing the environment could work wonders. In studies carried out by William Greenough at the University of Illinois, young rats raised in a complex environment together with other rat pups had a higher density of synapses than those placed in barren and solitary confinement. The creation of "smarter" rats made a memorable story—and not just for rodents. If mental gymnastics is good for young rats, the reasoning went, surely it would be helpful to human babies as well.[19]

None of these interpretations does justice to the nuanced nature of the findings, a point to which we'll return shortly. For now, what's important is how this research was presented in the media—not as a series of complicated and provisional results, but as proof that what happens in a child's first years makes all the difference in the world.

The pivotal importance of infancy to human development was hardly novel when, in the 1990s, Rob Reiner initiated his media blitz to popularize brain science. From Benjamin Spock to T. Berry Brazelton, one generation's child guru to the next, the significance of the earliest years had been the leitmotiv.[20] Appraisals of exemplary initiatives like Perry Preschool and the Abecedarian Project, as well as the nationwide evaluation of Early Head Start and generations of research in developmental psychology, have shown the value of early education. Still, none of those studies became the stuff of TV specials or *Time* magazine cover stories, while neuroscience seized the limelight.[21]

Why so?

Brain science is widely perceived as a "hard" science, with white-coated researchers beavering away in their laboratories, and that gives it special credibility. Neuroscientists don't talk about attachment or maternal bonding, concepts that sound like something lifted straight from the nursery. Instead they speak of neuronal connections, hard wiring, and brain architecture. Their poetry is the language of engineers—babies "wired to learn" and "computers made of neurons."

This vocabulary, and the cast of mind that it reflects, has intrigued a powerful new audience. Democrats had long monopolized children's issues—conservatives sneered at the field as the domain of the political ladies bountiful—but the seductiveness of brain science has attracted lawmakers from both sides of the aisle.

What's more, advances in technology have made it possible to visualize the brain at work. Since the earliest days of neuroscience, new techniques of visualization have stimulated new research. The neuron doctrine itself, the cornerstone of the discipline, was formulated in the wake of a technological advance. In the 1870s an Italian scientist named Camillo Golgi introduced a novel staining method for visualizing nerve cells, to stunning effect. Before Golgi came along, "The eye [was] in a tangled thicket where sight may stare and grope for ever fruitlessly, baffled in its effort to unravel confusion and lost for ever in a twilit doubt," rhapsodized Santiago Ramón y Cajal, whose Nobel Prize–winning research revolutionized the field. But with Golgi's new technique, "all was sharp as a sketch with Chinese ink on transparent Japanese paper."[22]

A century or so later, further new technologies excited the

neuroscientists and mesmerized the public.[23] CAT scans, PET scans, MRIs—these acronyms are now common parlance. CAT (computerized axial tomography) scans, a radiographic technique developed in the 1970s, enabled researchers to see images of the brain, though only anatomically. With PET (positron-emission tomography) scans and fMRI, or functional magnetic resonance imaging, neuroscientists could actually watch the brain at work. Suddenly it became possible to trace the neural correlates of human behavior.

This is when neuroscience entered the social mainstream, as vivid images of the functioning brain claimed a place in the popular imagination, akin to the way we reacted to the first photos beamed back from the moon. These brain scans do not unlock the ultimate mysteries of the brain. But, remarkably, they can show the biological responses associated with real experiences such as learning the way to San José, experiencing schadenfreude, sensing the touch of a lover's hand entwined in our own, and even the firing of single cells when we're presented with the image of a movie actress.[24]

In November 2006 CBS launched a TV show, *3 Lbs.*, about the travails of a brain surgeon, played by Stanley Tucci. The medical drama gave as much air time to close-ups of gray matter as to the doctors' soap operas. "The brain," a *New York Times* reporter observed, "has become a pop star."[25]

The market has cashed in on the belief that early brain development is the secret of success. At a time when parents are looking for every edge for their children, when preschools can charge more than universities—and have longer waiting lists—what's peddled as brain food flies off the shelves.

"Did you know that you can actually help to enhance the development of your baby's brain?" asks the copy on the back cover of a DVD titled *The Baby Prodigy*. "The first thirty months of life is the period when a child's brain undergoes its most critical stages of evolution." BabyPlus, a company that markets a prenatal sound-delivery system, claims that its product will help "babies and children reach their milestones earlier." Many parents have embraced the notion that, when it comes to the forming of the brain, there is a window of opportunity that closes early. As one well-educated, professional—and plainly fearful—mother told a writer for the *Atlantic Monthly*, "It sounds panicky, I know, but if those neurons are dying off. You have to get in there. If my baby doesn't use it with a stimulating game or class, he is going to lose it."[26]

The I Am Your Child Foundation's message, that the early years are forever, cuts two ways. It offers a promise that doing the right things from the start—classical music in the cradle, *Baby Einstein* DVDs for infants, and BabyPlus even before birth—will pay big dividends. But the threat that it's impossible to recover the lost ground of missed early opportunities taps into middle-class parents' fears of being insufficiently dutiful. *Everything I Need to Know I Learned in Kindergarten* has it all wrong, parents are being told, because by kindergarten it's too late. Use it—or else lose it, and try again with the next child.

The controversial 1994 book *The Bell Curve* makes an argument for *genetic* determinism—nature explains essentially everything—but, as we'll show later in this chapter, the racial and social-class overtones make genetics anathema to liberals.[27] The early education movement, though, which commands widespread allegiance from the political left, risks falling into the trap of what psychologist Jerome Kagan calls "*infant* determinism," the mistaken belief that everything that really matters happens early in life. This model of the mind, Kagan adds, also has a racial and class dimension: for genes, substitute parenting. "It is considerably more expensive," as Kagan writes, "to improve the quality of housing, education and health of children living in poverty in America than to urge their mothers to kiss, talk to, and play with them more consistently."[28]

Criticisms and Complexities

As predictably as the sequence of the seasons, hype generates counterhype. A book bearing the provocative title *The Myth of the First Three Years* made a splash when it came out in 1999. Its author, John Bruer, runs a foundation that funds psychological and biomedical research. A philosopher by training, he plainly relishes a take-no-prisoners style of argument. In his polemic Bruer skewers the birth-to-three movement for contending that "what we know about brain development during the first years of life [is] 'the key to problem solving at every level of society.'"[29] He derides Zell Miller's "Mozart for babies" campaign and lays waste to the work of Ron Kotulak, who, in a Pulitzer Prize–winning series in the *Chicago Tribune*, purported to locate in neuroscience an explanation for the genesis of everything from genius to criminality, Albert Einstein to Jeffrey Dahmer.[30]

The rats and the kittens, the orphans and the chimps: these studies have been treated as gospel, relied on as a scientific rationale for making a greater social commitment to the young. While Bruer's book goes too far in its emperor's-new-clothes rhetoric, it does offer necessary qualifications to the claims that were in widespread circulation. Just as Charles Nelson argued in his cautionary letter to Rob Reiner, none of the brain research bears the weight that the advocates were placing on it. Nor does it have anything to say to parents anxious to do the best by their kids.

Consider William Greenough's "clever" rats that supposedly made great gains when raised in a world of rodent wonders.[31] Contrary to the popular gloss, those studies do not show that enriched early experience is needed to accelerate brain development. Quite the opposite: they conclude that learning is a life-long process. Even the youngest rats in the experiment were adolescents, not babies, and when the adult rats were taken out of isolation and placed in normal rodent environments, their brains also developed new synapses. As Greenough himself has been at pains to point out, the study confirms the negative consequences of living in extreme deprivation—the equivalent, for rodents, of the Romanian orphanages—rather than the benefits of enrichment. The complex and communal settings in which the rats flourished more closely mimicked nature than the bleak isolated cages. Nor was the rats' brain development accelerated by being placed in the hyperstimulating environment: even when moved to the rodent equivalent of the University of Chicago's Lab School, they didn't become brighter any faster.

A considerable amount is understood about the emotional development of chimpanzees, and that work has been relied on in teaching parents how to do a better job of raising their kids. Experiments have demonstrated that baby chimps need a secure mother, or a supermom substitute, to develop normally, and brain scans have confirmed what observation has shown. But it's not evident how this pertains to bringing up kids, beyond the obvious point that they shouldn't be left home alone.

Nor can much be gleaned about the lives of normal children from the vividly evocative images produced by fMRI studies. Scientists have carried out brain scans on children with severe neurological impairment as a way of isolating, and eventually treating, the damage. But when it comes to peering inside the brain of the typical youngster, the researchers have, at least for now, bumped up against the limits of technology. The techniques used to generate such spectacular images in adults have only rarely been used on healthy children, either because they are too dangerous or because they require, implausibly, that kids cease their squirming for thirty or forty minutes at a stretch.

There are vital periods for particular aspects of brain development, as neural circuits develop their architecture based on experience. But these periods aren't here today, gone tomorrow; they taper off gradually, which is why scientists have come to call them *sensitive* periods, rather than critical ones.[32] What's more, these periods are implicated in determining basic brain functions such as sight ("experience-expectant" processes, neuroscientists call them), and in the normal course of a baby's life the brain will receive the needed stimuli.[33] The brain is hierarchical in developing skills. Sensitive periods for the acquisition of basic information end earliest, while more refined information reshapes the brain through the course of a lifetime. Only if parents seal their children in a dark closet—or, as scientists have done with kittens and monkeys, if they stitch their eyelids shut for the first months of their lives—will sight be forever impaired.[34]

Similarly, the evidence gleaned from studying the children from Romanian orphanages, settings in which infants were tethered to their bedposts, has at most limited relevance to ordinary youngsters' lives. By no stretch of the imagination can that nightmarish experience be likened to growing up helter-skelter in the inner city; any parent, rich or poor, who raised a child like a Strasbourg goose would be jailed for child abuse.[35]

Perhaps the most intriguing finding is that many of the Romanian orphans, especially those adopted and taken out of the orphanage very young, have shown remarkable resilience. The extent to which they have bounced back varies greatly, even among those who were removed from the orphanage at the same age. Some of the youngsters would be hard to distinguish from typical English teenagers, while others have languished; for others, emotional problems have emerged only during adolescence. These findings have a double-edged impact, suggests Eric Turkheimer, a psychologist at the University of Virginia. "On the one hand they contradict the direst predictions of those who contend it's all over at age three, while on the other they reinforce the environmental optimism of which the early education advocates and other progressives are so fond."

Extrapolating from the horrific to the typical is intellectually perilous. Despite the proliferation of "brain curricula," flash cards for reading and math, elaborate mobiles, and classical music CDs that fill the shelves of kids' stores, neuroscientists have yet to show that early enrichment does in fact produce baby Einsteins.

While *The Myth of the First Three Years* did a reasonably balanced job of summarizing the research, John Bruer's conclusion, that early brain development is merely a myth, exaggerated the point. Bruer went too far again when, in a 2002 article in *Nature Neuroscience* provocatively titled "Avoiding the Pediatrician's Error: How Neuroscientists Can Help Educators (and Themselves)," he instructed brain scientists to carefully qualify what they say, or else to shut up.[36] In *The Myth of the First Three Years*, Bruer took his marketing cue from the "early years are forever" advocates. He devised a catchy label to claim attention—"the myth of the first three years"—but it had the unhappy effect of replacing one misconception of early brain development—"use it or lose it"—with another. The predictable result has been mixed media messages and a justifiably perplexed public.[37]

Across the research domains "there is very strong empirical and clinical evidence that [birth to three] is a period of life when valuable pathways are laid down for cognitive and emotional growth," points out psychologist Samuel Meisels, president of Erikson Institute in Chicago. This more nuanced assessment of the importance of early development has been overshadowed by the advocates' assertions, as well as by the backlash from Bruer and his conservative fellow travelers, who have seized on *The Myth of the First Three Years* as a scientific rationale for opposing universal preschool. Yet nuance is what most needs highlighting.

With a handful of exceptions, like sight, early experience is *not* essential for later development. Still, it has considerable significance because it lays the foundation in a hierarchical process of development. "Although subsequent experiences can change the effects of early experiences," stresses Ross Thompson, a psychologist at the University of California at Davis, "it is usually difficult, expensive, and time-consuming to do so."

It's logical, then, for taxpayers as well as parents to pay close attention to children's needs, whether they are three- and four-year-olds attending a high-quality preschool or infants and toddlers at home or in good child care centers. Cognitive and developmental psychologists can cite chapter and verse on the benefits of early education, and so can researchers who follow the long-term impact of early education. There is remarkable agreement about this among behavioral scientists of all stripes, and the findings that have emerged from the neuroscience labs bolster that common understanding. It's this consistency across disciplines—importantly including brain science—that makes the strongest case for early education.[38]

When it comes to child rearing generally and preschool specifically, neuroscience hasn't even arrived at the end of the beginning. Although there have been great advances during the past generation, there's nothing solid that connects these studies with good prekindergarten. Early learning does matter greatly, since it is the scaffolding for all the learning that follows, and so it's sensible to focus on strengthening that scaffolding. But the life of the brain neither begins at birth nor ends at age three. The brain is more dynamic than that. While changes in its structure diminish by the third decade of life, its remarkable plasticity does not.[39]

Think of the brain as if it were an unfinished work of art. In the same way that the form a sculpture eventually takes is most influenced by the artist's initial creative choices, the brain is most affected by what happens early in its development. But neither the work of art nor the brain is immutable. In fact, it's hard for the artist (or the neuroscientist) to pinpoint when the creative process is complete. Just as Alberto Giacometti famously and endlessly reworked his paintings and sculptures and Rembrandt kept tinkering with his etchings, the brain continues to evolve, even into the last years of our lives.[40]

Because scientists have increasingly come to see the brain as a work in flux, they have been paying more attention to concepts like resilience—a measure of elasticity, or, put differently, a demonstration of how much of a work in progress the brain really is. Resilience matters because, among other things, it offers a way to understand the dynamic between deprivation and enrichment, pinpointing the boundaries of extreme deprivation and pointing toward effective intervention.[41]

Harvard's Charles Nelson has been studying resilience by examining the effects of removing children from the still-dreadful orphanages in Romania and placing them with Romanian foster families (an institution that didn't exist before Nelson and his team began working in that country). "Some things dramatically improve, while others don't," he says. "Depression and anxiety are cut in half, but attention deficit disorder isn't touched by foster care. IQ differences are associated with how long children spend in foster care and the age when they are placed there." Like those who were adopted by families from Britain (and other Western nations), the youngsters placed in foster care in Romania have reacted to their new environment in very different ways. The explanation for these differences lies partly in genetics, says Nelson, partly in the prenatal experience, and partly in the particulars of their days in the orphanage itself. What actually happened during their years in the institution or during their gestation? Will the imaging techniques of the not-so-distant future be able to reveal how the brains of children incorporate such episodes?

Neuroscientists and other child development researchers are beginning to understand how a stressful or toxic environment experienced during gestation can be associated with suicide and schizophrenia decades later.[42] The thinking used to be that the children's problems were all the fault of their mother, that it was the mother's drinking and drug use during pregnancy that did all the neurological damage. It's now plain that prenatal health care, nutrition, exposure to toxic environments, poverty, and the mother's psychological state all contribute substantially to fetal stress.[43] The mechanisms are not yet known, however, and—as is usually the case when it comes to altering the course of a life— there are no quick fixes.

Just as brain development doesn't begin at birth, it doesn't end at the age of three. The fixation on infancy, on the part of both the early education advocates and their critics, has obscured the remarkable adaptability of the adult brain. While scientists have long known that key components of cognition, including logical and mathematical abilities, do not fully mature until late in adolescence, the news is that the brain retains a remarkable amount of plasticity throughout life, just as it continues to generate new cells.[44] Intuitively, we have known that the brain can change dramatically, even late in life, but until recently scientists haven't understood how this happens. Now, because of ingenious investigations of such varying species as barn owls and London taxi drivers, we're beginning to find the answers.

Eric Knudsen and his colleagues at Stanford Medical School have been studying the neurobiology of barn owls. In one experiment, they placed specially designed spectacles on adult barn owls to shift their visual field artificially. Earlier studies had shown that juvenile owls could adapt to this change but adult owls could not. The young owls showed, as one would expect, significant brain plasticity, while the adult owls showed little to none.

The apparent implication was that, much as with those kittens that had one eye stitched shut, there existed a sensitive time period for the acquisition of vision—but this turned out not to be the case. In a later study, Knudsen trained the adult barn owls to adapt to their altered visual field by making the change in small increments, rather than all at once. "There is a substantially greater capacity for plasticity in adults than was previously recognized," the researchers concluded.[45] Not only had they found another instance of adult brain plasticity, they had also identified a learning technique that can tap into this capacity. While, as John Bruer would surely point out, it is always hazardous to draw conclusions about the human brain from animal studies, this cutting-edge research does offer ideas worth pursuing.

Taxi drivers in London provide an even more pertinent example of how the brain continues to adapt. London cabbies are required to have what's known as "the Knowledge," a mental map of every street in the city. Eleanor Maguire and her associates at University College London's Institute of Neurology were able to show that the posterior hippocampi of these cabbies, the part of the brain that's enlisted when navigational skills are required, are larger than those in the rest of us—and the more experienced the taxi driver, the bigger the hippocampus. As the scientists conclude, "There is a capacity for local plastic change in the structure of the healthy adult human brain in response to environmental demands." Lifelong learning, rather than being a marketing strategy to persuade septuagenarians to return to the campus, proves to have a basis in brain science.[46]

The London cabbie study, as well as recent research on activities as varied as piano playing and juggling, delivers a salutary reminder that mental life doesn't end at age three—the brain remains very much a work in progress throughout much of life.[47] Even training seniors to do basic aerobics helps the brain to function more effectively. There is yet a further layer of complexity in this account of brain development: how the brain processes new information varies with age. It is hard, but not impossible, for an adult to learn to speak a foreign language like a native or play a musical instrument like a pro—it just happens differently. Cognitive psychologists have charted variations in how infants and toddlers make sense of the world, and educators have stepped in with "developmentally appropriate" ways of teaching. If adults have neurologically different approaches to learning, then pedagogy needs to be tailored not just to babies but also to their parents, and to their grandparents as well.[48]

"The real question," as *From Neurons to Neighborhoods* notes, "is not which matters more—early or later experience—but how later experience is influenced by early experience." Childhood experiences are particularly pertinent, not because they provide an unalterable blueprint for adult well-being but because what is learned at the beginning of life establishes "a set of capabilities, orientations to the world, and expectations about how things and people will behave that affect how new experiences are selected and processed."[49] That's why the "words, words, words" approach that we witnessed at the Chicago Child-Parent Centers is right on target.

John Bruer begs to differ. He contends that five-year-olds—maybe fifty-year-olds too—can catch up quickly if they fall behind, so long as they are properly taught. In theory he's right, but what's theoretically possible isn't what's actually happening in school.[50] From kindergarten on, teachers impose expectations that, if not met, discourage and demoralize children. That's why adolescents' success in education is so readily predicted by the skills they demonstrated as kindergarteners. If high-quality preschool does nothing more than enable children to avoid this early heartache, it is worth the price.[51]

In domains that range from mental illness to Alzheimer's disease, neuroscience has made discoveries that are hastening the prospects for treatment and cure. Some day it may yield discoveries of comparable importance in early education. "The hope," as Charles Nelson says, "is that the tools we use to get into the brain can also be used to evaluate the efficacy of interventions. We still don't know why they work; by tracking them, we can get a sense of their plasticity."

If neuroscience didn't exist, good preschools would look exactly as they do now. We know from other research that a strong emotional attachment between an infant and a loving adult is important, and that four-year-olds figure out that others have opinions different from their own. "The very things you learn," observes Berkeley psychologist Alison Gopnik, whose book *The Scientist in the Crib* elegantly brings this work together, "enable you to learn new things."

Studying how and why behavior changes, and how learning best happens, is the ultimate object of the quest. If, despite the hopes of the advocates, the scientists aren't yet there, that's really to be expected, since the research is still in its infancy. As Nobel Prize–winning neurologist Gerald Edelman has noted, the human brain is "the most complicated material object in the known universe."[52]

This proposition also holds true for the new generation of research in genetics, which has played a far more modest role in the preschool debates. The universal prekindergarten movement has shied away from the field because of its long-standing embrace of heredity-based theories of intelligence, and the corollary belief that preschool is a waste of time. Small wonder then, that, following the principle "out of sight, out of mind," the pre-K advocates haven't said anything about genetics. But new work shows that the field has much to contribute to the argument for early education.

Genetics: Beyond The Bell Curve

When it comes to explaining the roots of intelligence, the fight between partisans of the gene and partisans of the environment is ancient and fierce. Each side has challenged the other's intellectual bona fides and political agenda. What's at stake isn't just the definition of good science but the meaning of the just society. The nurture crowd is predisposed to revive the War on Poverty, while the nature crowd typically embraces a more hereditarian perspective.

A century's worth of quantitative genetics literature concludes that a person's IQ is remarkably stable, and that as much as 80 percent of IQ differences between individuals can be attributed to heredity.[53] This is how IQ is widely understood, as being mainly "in the genes," and that understanding offers a convenient rationale for doing nothing about seemingly intractable social problems like the black-white school achievement gap and widening income disparity. If nature disposes, the argument goes, there's little to be gained by intervening.[54]

Prominent geneticists like Berkeley's Arthur Jensen have long contended that, since there is no way significantly to boost IQ, compensatory education is a bad bet. "The chief goal of compensatory education—to remedy the educational lag of disadvantaged children and thereby narrow that achievement gap between 'minority' and 'majority' pupils—has been utterly unrealized in any of the large compensatory education programs," Jensen argued some years ago, inciting a scientific and social donnybrook. "In other fields, when bridges do not stand, when aircraft do not fly, when machines do not work, when treatments do not cure, despite all conscientious efforts on the part of many persons to make them do so, one begins to question the basic assumptions, principles, theories, and hypotheses that guide one's efforts. Is it time to follow suit in education?"[55]

If the 1997 White House conference on brain development was the high-water mark for neuroscience in the public arena, the comparable attention-getting moment in quantitative genetics came with the ballyhooed 1994 publication of *The Bell Curve*. Its effect was to push policy thinking in precisely the opposite direction. While the neuroscience findings were touted as proof of the importance of early intervention in shaping the developing brain, thus helping to close racial and socioeconomic divides, *Bell Curve* authors Richard Herrnstein and Charles Murray relied on quantitative genetics to make the contrary argument, that the United States is a genetic meritocracy, and to urge an end to affirmative action. The book recycles the claim that genetically based IQ deficiencies explain African Americans' disproportionate rates of poverty and incarceration.[56] It garnered page-one reviews and sold more than half a million copies. Conservatives brandished it as a weapon in the culture wars. Liberals, obliged to play catch-up, scoffed at the ignorance of the authors (they were "a pigeon psychologist and a barracks economist," mocked one critic), pointed out flaws in the methodology, and attacked the recommendations as a ratification of injustice.[57]

Far more than science is implicated here. Because genetics has such an ugly political history—the American eugenics movement advocated sterilizing the "unfit" and Hitler's Germany used the research for unspeakable purposes—liberals have understandably downplayed genetic explanations of human behavior.[58] While contemporary geneticists weren't Nazis, their opponents felt that they *were* naïve about the malevolent uses to which their work could be put. When Tufts psychologist Richard Lerner wrote about the misuse of genetics, he pointedly titled his book *Final Solution*.[59] Yet intellectual life does abhor a vacuum: by dismissing or ignoring the importance of heredity, focusing instead on factors like poverty and stress, liberals had left a void in the public conversation on intelligence that *The Bell Curve* was able to fill.

In fact the heredity versus environment model, the intellectual framework for the *Bell Curve's* line of thinking, is itself wrong. A new generation of studies shows that genes and environment don't occupy separate spheres—that much of what is labeled "hereditary" becomes meaningful only in the context of experience. These findings give added scientific heft to the preschool research demonstrating the long-term effects of high-quality early education. The studies of Perry Preschool, the Abecedarian Project, and the Chicago Child-Parent Centers show that early educational experiences can make a major difference. Genetics, no less than neuroscience, helps to explain why.

"Feeble-Minded Love"

The debate about the roots of intelligence dates to the turn of the twentieth century, with the origins of the IQ test. Lewis Terman, who constructed the widely used Stanford-Binet IQ test, regarded it as a great sorting machine that could protect society against "the menace of the feeble-minded." However, to French psychologist Albert Binet, who had devised the first usable instrument a few years earlier, the test results were a diagnostic tool, not a life sentence. While working with retarded children, Binet had developed what he called "mental orthopedics," exercises that were designed to strengthen their intellectual abilities.[60]

Terman's views came to dominate American psychology, but in the 1930s a group of researchers from the University of Iowa's Child Welfare Research Station was able to put them to the test.[61] Nothing was known then about the molecular science underlying the interplay of nature and nurture—that would await the discovery of DNA—but the findings of the Iowa empiricists pointed the way. Their studies showed that altering the circumstances in which children grow up can have a powerful impact on their IQ.[62]

The Soldiers' Orphans' Home, a state-run institution in Davenport, Iowa, asked university researchers to assess the children living there, so adoptive parents wouldn't unknowingly take on a "feeble-minded" child.[63] When a young psychologist named Harold Skeels and his colleagues began testing the children, they stumbled on a way to test the theory of genetic determinism. Two girls in the orphans' home, both barely a year old, had been unable to adjust to orphanage life—"they were pitiful little creatures," Skeels wrote, "sad and inactive, they spent their days rocking and whining"—and they were given psychological examinations. The tests showed that their developmental levels were comparable to infants half their age, and so, according to protocol, they were sent to the Glenwood State School for the Mentally Retarded.

To everyone's surprise, the two girls thrived at Glenwood. Eighteen months after they arrived there, when Skeels gave them the same battery of tests again, their development was in the normal range. This finding was so unexpected that he administered the test once more, with the same results. After doing a bit of investigating, Skeels learned that, at Glenwood, the girls had been taken under the wing of two older mentally disabled women. They were returned to the orphanage, and were adopted soon afterward.

At this point, the psychologists decided to conduct an experiment. They selected twenty-five children from the orphanage. Twenty of the youngsters were illegitimate and had been surrendered by their mothers at birth, and the rest had been taken from their parents because they had been abused or neglected. Thirteen of the toddlers, all of them younger than three, were transferred to Glenwood. At the time their IQs ranged from 35 to 68, rendering their chances for adoption essentially nil. The other twelve, with a median IQ of 90, remained at the orphanage.

The babies sent to Glenwood were placed on wards with some of the older and brighter women there. On their own, these women started to mother the toddlers, in effect adopting them. They took great pride in being good mothers, giving the toddlers constant attention, talking to and playing with them, competing with one another to see whose child would walk or talk first. The youngsters also spent time with the matron who ran Glenwood. She grew attached to them too, and made sure they had lots of chances for interaction as well as the most up-to-date educational toys.

Fourteen months later, when the children at Glenwood were retested, their average IQ had risen twenty-seven points, from 64 to 91, and all but two of them had made gains of at least fifteen points. Meanwhile, the average IQ score of the children who had stayed in the barren environment of the orphanage had plummeted from 86 to 60, with one child's IQ dropping forty-five points. According to Lewis Terman's theories this wasn't supposed to happen, because IQ was essentially fixed from birth.

Their experience at Glenwood meant everything to those children. Two and a half years later, only one of them remained there; all the others had been adopted. At that point, the experimental group had an average IQ of 95.9—nearly normal. The biggest gain was recorded for a child placed with what was described as a "superior" family. "Feeble-minded love" had made all the difference, said *Time* magazine.[64]

Nearly thirty years later, in the early 1960s, Harold Skeels tracked down everyone who had participated in the original study. Almost all the children who'd been sent to Glenwood had gone on to have a normal life. They'd become, among other things, a staff sergeant, a housewife, a nursing instructor, and a real estate salesman; their incomes matched the state average. None of them showed any signs of antisocial behavior, none had ever suffered any mental illness, and none had ever been on welfare. Most of them had graduated from high school and five had gone on to college, one of whom did some graduate work—an academic track record that compared favorably with the typical Iowan of the day. All but two were married. Their spouses' occupations ranged from laborer and mechanic to dental technician and advertising copywriter. Their children had an average IQ of 104.

The story was totally, and dispiritingly, different for those who had stayed in the orphanage. On average they had stopped going to school after the third grade, and just one had gone beyond the eighth grade. Five of them had spent their entire lives shuttling among institutions. One had become a typesetter, a skilled trade, but the person with the next highest-status job was a dishwasher, and as a group they earned barely a third of the state average. Only one had gotten married. The state of Iowa, Skeels estimated, had spent five times more on these individuals, because of their continuing need for care, than on those who had been transferred to Glenwood.[65]

"Under present-day conditions," Harold Skeels wrote in 1966, "there are still countless infants born with potentialities for development well within the normal range, who will become mentally retarded and noncontributing members of the society unless appropriate intervention occurs." That's another way of saying that, while genes matter, the environment fixes the extent to which a person's genetic potential is realized. That message was heard by David Weikart, the founder of Perry Preschool, as well as by those who were designing the new Head Start program.[66] From the sterile Iowa orphanage in the 1930s to the loveless conditions of the Romanian orphanages under Nicolae Ceausescu— over the decades, researchers have repeatedly demonstrated the life-changing impact of being taken from a nightmarish world and placed in a nurturing setting.[67]

Stalking the Wild Taboo

Contemporary quantitative geneticists come from a distinct intellectual tradition.[68] Psychologist Harold Skeels and his colleagues, like those who have traced the life histories of the Romanian orphans, were moved by the impulse to rescue. Quantitative geneticists, in contrast, pride themselves on being disinterested scientists whose task is to parse statistical data on IQ. Their work, which focuses on adopted children and twins, has been taken to show the power of genetic explanations of intelligence, but a new body of research undermines those findings.

Studies of adopted children have found that their IQ scores are considerably closer to those of their biological parents than their adoptive parents, and that's consistent with the proposition that intelligence is mainly inherited. However, since poor families rarely adopt children, those studies have generally looked at youngsters placed with well-to-do families. What's more, most adopted children come from poor families; almost nothing is known about those whose biological parents are well-off.

What happens in these rare instances of riches-to-rags adoption? To answer that question, two psychologists, Christiane Capron and Michel Duyme, combed through thousands of records from French public and private adoption agencies.[69] "It was slow, dusty work," Duyme recalls. Their natural experiment mimics animal studies in which, for instance, a newborn rhesus monkey is taken from its nurturing biological mother and handed over to an uncaring foster mother. The findings are also consistent—how genes are expressed depends on the social context.

Whatever the background of the adoptive families, Capron and Duyme learned, adopted children whose biological parents were well-off had IQ scores that averaged sixteen points higher than those born to working-class parents. That figure represents the maximum difference that can be attributed to heredity—when children are adopted soon after birth, the main way that their biological parents influence their IQ is through their genes. (As we've seen, neuroscientists have found that the stresses of pregnancy can shape children's later development. While poor mothers are likely to have had a harder time of it during pregnancy than their more affluent counterparts—which is what Capron and Duyme have subsequently been investigating—this study didn't incorporate such data.)

What's remarkable is how big a difference the adoptive families' background made. The average IQ of children from well-to-do parents who were placed with families from the same social stratum was 119.6. But when poor families adopted such infants, their IQ was 107.5—twelve points lower. There was a similar variation for children born into impoverished families; youngsters adopted by parents of similarly modest means had average IQs of 92.4, while the IQs of those placed with well-off parents averaged 103.6. This research confirms that environment matters. The only, and crucial, difference between these children was the lives they had led.

A later study of French youngsters adopted between the ages of four and six points to the continuing interplay of nature and nurture. Those children, like the babies in the Iowa orphanage, had little going for them. At the time of adoption, their IQs averaged 77, which put them on the cusp of retardation. Most had been abused or neglected as infants, then shunted from one foster home or institution to the next.[70]

Nine years later they retook the IQ test. All of them did better—another rebuff to the traditional view that intelligence is stable. The extent of improvement was directly associated with the adopting family's status. Children adopted by farmers and laborers had later average IQ scores of 85.5; those placed with middle-class families had average scores of 92. The average IQ score of youngsters placed in well-to-do homes climbed more than twenty points, to 98—a jump from borderline retardation to a whisker below average. That's a huge difference—a person with an IQ of 77 couldn't explain the rules of tennis, while an individual with a 98 IQ could successfully analyze a championship match—and it can be explained only by variations in family circumstances and the plasticity of children's minds.

Unlike scientists who study the behavior of mice or chimpanzees, quantitative geneticists cannot fiddle with genes or radically change the environment. Twins—experiments of nature—are thus their best bet. Identical twins are clones who share all the same genes, while fraternal twins are just siblings who were born at the same time—only half of their genes are identical. If heredity explains most of the differences in intelligence, then the IQ scores of identical twins should be much more similar than the IQs of fraternal twins, and this is what the research has historically reported. It was thought that only when children spend their earliest years in the most horrific circumstances ("crack houses of inner cities" is the graphic example used by one eminent scientist) does the environment make a notable difference. Otherwise, genes rule.[71]

Then along came Eric Turkheimer to shake things up. Turkheimer is the kind of irreverent academic who gives his papers user-friendly titles like "Spinach and Ice Cream" and "Mobiles." The psychology professor also has a reputation as a methodologist's methodologist. In combing through the research, he noticed that the twins who had been studied all came from middle-class families. The explanation was simple—poor people don't volunteer for research projects—but he wondered whether their omission mattered.

Together with several colleagues, Turkheimer searched for data on twins from a wider range of families.[72] He found what he needed in a national sample, gathered in the 1970s, of more than

50,000 children—among them 623 pairs of twins—many from poor families, who had taken IQ tests at age seven. In a widely discussed 2003 article, he wrote that, as anticipated, they had found that virtually all the variation in IQ scores for twins with middle-class (or higher) parents could be attributed to genetics.

The big surprise was among twins from the poorest families. Contrary to what one would expect, among those youngsters the IQs of identical twins did not vary any less than the IQs of fraternal twins. It turns out that heredity explains almost none of the IQ variation in this case—the impact of growing up impoverished had overwhelmed the children's genetic capacities. In other words, home life is the key factor for youngsters at the bottom of the economic barrel. "If you have a chaotic environment, kids' genetic potential doesn't have a chance to be expressed," explains Turkheimer. "Well-off families can provide the mental stimulation needed for genes to build the brain circuitry for intelligence."

"This was the clearest result I had ever gotten," says Turkheimer. "I'm used to delicate results from complex statistical models, but this isn't delicate." He spent the next six months "trying to make the result go away by proving to myself that it wasn't a function of how I'd analyzed the data. In fact it is a great big effect."

This provocative finding has been amplified in subsequent studies carried out by Turkheimer and others. An analysis of the reading ability of middle-aged twins shows that, even half a century after childhood, family background still has a big effect—but only for children who grew up poor.[73] Turkheimer's colleagues have looked at a sample of twins who took the National Merit Scholarship exam, and the findings are much the same. Although these teenagers are among the academic elite, and mostly come from well-off homes, variations in family circumstances still matter; children from the wealthiest households have the greatest opportunity to develop all their genetic capacities.[74] The better off the family, the more a child's genetic potential is likely to be, as Turkheimer puts it, "maxed out."

Confirmation of these findings has also come from a wholly different domain—neuroscientists studying brain-behavior relationships in reading ability. A 2006 study carried out by a team at Cornell Medical Center, using neuro-imaging to measure brain behavior, has found that "individual differences in skill result in large differences in brain activation" in poor children. As in Turkheimer's work, the wealthier the child's family, the less variation is observed. Children who might otherwise have been poor readers "benefited from increased exposure to print, which served to 'buffer' their skills, leading to higher achievement," the research team concluded. "Cognitive, social, and neurobiological influences on reading development are fundamentally intertwined."[75]

While the likelihood that children will realize their IQ potential can largely be predicted by their families' socioeconomic standing, the mechanism isn't money or status. Those are just proxies for the time and energy adults expend to keep a youngster mentally engaged, and the social capital that helps steer a child to success. On average, well-off households have the resources required to provide better settings for the fullest development of a child's natural abilities.

In *Meaningful Differences in the Everyday Experiences of Young American Children*, University of Kansas psychologists Betty Hart and Todd Risley write that, by the time they are four years old, children growing up in poor families have been exposed to 32 million fewer spoken words than those whose parents are professionals. Four-year-olds from professional families have larger vocabularies than the *parents* of the poorest three-year-olds. This language gap translates directly into stunted academic trajectories when the children enter school.[76]

The "Flynn effect," named for James Flynn, the New Zealand–based political philosopher who first spotted it, also poses a major challenge to the genetic orthodoxy. Flynn picked up on the fact that, since World War I, every generation has had a higher IQ than its predecessors. This pattern, a gain of eighteen to twenty points a generation on "culture-fair" tests that are supposed to measure "pure" intelligence, is consistent in the data from countries around the world that have a history of doing mental testing for military service.[77]

There is no conceivable genetic explanation for this result, no reason to believe that one generation is innately smarter than its predecessors. Most likely the Flynn effect reflects a feedback loop. Changes in the environment, ranging from better nutrition to urbanization, lead to higher IQs, which in turn lead to ever-more-demanding environments.

"People who have an advantage for a particular trait will be matched with superior environments for that trait," argues William Dickens, a senior fellow at the Brookings Institution who works with Flynn. "Genes can derive a great advantage from this because a genetic advantage remains with you throughout life, while environmental differences come and go."[78]

Taken together, the studies of twins, the neuro-imaging research, and the Flynn-effect findings pose a fundamental challenge to the classic contention that IQ is overwhelmingly genetic. "Quantitative geneticists like Arthur Jensen credit genes for all the potent environmental differences that twins share," Dickens says, "but that's wrong—the twin studies hide the potency of environmental influences on IQ." By taking yet another intellectual route, Dickens and Flynn wind up at the same place as

Turkheimer and the Cornell neuroscientists: life outcomes are decided at the intersection of nature and nurture.

The recent twin and adoption studies, as well as the Flynn effect, come down squarely on Albert Binet's side of the century-old argument with Lewis Terman. If heredity defines the limits of intelligence, experience largely determines whether those limits will be reached. The interesting question isn't *whether* the environment matters, but *when* and *how* it matters. That's why "mental orthopedics"—early childhood education, in modern parlance—can be so important.

Opening the Black Box

Quantitative genetics statistically partitions the relative strengths of genetic and environmental factors. Molecular genetics opens up the genetic black box to identify the biological causes.[79]

Much of the work in this field aims at specifying the genetic foundations of diseases ranging from cancer to Alzheimer's, with the goal of finding a cure. There is also an ongoing search for the "intelligence gene," or cluster of genes, that can explain variations in intelligence—a hunt for the biological source of what quantitative geneticists call "g," or general intelligence. But that research seems likely to confirm what the recent twin and adoption studies have shown: it's the intersection of heredity and environment that really matters.

Molecular genetics has mainly focused on finding "candidate genes," the genes *for* specific conditions. There have been a few successes, Alzheimer's disease among them, and some spectacular failures, such as the "manic depression gene" that researchers claimed to have identified among the Amish.[80] As Sir Michael Rutter, a polymath whose interests range from the well-being of Romanian orphans to molecular genetics, points out, "It is all too tempting to conclude that once there is a solid confirmed finding on a gene that is associated with some behavioral trait or disorder, then that gene is necessarily involved with the cause of that feature." Not so fast, says Rutter. "Identifying a gene is only the first step in establishing the pathway to any condition. Specifying that pathway requires identifying the environmental influences on gene expression, the key process that determines the functional operation of genes."[81]

Many scientists are now shifting gears. "Rather than trying to find the gene that causes a particular outcome, we said, 'Let's think about how it's mediated through environmental risk,'" notes Thomas O'Connor, a psychologist at the University of Rochester Medical Center who is conducting research on the long-term impact of prenatal stress. "Rather than, say, trying to link a serotonin transmitter directly to depression, it makes better sense to think about a genetic predisposition that's literally turned on or off by life risks." That's a restatement, in a different scientific vocabulary, of Eric Turkheimer's research on twins, with "life risks" substituted for poverty.

Groundbreaking recent studies have shown specific instances in which variations in the environment determine actual "gene expression," meaning the form, or allele, that the gene takes.[82] Avshalom Caspi and Terrie Moffitt, psychologists who split their time between the University of Wisconsin and the University of London, have demonstrated that the gene MAO, linked to aggressive and potentially violent behavior, is effectively deactivated when an individual grows up in a caring and intimate family. They have also found that a relatively stress-free home life has the same benign effect on the 5-HTT gene, which helps regulate the brain's production of serotonin, a neurotransmitter thought to play a major role in the biochemistry of depression. Similarly, psychologists at the University of Helsinki have established that a child's environment can moderate the effect of the gene DRD4, which is linked to thrill-seeking behavior.[83]

These studies offer genetic substantiation of earlier research that relied on clinical assessments to show that parents have a big influence in structuring their children's world—and that those early experiences have a potent, long-lasting impact on children's resilience in the face of many kinds of stress. A thirty-five-year follow-up study found that, by the time they were middle-aged, undergraduates who described their relationships with their parents as cold and detached were four times likelier to suffer from chronic illnesses ranging from alcoholism and depression to diabetes and heart disease. A good family life has the opposite impact—it's a source of strength in the face of chronic stress.[84] "In our study," says Terrie Moffitt, who has been studying a large group of individuals from the New Zealand city of Dunedin, "we're learning that it doesn't matter whether we're looking at gum disease, heart disease, cancer, depression, or risk-seeking. There's no straight genetic effect—the vulnerability emerges only in circumstances of environmental risk."[85]

Scientists have begun to trace these vulnerabilities back to the womb. "We're showing the persisting effects of stress in pregnancy on kids," says Thomas O'Connor. Christiane Capron and Michel Duyme's hunch—that greater stress in poor households accounts for some of the seventeen-point difference in IQ between children born to poor parents versus rich ones—is being scientifically borne out. "We have been desperate to treat anxious, pregnant women, to see if making them less anxious will have an effect on the kid," O'Connor adds. "If responses to stress are tied to the immune function, psychological outcomes, maybe intelligence, then all bets are off. We could save the world by making moms less stressed in pregnancy."

Since the early 1990s scientists have been on a quest for the gene, more likely the cluster of genes, for IQ. So far they haven't been successful. Finding a gene that significantly contributes to even a well-defined disorder is hard enough, because of the interactions between nature and nurture that the studies on thrill seeking and depression have confirmed. The more sophisticated array of interactions affecting the intellect makes the quest for an "intelligence gene" appear quixotic. What's more, even if a gene cluster was found to be associated with IQ, what to make of that finding isn't obvious. It would not show definitively that IQ is "real." After all, as Eric Turkheimer points out, "you could make up a concept, like being a good speller with big feet, and find genes that are associated with it." Complex social and biological concepts like intelligence don't allow for easy answers.

The intelligence-gene research, like the hyping of the "gay gene" and claims of other "genes for" sightings, including a divorce gene and one for religiosity, has commanded outsized media curiosity. As with much of the coverage of neuroscience, the reporting has stressed the sensational and downplayed the complexities.[86]

In 1998 Robert Plomin, an internationally renowned molecular geneticist, and his research team at the University of London thought they had solved part of the intelligence puzzle when they located a gene that was statistically associated with high SAT scores.[87] Although that gene accounted for just 2 percent of the variance in SAT scores, the report made a splash. As Michael Rutter bitingly points out, "Academics made astonishing statements that this revolutionized our thinking about the importance of genetic factors in intelligence."[88] But four years after the SAT study, when Plomin published a follow-up paper reporting that he couldn't replicate his earlier result, that article got no notice. Finding an IQ gene was news; failing to do so wasn't.[89]

In the quest for genes linked to intelligence, failure has generally been the order of the day.[90] It's a "hard slog," Plomin acknowledges. To a thoughtful skeptic like Eric Turkheimer, "rooting around in the brain to find [a gene for intelligence] is a mistake." University of Sydney psychologist Dennis Garlick adds that, even if such genes were to be identified, "it is still a long road from identifying the genes responsible for intelligence to actually understanding what they do, and hence understanding how intelligence is inherited."[91]

That road is not only long but also incredibly convoluted. "Some genetic influences operate only on fathers but not mothers, on warmth but not on conflict," notes David Reiss, a psychoanalyst at George Washington University Medical School; in his book *The Relationship Code* Reiss analyzes the genetic and social influences on adolescent development. "You have to reconceptualize the gene as part of a social nexus—to think of the field as 'sociogenetics.'"

"You can predict whether a nine-month-old will smile and laugh by knowing the sociability of the birth parents," Reiss points out—but only when the adopting parents are depressed. "When they're not depressed, the parents' genotype has no influence. Those kids smile and laugh like normal kids. It takes an anxious climate for those genetic influences to show themselves on an important behavior in a nine-month-old—the capacity to engage a parent!"

Appreciating how genes do their work lies at the heart of the matter. This is where the infinitely intricate interplay between nature and nurture—"the nonlinear, uncontrolled developmental process that is a human life," as Turkheimer describes it— once again claims center stage. "Everything interacts with everything else."

Genetics has traditionally been the redoubt of the hereditarians, who imagine a straight-line march from genes to physiology to phenotype, but science is painting an entirely different picture. "I am skeptical that genetic work ever will provide an understanding of the basis of intelligence," says Michael Rutter. "It doesn't really matter whether the heritability of IQ is this particular figure or that one. Changing the environment can still make an enormous difference."[92]

All Together Now?

Across a wide array of disciplines in the natural and social sciences—developmental and behavioral neuroscience, genetics, medicine, and cognitive and developmental psychology among them—researchers are converging on a new understanding of human development, one that emphasizes the interplay of nature and nurture. "The concept of gene-environment interaction is all over the place," says David Reiss. "It's the watchword of a new faith, on every NIH tongue, in every psychiatry grand rounds presentation."[93]

The links between neuroscience and molecular genetics are especially tantalizing. Brain science focuses on the pathways of the brain, while molecular genetics looks at what's being transmitted along those pathways. "Of all the developments that have contributed to neuroscience in the past two decades," observes Nobel Prize–winning neurophysiologist Eric Kandel, "none has had a greater impact than the application of molecular genetics. It is becoming increasingly evident that, in the near term, the extension of genetic approaches to clinical neurology and psychiatry holds greater promise than any other approach for our understanding of the etiology of various disorders and for their diagnosis."[94] Terrie Moffitt sees the intersection of these fields shaping the research agenda. "We have to link molecular genetics and neuroscience. We need to get DNA on the people in the neuroscience studies, and we need to import neuroscience into our own work, to encourage cross-talk between these sciences."

Eventually that synthesis will have to reach beyond science, with its promise of elegant answers, to take account of the blooming complexities that life inevitably introduces into the mix. Or so Harvard biologist Edward O. Wilson believes. In *Consilience: The Unity of Knowledge*, Wilson argues that science is on the brink of a development that has been the dream of researchers and philosophers since Francis Bacon. "The momentum is overwhelmingly toward conceptual unity," Wilson writes. "Disciplinary boundaries are disappearing, in favor of shifting hybrid disciplines in which consilience is implicit."[95] Brain science is crucial in this context, for it forms a bridge between biology and the social sciences.

This is the ultimate promise in research—tying laboratory results to the processes of brain development over the course of a lifetime. If that day comes, the brain scientists and geneticists will be able to speak with specificity to parents and educators about the circumstances in which their young charges are most likely to thrive. Meanwhile, their findings buttress what other scientists, using other tools of research, have demonstrated about the profound impact of early education.

F · I · V · E

Who Cares for the Children?

David L. Kirp and Deborah Kong

IN THE mid-1990s universal prekindergarten was relatively low on the wish list of children's rights advocates. The big-ticket item was more and better child care, a goal that seemed well within reach.

After the long dry spell of the Reagan years, the federal child care budget started to expand, and a radical shift in welfare policy made further expansion a practical necessity.[1] In 1996 the Temporary Assistance for Needy Families (TANF) program made good on President Clinton's pledge to "end welfare as we know it"—with a vengeance. Millions of mothers, many of them with infants and toddlers, were lopped from the welfare rolls and pushed into the job market. They joined the tens of millions of working- and middle-class women who were already working to pay the household bills. Someone had to take care of all these babies, and there simply weren't enough grandmothers around.

In her 1996 best-seller, *It Takes a Village,* First Lady Hillary Clinton wrote glowingly about the French crèches and *écoles maternelles* to which all families could send their youngest children.[2] Could America move in that direction? The child advocates' aim was "early care *and learning*," not conventional babysitting or child minding.[3] In the 1960s and 1970s feminists had promoted child care for the sake of women, to free them from the burdens of domesticity, but these new activists were fervent about the children themselves. They had in mind a program of high quality, patterned after the then-new Early Head Start program.

Bigger but Not Better

Expansion—but not quality—is what actually emerged from Washington. Using some of the savings generated by the TANF cuts in welfare payments, the child care budget ballooned from $750 million in 1991 to more than $11 billion in 2003, and tax credits added another $2.7 billion.[4] But with rare exceptions, little attention has been paid to the youngsters' needs. Washington decided against setting standards for the quality of child care, leaving that to the states. At the state level, a "workforce commission" usually manages the program, and the name aptly describes its priorities—a focus on working mothers, not their kids.

Policymakers perceive a sharp distinction between prekindergarten and child care. Pre-K, to their way of thinking, is tied to education. It comes with the backing of leading economists and neuroscientists. It's supposed to prepare youngsters to succeed in school, and there is considerable evidence that good preschools can do just that. Child care, by contrast, isn't usually regarded as preparing infants and toddlers for anything. It's a fill-in for parenting, a way of getting, and keeping, mothers on the job.

With the help of tax credits, well-off parents can hire nannies or send their offspring to the best nursery schools. Only a minuscule fraction of poor families—fewer than three in a hundred—

have access to an Early Head Start program or one of the handful of Educare Centers patterned on the Chicago model for early education and infant care. Most early child care is mediocre or worse—toddlers taken "straight from the car seat to the pumpkin seat until they scream their heads off," as one veteran operator of a chain of day care centers describes the drill.[5]

"Sitting at the policy table," says Matthew Melmed, the executive director of the national advocacy organization Zero to Three, "my role is to cry about why we aren't paying attention to babies."

The characteristic political response is a shrug-of-the-shoulders belief that, somehow, today's families are making do. "We're pretty much in denial about the demographics of our workforce," observes Donna Klein, the president of Corporate Voices for Working Families.

"Society has convinced us that it's a personal issue," says Joan Lombardi, who shaped federal child care policy during the Clinton administration. "You go and deal with it by yourself. You go and figure out what to do."

The rules of the child care game reflect a deep, widespread, and enduring cultural belief that mothers really should be staying at home. Never mind the facts of economic life that send them to work. Ignore, as well, the fact that paid family leave, available in every postindustrialized country except Australia and the United States, logically ought to be on the books; it's a policy that should appeal to social conservatives as well as liberals, and many working parents would welcome the chance to stay home with their newborn babies.[6] The 1950s are long gone, but *Ozzie and Harriet* values remain imbedded in the American psyche.

Child care may be accepted as a necessity today, but it's seen as a *regrettable* necessity. In a 2002 poll, 42 percent of men—and nearly as many women—agreed that, ideally, the man should be the breadwinner while the woman takes care of the home. "Ambivalent feelings," says Ellen Galinsky, executive director of the Families and Work Institute, "are still alive and well."

What If?

Imagine a counterhistory in which the country decided to make the best early education and child care widely accessible. Such a project was actually up and running in the Portland, Oregon, shipyards during World War II. But when the war ended, so did the program. Those Portland child care centers represent a remarkable accomplishment as well as a lost opportunity. This mostly forgotten chapter in our history helps to clarify why pre-K, not child care, has become the centerpiece of a nationwide movement.

Edgar Kaiser had a war to supply—the government wanted a "bridge of ships," including tankers, Liberty ships, Victory ships, and attack transports—but with millions of men away fighting the war, he needed women workers to help do the job.[7] Sixteen thousand women came to Portland to work in Kaiser's shipyards, and a quarter of them had young children. Lots of companies were in the same situation, of course, and so for the first time Washington found itself paying for nurseries. But getting one of those federal centers up and running took months, and Kaiser didn't have time to waste. He went straight to the U.S. Maritime Commission, which had ordered the ships, and negotiated a contract that included the cost of running company child care centers.

This news didn't please the citizens of Portland. River City, as it was called, was an insular place, disdainful of the women its residents referred to as "riff raff," who carted their young children halfway across the country to make money. For their part, the city's social workers feared that the company, intent at all costs on keeping the women on the job, would exploit their children, and the decision to locate the centers at the gates of the plants only reinforced those suspicions.

Like most businessmen, Kaiser initially assumed that anyone could look after little children, but when confronted with the hostile citizenry he put himself through a crash course in child development. Kaiser concluded that offering the best care possible was the right thing to do and, pragmatically, the best way to minimize absenteeism. "He saw child care in a professional light, as integral to young children's development," said Lois Meek Stolz, who directed the centers, and the fact that Stolz, the longtime director of the Child Development Institute at Columbia University's Teachers College, was recruited to run the nurseries after a nationwide search signaled the company's seriousness.

"In the past, good nursery schools have been a luxury for the wealthy," said James Hymes, Jr., Stolz's deputy, who went on to become a major figure in early education. "The Kaiser Child Centers are among the first places where working people of average means have been able to afford nursery education for their children."[8] The women who came to Portland for the ship-building jobs were initially reluctant to entrust their children, some as young as eighteen months, to strangers; in their experience, that happened only when youngsters were sent to the county orphanage. But what they saw in the company's new Child Centers won them over.

In designing the centers Stolz and Hymes paid attention to the particulars—everything from the colors of the rooms (light pastel shades) to the menu of real afternoon snacks rather than just milk and cookies. Because Kaiser's shipyards were as immaculate as office buildings, they felt it made sense to locate the centers right next to them, so that mothers could drop off their kids as they arrived at work.

At their peak the shipyard centers enrolled 1,005 youngsters—they were the biggest child care centers in the country—and since the plants were running twenty-four hours a day, they were open around the clock.[9] But what they offered was far from the impersonal, mass-produced care that today's child care chains, like Teddy Bear in Chicago, deliver. Perusing the old photos is like entering a world calculated to please and excite the very young. All the furniture was kiddie-sized (Kaiser had it shipped from New York), and so were the sinks and toilets. The rooms were spacious, stocked with picture books and carpentry equipment, musical instruments and easels, and they opened onto a central courtyard crammed with jungle gyms, sandboxes, and swings. The daily schedule—story time, play time, meal time, nap time—was arranged to match the rhythms of a child's day.

"There was real excitement" about the centers in the leading teachers' colleges, Stolz recalled, "which had never before known any hue and cry about nursery school teachers."[10] Two teachers were assigned to each classroom; all the teachers had college degrees, and the lead teacher for each class had to have taught in a nursery school. The innovativeness of the venture was a draw for teachers, and so was the salary, which was considerably higher than what they were used to earning. This was the market at work: if they were paid less, Kaiser figured, they would be stolen away by the shipyards. The children's meals were planned by a nutritionist—cod liver oil, mixed in the morning orange juice, strikes the single anomalous note—and the infirmary was staffed with registered nurses.

The centers were as attentive to the mothers' concerns as to the children's. (Stolz later said that a better name for them would have been the Child *and Parent* Service Centers, to reflect this dual emphasis.) Fees were kept affordable: seventy-five cents a day for one child, about eight dollars in 2006 dollars, and fifty cents more for each additional child in the family. At the end of their shift, mothers could pick up a hot meal to serve their children at home, and they could even drop off socks and shirts for mending. The teachers took endless photos of the kids, which the mothers sent off to their husbands in the military.

Infants, toddlers, preschoolers, kindergarteners—all were included in the mix, and plans were in the works to add babies as young as six months. This wide age range makes a hash of the familiar dichotomies: babysitting for infants and toddlers versus education for the three- and four-year-olds; child care versus preschool and kindergarten. The centers offered the nurturing as well as the education best suited to the age-specific ways that children make sense of their world. "Every day care center is a school," James Hymes wrote years later. "The choice is never between custodial care and education. The choice is between unplanned and planned education, between conscious and unconscious education, between bad education and good education."[11]

The Kaiser centers provided "probably the best child care being offered in the country," Stolz and Hymes stated in their final report.[12] They had "experimented in the development of programs which have importance to the future of nursery education," including "a program of growth and development for groups of children under two years of age." Mothers had seen the positive effects. Their children's "language grows," they had reported, and the kids also became "more self-reliant."[13]

Thirty years later, Lois Stolz mused about whether the experiment should have become a national model. "Can an industry carry out a program that is good for children, good for their families, as well as good for itself?"[14] Since Washington had paid most of the tab, the better question is whether government and business should collaborate in delivering Kaiser-quality care.[15]

Not until 1965, when the Head Start program began, would three- and four-year-olds receive federally supported education even remotely comparable to what the Kaiser centers offered. And not until 1994, with the launching of Early Head Start, would Washington pay for good infant and toddler care. And while Head Start and Early Head Start are meant only for families living in poverty, the shipyard nurseries were aimed at the working class, which actually has the fewest options when it comes to finding decent and affordable child care.[16]

If the Kaiser Child Service Centers, cod liver oil and all, were now operating nationwide, no one would be fretting about the quality of child care, and universal preschool would have become a staple long ago. One reason that didn't happen is how the Kaiser project was sold to the public—not as a way of cultivating young minds, but as the helpmate to industry during a moment of unique need.

"Never before has American industry cried out for womanpower as it is doing today." When Lois Stolz wrote about the Portland shipyard centers in a *New York Times Sunday Magazine* article, she didn't play up their caliber.[17] Instead, she stressed how "day care"—a term associated with babysitting—enabled mothers to help the war cause. "If the mothers have no conveniently situated, capably run place in which to leave their young children during working hours," she noted, "they will not stick loyally at their war jobs." Deep into the article Stolz made passing reference to the fact that the education being provided at the Kaiser centers was "aligned with the best practice in the field of child development." But she, or more likely her editors, must have appreciated that, to the readers of the *Times*, this fact didn't count for much.

Casting the argument for child care this way—not as an end in itself but rather as a means of making the economy hum more smoothly—set the stage for everything that followed. When the war ended, the Kaiser centers, like other government-funded programs across the country, were shuttered. Women were no longer needed in the workplace, the thinking went, so they could go back to staying at home with their babies. The idea that poor and working-class kids might thrive if they could spend some time in such places—that they might benefit from the kind of experience that, as James Hymes pointed out, the well-off took for granted—wasn't even on the radar screen.

Less than a generation later, in 1962, the Perry Preschool opened its doors. In scope, Perry was smaller and less ambitious. The Kaiser centers used state-of-the-art pedagogy to educate thousands of children from the working class—a group that, like the Perry preschoolers, had been regarded as unable to absorb such a regimen.[18] But while the shipyard centers were always regarded as a wartime expedient, Perry was designed as an experiment that the nation could learn from, and that turned out to be the consequential difference.

Moreover, even while the Kaiser centers were operating, psychologists were furiously arguing about the Iowa orphans study—whether taking children out of an orphanage, and so radically changing their milieu, could transform their lives. Although evidence about the Child Service Centers' impact would have made a contribution to that debate, the project was never considered in that light.[19]

Out of Harm's Way

During the Kennedy administration, the federal government once again began to underwrite child care. Ever since, says Ron Haskins at the Brookings Institution, "The big policy idea has been that the federal government would accept major responsibility for day care if government encouraged or, as was eventually to happen, required welfare mothers to work." But if expanding the workforce is paramount, then the quality of the care isn't a priority.[20]

The closest that Washington has ever come to taking a kid-centered approach was the 1971 Child Development Act.[21] That legislation looked to be the obvious next step after Head Start. It was promoted not as a way to nudge mothers off the welfare rolls—Richard Nixon had earlier mandated such a work requirement, which incorporated child care—but, like Head Start, as a way to make children's lives better.

President Nixon vetoed that legislation in memorably nasty language. "For the Federal Government to plunge headlong financially into supporting child development," he declaimed, "would commit the vast moral authority of the National Government to the side of communal approaches to child rearing over and against the family-centered approach."[22] That veto effectively buried the issue for a generation.

"Family" versus "communal" approaches to child rearing—there is no rationale for defining the issue in these either-or terms, but the dialogue has seldom been strong on logic or nuance.[23] Consider the arguments advanced during a segment on *The NewsHour with Jim Lehrer* that aired in October 1997. That PBS show has a reputation for sweet reason, to the point of ennui, but this exchange was hardly staid.

Former Reagan administration official Charmaine Yoest found

inspiration in Alexis de Tocqueville's classic, *Democracy in America*, for her claim that government should keep its hands off. "You know, one hundred fifty years ago Tocqueville said that the strength of America lay in our voluntary associations and the strength of Americans to be self-reliant. As we talk about the federal government coming in and trying to solve these kinds of very personal, intimate problems for people, we are going against the grain of what we need to see happening, of emphasizing community solutions, of parents solving their own problems." Psychiatrist Stanley Greenspan chimed in with a hypersimplified version of neuroscience, insisting that the home, rather than child care, was the right place for young children to acquire the "six key experiences" that promoted "intelligence and emotional growth."

Ellen Galinsky of the Families and Work Institute, cast as the lone child care advocate, thought she was having a *Groundhog Day* moment: "We're having this discussion as if it were like 1971, when we were talking about creating a federal system of child care, which of course didn't happen." Yoest insisted that to enact the Clinton administration's proposals meant embracing something akin to the "communal child rearing" that Nixon had meant to bury. "No we're not," replied Galinsky. "Most of the [federal] spending goes to give families money to help support their choices." But Yoest wasn't buying it. "Federal money always comes with strings," she contended, to which a frustrated Galinsky countered that "it actually doesn't."

The *NewsHour* segment was timed to coincide with what was supposed to be a watershed event for child care. After wandering in the desert for years, advocates had finally gotten the attention they craved, a day-long White House Conference on Child Care.[24] Standing under the massive crystal chandeliers of the East Room, First Lady Hillary Clinton spoke of a "silent crisis" in child care.

Such events are often gabfests, feel-good moments for the faithful, but this time there was reason to anticipate concrete results. Although the 1971 veto hovered over the proceedings like Banquo's ghost, a lot had changed since then. The migration of mothers into the workplace, which had earlier been described as a "subtle revolution," wasn't so subtle any more. Most mothers were employed, including more than 60 percent of those with preschoolers. The nation, wrote *Boston Globe* columnist Ellen Goodman, had arrived at "the end of a long cultural debate about motherhood as we know it."[25]

In the wake of the White House event and the news stories that it generated, improving the lives of young children held the promise of becoming the next big idea on the domestic policy front—"moving out of the ladies' department," as social commentator Jonathan Alter wrote in *Newsweek,* and "into the macho world of big-time, bone-crunching legislation."[26] President Clinton promised to make the topic of "affordable, accessible and safe" day care a centerpiece of his 1998 State of the Union address.[27] But in politics, as in life, timing is everything. Even as he was putting the finishing touches on that address, the Monica Lewinsky scandal was beginning to seep out, and for the rest of the Clinton years matters of policy took a backseat to the debacle of impeachment.

Meanwhile, Clinton's 1996 welfare reform legislation has "turned out to be a money machine for child care," says Ron Haskins. Eligible parents receive child care vouchers, and one of the few stipulations in the law is that they be told that they may select anyone, whether licensed or not, to take care of their kids. Most rely on informal, unlicensed care—offered by the ladies in the church basement, or Grandma, or the neighbor with young children of her own, a TV set tuned to *Sesame Street* or the soaps, a few coloring books, and maybe a sandbox in the backyard.

The fact that most parents have relied on that option is sometimes cited as evidence that the system is working. "Parents like to choose their own care, and lots of parents like care in church basements and in their neighborhoods," Haskins contends. "Many Americans are wary of government regulations, especially federal regulations."[28] But because most states don't inform parents about variations in the quality of what's on offer—many don't even assess whether the informal settings are safe, let alone how good they are—it is hard to say that families are making an informed choice. And for many parents, the cost of child care at a licensed center is out of reach. The average cost of full-time care is more than $5,000 a year—that's more than the tuition at many public universities—and parents of infants pay about $1,500 more.[29] As Hillary Clinton said at the 1997 White House conference, "It is difficult to think of a consumer situation in America where so many people are paying so much and often getting so little."

Neighbors who take care of others' kids presumably like children, and they understand the time binds on working parents. Such loving-kindness and flexibility, though not amenable to evaluation, is worth a lot, since among most couples earning less than $50,000, at least one spouse isn't working nine to five.[30] "Have you ever seen the schedule that parents who work in the big-box stores have to meet?" asks Maria Whelan, president of the Chicago-based advocacy group Action for Children. "They're on swing shift one week, graveyard shift the next, their days off keep changing every week—who else is going to be that flexible?"

In a kinder, gentler world, companies like Wal-Mart and Target would behave like Henry Kaiser, lessening the stresses they inflict on their workers' home lives. As things stand, though, most businesses duck this responsibility and families are left to fend for themselves.

Child development experts don't know much about what these neighbors and relatives are doing while minding others' children, although they have their suspicions (watching TV comes high on the list).[31] For years, however, they have been studying licensed centers and family-care homes. What they've seen hasn't been pretty, and as the need for day care has burgeoned, things seem to have gotten worse.

A nationwide survey carried out in the early 1970s showed that most child care centers were pedestrian at best. A generation later, with many more children needing care, a similar survey found that the situation had deteriorated: three-quarters of licensed centers were mediocre, and one in eight was providing "less than minimal" care.[32] Few states require providers to have any training. Child care workers—the label "worker" is itself telling—are paid about as much as burger flippers at Jack in the Box, about $5.15 an hour; their current wages, adjusted for inflation, are about $1.00 an hour *lower* than they were in 1977; and among all occupations, only gas-station attendants are more likely to switch jobs.[33]

"The old saying," says Marcy Whitebook, longtime director of UC Berkeley's Center for the Child Care Workforce, "is 'Parents can't afford to pay, teachers can't afford to stay—there's gotta be a better way.'"

With federal child care regulation off the table, and most states doing little, the National Association for the Education of Young Children, the biggest private organization of child care professionals, stepped into the breach. Its most recent standards, adopted in 2005, "lift up the role of the teacher as a teacher, not just someone who is nice to children," says Sue Bredekamp, who directed NAEYC's professional development program. "This will challenge even the best programs." Teacher qualifications have been stiffened as well—by 2020, child care teachers in participating centers must have a two-year associate's degree and be on their way to earning a BA.

The NAEYC wants to erase the line between day care and preschool—to turn former Clinton administration official Joan Lombardi's vision of "good education" for children of every age into practice, not with government regulation but through private suasion.[34] How well the teachers are trained, how responsive they are to children's needs, what the ratio is of teachers to kids, how inviting the classroom and the playground are—the organization's standards coincide with what any thoughtful parent would be looking for in either a child care center or a prekindergarten.[35]

But NAEYC accreditation is entirely voluntary. Nationwide, less than a tenth of the 125,000 licensed centers have secured it—not enough to put substantial pressure on the child care marketplace. Among those who run the accredited centers, perpetually strapped for funds, there's also considerable grumbling about the feasibility of putting the 2005 requirements in place.

What is to be done? Economists talk about making the child care market work more efficiently by offering better information to families. Child development specialists emphasize the need for tighter regulation and more publicly run programs like Early Head Start. Most of the experts agree on two things: the system is broken, and it will cost a lot of money—estimates range from $12 billion to more than $100 billion—to fix it.[36]

Thinking big was the order of the day after the 1997 White House Conference on Child Care: expanding Early Head Start and Head Start to include working- and middle-class families, or helping parents to become better consumers of child care, or adopting nationwide quality standards, or maybe even enacting a version of the fabled 1971 Child Development Act. Since then, however, child care has once again slipped below the policymakers' radar. Decentralization, deregulation, and privatization, rather than quality, remain the guiding criteria.[37]

"You have to ask yourself, 'What are the Democrats doing?'" economist Barbara Bergmann, the author of *America's Child Care Problem: The Way Out*, inquires pointedly. "'What did they do all during the Clinton administration?' Not a goddamn thing. They got scared on health insurance." Matthew Melmed at Zero to Three muses that "if we had people like Hillary today, we could go to the foundations. But Hillary isn't touching the issue." Apparently the senator with ambitions has calculated that, despite the economic and demographic realities, child care remains just a women's issue.

When Barbara Reisman was running Child Care Action Campaign, a lobbying group, in the 1980s, she formulated the argument that spending money on good child care would produce substantial returns down the road. "We really wanted to move child care away from being perceived as a women's issue, because women's issues aren't taken seriously," Reisman explains. "They are seen as soft or private, not as important as other things like economic development. So our goal was to show the links between economic development and the availability of high-quality child care. We also recruited men to make the case—when you have unexpected messengers, people pay close attention."

This argument has worked well for preschool advocates. But for child care, the stunning cost-benefit analyses on which pre-K supporters have relied aren't to be had. Also missing is any evidence that the Kaiser shipyard centers (or any other child care center, for that matter) had noteworthy long-term effects comparable to Perry Preschool or Chicago's Child-Parent Centers.[38]

What's more, talking about infants and toddlers in the language of "investment" evokes a familiar Dr. Laura–esque ambivalence about who bears responsibility for bringing up the next generation. "If you use the term 'child care,' people think of it as 'that's for working parents,' and preschool means something different," says Child Care Action Campaign's Reisman. "We can talk until we're blue in the face about how the two are related and they're not mutually exclusive. But it's what people hear."

The argument for preschool is much simpler—every child should come to kindergarten ready to learn. "You can put pre-K in a box, you tie it up, and you put the bow on it," says Helen Blank, formerly at the Children's Defense Fund. "Parents can see a classroom of four-year-olds. Child care is birth to thirteen. It's pretty messy. It's neighbors . . . it's people working off hours . . . it's everything. With pre-K you can really feel good. You get the four-year-olds, they're in their classes, and you did it—education. They're all going to grow up successful."

By 2001 preschool seemed a more promising arena for reform. The White House Conference on Child Care was only a receding memory. The Clintons were gone, George Bush occupied the White House, and for all his talk of compassionate conservatism, there would be no revisiting of the topic of child care—that was the states' affair, and the states viewed child care largely in workforce terms.

"Public school officials said, 'Prekindergarten, we'll buy into this,'" says Dana Friedman, cofounder of the Families and Work Institute. "They saw potential for the big money that 'child care' has never been able to get, and everybody said, 'Yeah, let's ride that train.'" When two foundations with an activist bent, the Pew Charitable Trusts and the Packard Foundation, set out at the start of the new century to define their institutional agendas for the coming years, each of them laid out a ten-year plan to promote universal preschool. Those decisions have contributed to shaping a movement.

S · I · X

Jump-Starting a Movement

BEGINNING in the 1970s, when the idea of publicly funded early education, not just for poor children but for all kids, was first being bruited, the right was motivated to mobilize. Conservatives were deeply antagonistic toward what was regarded as a quintessentially nanny-state project. That instinctual distaste lingers: wherever state-supported prekindergarten appears on the legislative agenda, a reactionary lawmaker will invariably fulminate about "ripping infants out of their mother's arms."

Over the years, however, many conservative organizations have developed a pitch that's both more sophisticated and less overtly ideological. It is not that the ideology has changed, just that the tone of the message has been softened. These groups have ventured into the research business, attacking the empirical justifications for prekindergarten. The formation of a confederacy of like-minded organizations has helped to magnify their voice.

Those on the other side of this great social divide—for whom the welfare of children isn't just a family affair but is also a public responsibility—have been engaged in a long-running, high-stakes game of political and policy chess with the right. While conservatives present a clear set of principles for children's policy—less government, family values, and lower taxes—liberals are, as ever, a house divided. Such foundations such as the Pew Charitable Trusts and the Packard Foundation, which have supported efforts to attain the readily defined goal of universal preschool, find themselves at odds with advocates dedicated to advancing a far broader array of claims, and the arcane art of how best to "frame" these issues has been absorbed into the intramural dialogue. The account of these ideological and tactical fissures isn't just inside baseball, of interest only to the cognoscenti—how it plays out affects not only the nature and quality of the preschools that taxpayers support but also the prospects for a wide-ranging children's movement.

Almost a Revolution

In the mid-1990s, after decades of spoiled dreams, a sea change in politics, one that would situate children at the political forefront, seemed finally to be taking place.[1] As we've seen, child care was a part of the story. But it was only a part—everything from health insurance to infant and toddler care was on the table.

The first signs of this shift could be glimpsed several years earlier. In 1987 Democratic strategist Stanley Greenberg wrote a widely circulated memo arguing that an emphasis on children's needs could bring fallen-away party members back to the fold. "When candidates talk about kids, they are talking about the fundamental economic and social terrain on which Democrats must run," Greenberg maintained, and children's issues could become a way for many Americans to "rediscover government."[2] Republicans made a similar calculation, and so, suddenly, politicians from both parties were outbidding one another in their generosity toward the young. In 1991 George Bush billed himself as the "education president," and Bill Clinton pushed the National Governors Association to focus on education. Not surprisingly, education figured prominently in the 1992 presidential campaign.

This was a moment when the righteous claims of children momentarily rose above partisan calculations. Also in 1991, amid considerable hoopla, the National Commission on Children emerged from fifteen months of site visits and town meetings, including a reenactment of Robert Kennedy's "poverty walk" in the West Virginia hollows, with a bill of particulars covering everything from health and family-support initiatives to early education and family values. Especially remarkable was the fact that a committee whose members ran the ideological gamut from the unreconstructed antipoverty warriors at the Children's Defense Fund to the hyper-traditionalist Family Research Council could produce a unanimous document. Pointedly contrasting its intention with all the earlier futilities, the commission titled its manifesto *Beyond Rhetoric*.[3] The Carnegie Corporation's 1995 report, *Starting Points,* sparked interest with its talk of a "silent crisis" that faced young children and their parents, and its references, new at the time, to the importance of the early years for the development of the brain.[4]

This was a propitious moment for the Pew Charitable Trusts, a foundation that searches for problems on which it can have a direct impact, to enter the arena. Pew proposed a decade-long effort, immodestly intended to reinvent the system of child care and early education. It envisioned bringing together all the state agencies that served the young—whether in the health, education, or social services arena—tracking what was happening on the ground, saving money by combining efforts, and thus leveraging better outcomes. Five states signed on, and the cumbersome, painstaking work of bureaucratic coordination began.

Eighteen months later, Pew decided to pull the plug. "It broke my heart," says John Love, a senior researcher at Mathematica Policy Research who had participated in designing the evaluation. While this is not how policy wonks usually talk, Love remembers the months he devoted to the venture as the most exciting time in his professional life. Nearly a decade afterward, when Love went to Georgia to meet with senior managers in that state's recently created Department of Early Care and Learning, he found that "the remnants of the project are still there, and they are having an impact on how people talk with each other."

The decision not to go forward was a hard call for Rebecca Rimel, who has been at the helm of Pew since 1988. But the initiative had proved "too complicated to manage," she says. "The politics were too deep. And how do you measure success?"

When *Philadelphia* magazine profiled the city's single most powerful individual in 2005, it didn't select the mayor or the CEO of Sunoco or the owner of the Phillies. Instead it chose Rebecca Rimel. One reporter observed, wonderingly, that "what she wants she usually gets," whether that is completing the long-stalled Independence Park Mall, the new home of the Liberty Bell, or a massive get-out-the-vote initiative during the 2004 campaign, aimed at bringing politically disaffected young adults to the polls.[5] "I'm a heat-seeking missile in getting to the goal," she says.

In 2000, as Rimel and Susan Urahn, the managing director of state policy initiatives at Pew, were pondering their next moves, Rutgers University economist Steven Barnett came calling.

Barnett, who since the early 1980s had been tracking the Perry Preschool children, made a strong case for focusing Pew's efforts on prekindergarten.

The timing was propitious. Rimel had concluded that higher education was "impermeable to outside influence," and Pew's involvements in primary and secondary education had amounted to "two steps forward, one step back." Good pre-K was a worthy aim because it could "give kids a fighting chance." There was good evidence—better evidence, indeed, than for any other child-related venture—that prekindergarten, when done right, could have a powerful effect.

Universal preschool was also an excellent fit for the foundation. "We pick issues that are ripe, where the facts are clear and where we can bring change in a short time," says Rimel. The objective was understandable and readily specifiable—high-quality, voluntary preschool for all three- and four-year-olds—and an infusion of foundation money could swing the momentum in that direction. Although more than thirty states were already underwriting preschools when Pew entered the picture, only two, Georgia and Oklahoma, had a universal program up and running; elsewhere, classes for three- and four-year-olds were modest in number and spotty in quality. No other major foundation had staked a claim to the issue.[6] What's more, unlike the public schools, prekindergarten had neither a bureaucracy nor a teachers' union to mollify. It seemed a tabula rasa on which Pew could leave its mark.[7]

In 2001, one week after 9/11, Pew's board of trustees gave its approval to the preschool initiative. This wasn't going to be a 1960s-style civil rights campaign driven by the justness of the cause and the evilness of the adversaries. The 1960s are ancient history at Pew, where the model is unapologetically corporate.

Pew is in the philanthropy business. As with its other ventures, the tools of contemporary politics were brought to bear—polls, focus groups, targeted marketing, clear "messaging," grassroots organizing, and the cultivation of influential supporters, especially from the business sector.

"The stars were aligned: politics, policy, and advocacy," Susan Urahn notes. The size of the projected investment—$10 million a year over the course of a decade, to underwrite policy-driven research and advocacy—coupled with Pew's desire to promote universal preschool across the country, made it the biggest player in the field.

It was also the most controversial.

In many fields Pew has the money to attract the best talent in the trade, nudging them into making its priorities their own.[8] That doesn't make it very popular. "Pew always does a diagnostic, finds the existing organizations to be deficient and then creates its own," says a marketing specialist who insisted on speaking off the record. "That's why it's widely disliked."

Pew doesn't shy away from underwriting advocacy, something that gives most foundations hives. By law, while foundations may support advocacy, they are required to stay clear of lobbying for a particular piece of legislation, a line that can come to seem awfully fine. Pew is different. In 2004 it changed its legal status, becoming a public charity; as such it can use up to 5 percent of its funds directly for lobbying and can also run its own programs.

"I'm a raging incrementalist," says Rimel, who has scoped out the Pew Trusts' end-game for preschool. "If ten states adopt universal pre-K [by the time the decade-long commitment ends], then the advocates will pick this up and we'll move on. Even if three of the programs are cruddy, it's a win. If the figures are reversed, we'll keep funding the advocacy organizations."

Total: 39.70
Tip: 7.00
Payment Amount: 32.70

Ticket Name: Table 2
Server: stephanie
Authcode: 021802
Reference: 12814
CC Num: XXXX XXXX XXXX 1313
CC Type: Mastercard
Name: CORTES/WILLIAM
Credit Purchase

Amount Due: $32.70
Grand Total: $32.70

Sales Tax: $2.70
Subtotal: $30.00
Enchiladas   1 $18.00
Sausage from Brazil 1 $9.00
White Sangria   1 $3.00

ITEM   QTY PRICE
02885050 # 4 10-18-17 W9 10:18:47 #102AVR/01
stephanie SERVER JANICE SHOP
TABLE: Table 2 - 2 Guests
Division for Day Abuna

PH (P1) 535-1500
BROOKLINE, MA 95442
532 MANHATTAN ST.
EL CENTRO

EL CENTRO
236 WASHINGTON ST
BROOKLINE, MA 02445
ph (617)232-4200

Thank You for Visiting
TABLE: Table 2 - 2 Guests
Your Server was alejandra
10/9/2013 7:19:07 PM - ID #: 0059620

ITEM	QTY	PRICE
White Sangria	1	$7.00
Sangria Roja Glass	1	$7.00
Enchiladas	1	$16.00
Subtotal		$30.00
Total Taxes		$2.10

Grand Total $32.10
Amount Due: $32.10

Credit Purchase
Name: CORTES/YLIANA
CC Type: MasterCard
CC Num: xxxx xxxx xxxx 1217
Reference: :46814
Approval: 081902
Ticket Name   :Table 2
Server   :alejandra

Payment Amount: $32.10

Tip: 7.00

Total: 39.10

X _____

Please Come Back!

Polling and "Messaging"

Pew believes in polls—it has long supported an array of public opinion research, on everything from presidential politics to global warming—and every poll conducted on the topic in recent years has confirmed preschool's popularity.[9] In a few states, Illinois and California among them, advertising campaigns underwritten by foundations and state agencies have extolled the virtues of good preschool. Those efforts doubtless made some difference—popular support for pre-K increased there—but even where pre-K hasn't been deliberately promoted, enthusiasm has run high. As Steven Barnett pointed out during his meetings with the Pew staff, on this issue the citizens have been leagues ahead of the politicians.

By better than two-to-one margins, voters support quality pre-kindergarten for every four-year-old. What's more, preschool ranks high on their list of public priorities—higher than reforming the public schools or cutting state taxes. More than half say they'd be more likely to support a candidate for governor or a legislator who favored preschool for all, and they express their willingness to pick up the tab, even if that means a tax hike. The public has embraced the conclusion that pre-K is a way to get four-year-olds ready for school. But including three-year-olds in the program is considerably less popular. And to the dismay of those whose main concern is the welfare of babies, there's considerably less popular support for educating infants and toddlers.

Frank Luntz, a Republican pollster, was drawn into the preschool orbit by Hollywood actor-director Rob Reiner, an ardent enthusiast of early education, who convinced him with arguments about the importance of early brain development. In 2005 Luntz, widely credited with coming up with "the death tax," the phrase that killed off the estate tax, surveyed Ohio voters. "If you can provide children from birth to age six with fair chances and their parents with good choices, an early care and education campaign will be a success," he concluded. Luntz was surprised that pre-K would be so popular. "Republicans favor these programs at a much higher rate than we expected, and Democrats are already on board."[10]

"The polls tell you where you are," Steven Barnett observes, "but that doesn't mean you can't change things." Barnett was the obvious choice to conduct the preschool policy research that would underpin Pew's "evidence-based" initiative, since this was what he was already doing in New Jersey. There, the state's highest court had ordered lawmakers to give children living in the worst school districts a high-quality early education, and it was Barnett's job to attach specifics to the all-important concept of "quality."

"Those kids were getting terrible pre-K and they were coming to kindergarten way behind," says Barnett, who proposed that Pew emphasize similar issues all across the country. The National Institute for Early Education Research (NIEER), conceived and underwritten by Pew and directed by Barnett, had received more than $20 million by 2006. "What attracted the foundation," Barnett believes, "was the model of using research to move a public policy agenda, providing information in a way that the media would cover it and the public would know about it."

The institute works in tandem with Pew, and the research priorities are selected to coincide with what's on the minds of policymakers. NIEER prepares state-by-state reports on the anticipated payoff from universal preschool—consistent with other research, those analyses generally estimate a three-to-one return on a state's investment. It has prepared studies showing that teachers who have a bachelor's degree do the best job of preparing preschoolers for later success and that running preschools for all children, not just the neediest, makes the best sense. While these findings don't go uncontested, Barnett vigorously defends NIEER's research. "Academics usually aren't willing to speak up for their work," he says—"it's 'I did the study, it's published, end of story'"—but he seems to relish taking on his critics.

NIEER's annual yearbook, the *Consumer Reports* side of its work, uses a ten-point rating scale to measure the quality of a state's prekindergarten initiatives, with points awarded for small classes, teachers with college degrees, and the like. The yearbook shines a spotlight on states that are doing well, as well as on those that aren't. "Whether the publicity is positive or negative, it has an influence," says Barnett. "Oklahoma didn't know it was the nation's leader until our report appeared. Then politicians in other states started saying, 'If Oklahoma can do it, so can we.'" To make sure that word gets out, Barnett reviews the findings with lawmakers and advocates. "We get calls from governors' offices," he says, when asked about the direct impact of NIEER's efforts: "'We're working on a new pre-K program. What do we need to do to get credit?'"

Research is just one part of Pew's strategy. The foundation recognized that, to carry the day, endorsements were needed not just from the old-line children's advocacy groups but also from unanticipated sources. "We found champions from many sectors—police chiefs, business leaders, seniors, physicians, school board members—who weren't the usual suspects, and who were willing to say that prekindergarten is essential to helping children succeed," says Sara Watson, who has managed the pre-K project since its inception. "The idea was to figure out whatever local advocates need to get the message across, then work from the top down and bottom up to make that happen."

Pew also wanted to support the work of advocates in states where universal preschool seemed viable, but that was more easily said than done. The foundation's initial foray proved a false start. The Trust for Early Education, established in 2002 with substantial Pew backing, had a hard time turning its gaze away from the doings (more precisely, the *non*doings) in Congress and toward the state capitals. Washington is the domain its executive director, Amy Wilkins, knew intimately—she had earlier worked at the Children's Defense Fund—but all the action was elsewhere.

The second try—Pre-K Now, largely a Pew creation—has turned out to be much more successful. Pre-K Now works closely with NIEER, marketing the research message and sustaining on-the-ground maneuvers in some fifteen states. Like NIEER, it was set up as a single-purpose organization. It's the other major recipient of Pew's preschool largesse, having received $20 million as of 2007, and much of its money is funneled directly to state-based activists.

Libby Doggett, the executive director of Pre-K Now, has long lived in the world of advocacy. For many years she worked in Texas, negotiating with conservative lawmakers to expand entitlements for disabled children, and later she was on the staff of the National Head Start Association. As the wife of Texas congressman Lloyd Doggett, one of ex-House of Representatives majority leader Tom DeLay's perennial redistricting targets, she knows the ins and outs of campaigns.

"Picking the states in which to invest was almost a science," Doggett says. "We had reams of data on the political climate, the budget situation, the child advocacy organizations. I was looking for two things: experienced advocates and someone high up in government who could make something happen." States like Illinois and New York were easy, since both the activist network and the supportive politicians were already ensconced. Kansas was a long shot—the perversity of a poor rural Kansas county's support for conservative Republicans is the theme of the best-selling political exhumation, *What's the Matter with Kansas?*—but the enthusiasm of the Greater Kansas City Community Foundation, which has made a twenty-year commitment to reforming public education, convinced Doggett to get involved.[11] That bet paid off. In 2006 Kansas joined the preschool movement when its lawmakers approved a $10 million pilot prekindergarten project.

The Golden State

Even as the Pew Charitable Trusts entered the preschool domain in 2001, in Silicon Valley the Packard Foundation found itself forced to confront hard questions about its future.[12] The foundation's endowment, heavily invested in Hewlett-Packard company stock, had lost nearly half its value in the wake of the high-tech collapse. Such a dramatic reduction concentrates the attention mightily.

Since its founding in 1964, children's issues had been one of the foundation's priorities (it has also concentrated on conservation and population). Packard had scattered its largesse broadly, but when the foundation's entire budget for children's programs was cut from $30 million to $18 million as part of the overall reduction, this fuzziness of focus became an unaffordable luxury.

Recruiting Lois Salisbury to head the program signaled a new direction for the foundation. Salisbury had spent more than two decades working as an attorney at Public Advocates, a public-interest law firm, and later became the executive director of

Children Now, California's major lobbying group for youngsters. She brought the no-nonsense perspective of an activist to the foundation. The analysis that led Packard to make universal preschool in California its marquee children's project paralleled the thinking that had taken place at Pew.[13]

This division of the world—a single state, California, for the Packard Foundation and the rest of the country for the Pew Charitable Trusts—was as logical as the remapping of Europe at the 1815 Congress of Vienna. Pew had already determined that it would stay clear of California. The Golden State is the preschool movement's biggest prize. One out of every eight three- and four-year-olds in the United States lives there; there are more young children in Los Angeles County alone than in any other state. But California is simply too big and complex, its politics too Byzantine, the price tag of persuading the voters and the power brokers too high, to be just one among the multitude of states in which Pew could productively invest.

The Packard Foundation was much better suited to the task. It has a long history of funding early childhood initiatives in the state, and by announcing its intention to spend nearly as much money to promote pre-K in California as Pew was spending nationwide, it immediately became a force to be reckoned with. Even before taking up the preschool cause, Packard had developed a solid working relationship with the state's First Five Commission, established by the voters in 1997 and headed at the time by Rob Reiner. By 2002 the commission had decided to concentrate on universal preschool. Packard could piggyback on its Hollywood-sophisticated promotion campaign, linking its efforts to the matching grants the First Five Commission was giving to communities committed to expanding preschool. Moreover, there were economies to be realized: with Pew's support, NIEER was already developing the economic case for prekindergarten, so Packard didn't have to duplicate that costly research project.[14]

The Packard Foundation developed a "logic model" laying out the first five years of its planned decade-long campaign. On paper the multicolored depiction resembles the map of the London Underground, with lines running every which way to show how strategy X is supposed to lead to output Y and, in turn, to outcome Z. Yet such easily caricatured complexity captures what the foundation is trying to do—its "theory of action."[15] The plan earmarks big chunks of money to obtain the support of key constituencies like the teachers' unions, as well as to recruit "nontraditional allies" like local chambers of commerce and police chiefs. Those mobilizing efforts are complemented by grants to communities that are setting up flagship preschools, on-the-ground demonstrations of what "quality" pre-K means, with the hope that those early adopters will encourage others to follow suit.

Just as Pew launched Pre-K Now to spread the preschool gospel, the Packard Foundation started Preschool California to move the topic to the front burner there. Early education is a crowded and contentious field in California, and Packard's involvement wasn't always welcomed. "Ideally, initiatives come from the bottom up," acknowledges Maryann O'Sullivan, Preschool California's founder and CEO, who had earlier worked to support afterschool programs, "but this one came from the top down. Because we had to make our intentions clear, we spent a lot of time during the first two years holding meetings across the state, explaining what we were about and enlisting support."

Focusing entirely on a single state, like investing all your money in a single company, is an inherently high-risk strategy. In 2002, when Packard's trustees gave the go-ahead for the ten-year effort, no one could have anticipated that California would soon confront a structural budget deficit that would put most new policy ideas on hold, or that Gray Davis, the Democratic governor, would be recalled, replaced by the Republican Arnold Schwarzenegger.

Most important, no one could have predicted that major decisions about how best to promote the cause of universal preschool would be made by Rob Reiner. As discussed in the next chapter, which takes a close look at prekindergarten politics in California, Reiner had his own theory of action—a statewide ballot measure mandating preschool for all—and that's the direction in which policymaking headed.

"We can't control who enters the field," says Packard Foundation president Carol Larson, who has spent most of her career working on children's concerns. "Whatever the issue, whether it's kids or conservation, we want to build momentum."

Although the ballot initiative ended up being resoundingly defeated in 2006, enrollment in publicly supported preschools has continued to expand in California, and Packard deserves some of the credit. Larson points to a map of the state showing the growing number of counties that have opened their own pre-K programs. In 2005, $160 million was in the pipeline, a figure that keeps growing as new entrants signal their interest. The Packard Foundation is in it for the long haul, says Larson, and "even if state policy doesn't change, there's a good chance that preschool is sustainable." Adds Packard's Lois Salisbury, "We're poised like a surfer who's ready to ride the big wave when it comes."

Thunder on the Right

The campaign for universal preschool is a red flag for conservatives of various stripes, those anxious to defend the prerogatives of what they perceive to be the endangered family and those whose fondest dream is to expand the market and starve the beast of big government.

For hard-core social conservatives, public prekindergarten evokes the dread fear that government is stealing babies from their cribs. Over the years, however, many on the right have toned down their rhetoric, becoming more nuanced and sophisticated in their approach in order to woo new supporters.

An antigovernment message has been crafted by a nationwide web of organizations that share a libertarian philosophy. Prominent among them are the Washington, DC–based Cato Institute ("promoting an American policy based on individual liberty, limited government, free markets"); the Goldwater Institute ("unrestrained government has proved to be a chief instrument in history for thwarting individual liberty"); the Reason Foundation ("free minds and free markets"); the Texas Public Policy Foundation ("individual liberty, free markets, limited government"); the Oklahoma Council of Public Affairs ("free enterprise, limited government and individual initiative"); and Freedom Works, founded by former Texas congressman Dick Armey ("lower taxes, less government, more freedom"). They take up the cudgels on a wide array of causes, from property and eminent domain to global warming and the federal No Child Left Behind legislation. State preschool is on their "not-to-do" lists.

These groups have tried to discredit the main calling card of the prekindergarten advocates—the proposition that the benefits of early education have been confirmed by research. It's an uphill struggle to upend the findings of modern neuroscience, the results of studies like Perry Preschool, and economic analyses done by the likes of James Heckman, but the conservatives mine the evidence, picking out what they see as confirming their predilections. To show the inefficacy of early education, they cite studies that conclude, controversially, that the achievement gains recorded among four-year-olds later fade away. Ignoring the evidence from NIEER's five-state study and research on Tulsa's preschools, described in Chapter 2, they contend that the paucity of evidence demonstrating the value of preschool for middle-class youngsters means public subsidies should be limited to the children of the poor.

At the Goldwater Institute, president and CEO Darcy Olsen turns out opinion pieces critical of pre-K that run in newspapers across the country. To make the conservatives' position look more respectably mainstream, Olsen has sought to enlist the preschool intelligentsia. In a 2005 paper, "Assessing Proposals for Preschool and Kindergarten: Essential Information for Parents, Taxpayers, and Policymakers," she misrepresented Yale psychology professor Edward Zigler, the doyen of early education, who has championed universal preschool for more than forty years, brazenly claiming that he opposes the idea.[16] When she suggested to NIEER's Barnett that they explore areas of policy agreement, he declined. "There are no areas of agreement," he tartly responded.

Olsen fared far better with Art Rolnick, the director of research at the Federal Reserve Bank's Minneapolis branch and a luminary in the prekindergarten movement. Their 2005 dialogue, published online by the American Experiment, a Republican think tank, sounds like an Alphonse-and-Gaston routine. "Darcy has done a nice job of laying out the problems with universal, rather than targeted, preschool," Rolnick said, responding to an opening gambit about which positions they shared. "I have a strong belief in the market mechanism," he added, another point of seeming consensus. "I'm a bit indifferent about whether the funding comes from the state or private."[17]

Throughout the conversation the point that eluded Rolnick is that he and Olsen differ fundamentally in their beliefs about government's responsibility. Despite his profession of indifference to public involvement, Rolnick has an activist's temperament—he has urged the Minnesota legislature to increase its spending on poor children. For him, the market—publicly subsidized and closely monitored—is a means to an end, a mechanism to achieve good early education for the least well-off. In contrast, Olsen's hobbyhorse contention is that it is premature to consider expanding preschool when K–12 education is in such terrible shape. That's a plausible position—but not when it's being advanced by the president of an institute resolutely opposed to generating the necessary revenue. For Olsen, this dialogue wasn't an affable intellectual exercise but a way of claiming a prominent convert to the anti-preschool cause.

Purporting to rely on research rather than raw emotion is a tactic that many of these organizations use. Vermonters for Better Education, a subsidiary of Freedom Works, used Olsen's 2005 paper to back up its opposition to prekindergarten for all. In California, the Reason Foundation recruited two conservative economists to dispute a 2005 Rand Corporation study underwritten by the Packard Foundation. The Rand report had found that, over the course of a generation, the benefits of good preschool to California's taxpayers would outweigh the costs by nearly three to one. The Reason Foundation's critique, though imbalanced, wasn't outrageous, since like most research, the Rand study was vulnerable to criticism on methodological grounds.

Lisa Snell, who runs the education program at the Reason Foundation, is candid about why she commissioned the rebuttal paper. "We don't put much credence in cost-benefit analysis, because it's so easy to manipulate the data by deciding which factors to include and which to leave out," she says. "We did the flip—we included more costs and were more skeptical about the benefits."

The Reason Foundation's report came in handy during the successful fight against California's 2006 universal preschool ballot measure. And Snell has been asked to testify by lawmakers in several states where preschool has been up for a vote. "Success brings scrutiny," acknowledges Libby Doggett at Pre-K Now.

Framing the Issue

"The success of pre-K has made the child care advocates nervous," says Doggett. That's putting things mildly. Despite thirty years of attempts to cajole the federal government into recognizing that the welfare of babies matters, the caliber of child-minding options remains abysmal. Meanwhile preschool is thriving, and Pew has borne the brunt of the child care advocates' frustration.

The complaint is that prekindergarten is diverting funds from infants and toddlers, paying teachers higher salaries and so making it even harder to lure teachers to work with babies—"robbing Peter to pay Paul" is the oft-heard lament. Matthew Melmed, executive director of the national lobbying group Zero to Three, assails the pre-K movement as "philanthropic hubris. They say that pre-K is saleable, but I could sell anything with the money they are pouring into it."

At the Packard Foundation, Lois Salisbury wonders why advocates for babies sometimes cast themselves as antagonists. "You need a long-term perspective," she argues, "rather than seeing things in *Sophie's Choice* terms of 'early education versus pre-K.'" Yet because public dollars are limited, choices do have to be made, and prekindergarten has ruled.

"We need a different frame for infants and toddlers," Melmed concludes, assessing why those who lobby on behalf of babies have had a hard time moving their agenda forward. "It's really the pre-K frame, 'brain development' and 'invest now.' Preschool stole our frame."

In no time flat, "framing" went from being insiders' lingo to buzzword to cliché. The terminology may need refurbishing, but the concept is a useful one. "People aren't rational actors," writes Matt Bai, summarizing the research. "Cognitive science proves that we are programmed to respond to frames deep in our unconscious minds—facts that don't fit we reject." To alter those frames, Bai adds, brain has to be "unlocked."[18]

This notion has become fashionable in politics, where competing frames are insinuated into everyday political discourse: "Social Security privatization" versus "individual savings accounts"; "illegal alien" versus "undocumented immigrant"; "entitlements" versus "government handouts." The right has been especially adept at the enterprise, treating as gospel conservative pollster Frank Luntz's list of the "fourteen words we never use."[19]

Critics contend that this manipulation of language cannot substitute for a paucity of ideas. But those who are in the trade insist that framing is not just a fancy word for spinning. It's a research-driven enterprise that aspires to make sense of how individuals process information—and, in the public arena, to use that knowledge of the subconscious mind to alter the frames on which people rely.[20] Linguists, anthropologists, and social psychologists have been attracted to what they see as an emerging science.

What moves the needle on a public problem? The early childhood research is compelling, says Susan Bales, president of the Frameworks Institute, which applies the models of framing to an array of policy problems, but it's essential to get the overall concept right if the message is to be effectively communicated. She offers as an illustration the way to talk, and not to talk, about the brain: "'Brain architecture' evokes concrete images of scaffolding and building, while 'brain development' draws a blank." It's difficult to educate people, Bales acknowledges, but she's convinced it is worth the effort. Once a concept like "brain architecture" is understood, then support for everything relating to early childhood, from nurses' home visits to young parents to good preschool, naturally follows. "The category is child development, not health or education. We don't get a lot of the public attention. You can't do it over and over. We'd be better off to shift the larger conceptualization, then to map a series of policies to be promoted over time."

Like many who study framing, Bales believes that the Pew and Packard foundations have made a costly mistake. Rather than fixating on preschool, they should be tackling the longer-term assignment of educating Americans about how children grow and develop. Even if the pre-K campaign succeeds, Bales contends, children's advocates will again have to start from scratch to inform the public about whatever comes next on the political agenda.

"Americans struggle for working models of child development," a "message memo" from the Frameworks Institute concludes:

> People talk about children as sponges, blank slates, precious objects, empty vessels to be filled. They concentrate their attention solely on the domain of the family and cognitive development. They don't see daycare as development but rather as a soft, safe container, and they misunderstand what's happening to the brain, perceiving it as ingesting information,

not wiring the circuitry. School readiness isn't yet an effective organizing principle. If communications are misdirected, school readiness can be interpreted pejoratively as hurrying children or the misguided practice of 'fancy' parents. The phrase 'hearts, souls and minds' is more effective in setting up a discussion of the developing child than are explicit school readiness and brain development messages.

"People resonate to the theme of stewardship," Bales adds. "They want kids to grow up to be good people. They want to leave the next generation a legacy." That's why the economic benefits of early childhood development must be laid out in a different language, says Lori Dorfman at the Berkeley Media Studies Group, whose work builds on the Frameworks Institute's approach.[21] Economists are potentially powerful messengers, precisely because their vocation *isn't* the welfare of kids; they are presumed to see things as they are, not as they should be. But Dorfman contends that economists shouldn't be talking in dollars-and-cents terms. The more persuasive terms are "reciprocity"—"What we give to children we get back in spades"—and "democracy"—"Support our youngest citizens."

"Politicians and businesses don't need theory," says Lawrence Aber, professor of applied psychology and public policy at NYU, "because they can throw money at a message: vote for candidate X, buy cereal Y. They are skeptical of eggheads. Pew has bought into this model. But public issues are different. These are testable insights, and we can't afford *not* to have good theory. We don't have the money to do brute work. We need back-office theoreticians doing basic research."[22]

Both Packard and Pew were initially intrigued by this line of reasoning—Packard paid for a chunk of the Frameworks Institute research that purports to show foundations the error of their ways—but they rejected the institute's recommendations. Unlike other foundations, they don't see their role as subsidizing scholars whose studies are oriented toward building an enduring knowledge base. They are entrepreneurs in the land of policy, searching for the main chance.

"To improve kids' opportunities you need to start with four-year-olds and work down, rather than diluting the effort and being unsuccessful, as we've always been," contends Lois Salisbury at Packard. "Preschool is a strategic choice, informed by twenty years of doing it the other way." At Pew, Susan Urahn says much the same thing. "Trying to build support for broad values without a specific objective will have no lasting impact. By focusing narrowly, and succeeding in changing policy and practice, the public will be more receptive to the next message. Each success is a building block."

"At some point smart people have to decide on a theory of change, on how the world works," counters Susan Bales. "These efforts are either run in media campaigns or behind closed doors. We're not getting into the places where people learn stories, the places of faith and the town hall meetings." It's a splendid vision of Americans "bowling together." But what's lacking is a way to make it come to life—to give these storytellers a setting in which to tell their tales, and to show how anyone, other than those paid to participate in research conducted at places like the Frameworks Institute, will listen to them.

The Frame of the Future

Ever since the Pew Charitable Trusts made preschool a priority, the foundation has largely masterminded the national early education agenda. Like the Packard Foundation, Pew has done a good job of leveraging its investment. It opted to back advocates who appreciate the arts of horse-trading and gentle arm-twisting, the kind of work that frightens most foundations. With its help, the activists have developed a national network of the like-minded, as well as tools more sophisticated than they could have devised on their own. Pew has woven sporadic and disjointed efforts into a semi-coherent whole, with a community of activists and champions to sustain it and a research base in neuroscience, evaluation, and economics.

Money talks—the entrance into the field of other well-endowed foundations with different priorities may shift the balance away from preschool and toward a broader children's agenda. In 2006, in an act of generosity unparalleled in the annals of philanthropy, Warren Buffett made a commitment of more than $30 billion to the foundation established by Microsoft's Bill Gates, and in so doing doubled the Gates Foundation's endowment. Buffett's daughter, Susan, had been operating the Buffett Early Childhood Fund, a small foundation that has supported initiatives such as Chicago's Educare Centers, that enroll poor infants and toddlers, Because of her family's largesse, the Buffett Early Childhood Fund became, in 2006, a force to be reckoned with—a multibillion dollar presence committed to helping the very young.

In 2005 the Gates Foundation inaugurated a program called Thrive by Five, a ten-year, $90-million effort to deliver children's services across its home state of Washington. At the foundation, Greg Shaw, the director of education, saw the wisdom of developing the potential of children who were growing up in vulnerable communities, while bringing community leaders into the conversation about what was most needed. Like many others, he was impressed by the Perry Preschool and Abecedarian studies, as well as by research showing the value of nurses' home visits for young mothers. "Can these studies be brought to scale?" Shaw wonders. "Is there support from the communities, and from business leaders?"

This "selective universalism," putting the worst-off neighborhoods first, departs from the philosophy of Pew and Packard, which emphasizes the importance of reaching all children.[23] It also differs from the Educare model, which concentrates on the needs of vulnerable babies rather than the ecology of their neighborhoods.

The Gates Foundation habitually thinks big, and some day it may decide to roll out its model nationwide. For the foreseeable future, however, the challenges of a single state look sizable enough. Shaw, who had earlier worked at Microsoft, doesn't come to his job burdened by what he calls the "quandary" of "zero-to-three versus pre-K." The real issue, he says, is "whether a comprehensive, complex early learning program for all families can come to scale and be effective." Daniel Pedersen, president of the Buffett Early Childhood Fund, translates this vision into a concrete legislative goal. "I want to see the country look more like Illinois, with universal preschool and birth to three as well, with eleven cents of every dollar going to infants and toddlers."

Placing the broad and amorphous needs of the most vulnerable young children at the center stage of policy, rather than homing in on a more fine-grained target like preschool, has often been attempted, most recently in the mid-1990s, and the results have generally been disheartening. Still, the Gates and Buffett foundations have much deeper pockets than old-line advocacy organizations like the Children's Defense Fund. Will that make the critical difference?

There is evidence that popular attitudes are shifting, away from a laissez-faire view of the state's role in the lives of the very young and toward an acceptance of greater public responsibility. In 2006 Denver, Colorado, voters increased their sales tax to underwrite universal preschool. The electorate in Nebraska and Arizona, two socially conservative states, approved modest boosts in state spending to expand an array of early childhood initiatives.

In Nebraska, as in Oklahoma, where the legislature approved a similar measure, the state's contribution must be matched by substantial private support. Not coincidentally, both of these states have enormously wealthy philanthropists with good political connections and a passion to help children: Susan Buffett in Nebraska and multibillionaire George Kaiser in Oklahoma. Earlier they had brought to their home states the Educare model of intensive child care and early education for poor infants and toddlers, developed by Irving Harris's Ounce of Prevention Fund in Chicago. The new laws enable them to promote that model more broadly.

Forbes magazine ranks oil and banking entrepreneur George Kaiser, Oklahoma's early education angel, as the twenty-seventh richest American, with a fortune estimated at greater than $8 billion. Susan Buffett's father is number two, and Washington's Bill Gates, of course, tops the *Forbes* list. But despite Gates's $53 billion, not even he can improve the quality of children's lives across the country single-handedly. His foundation's annual budget, though more than three times bigger than Pew's and Packard's combined, is a pittance compared with the hundreds of billions of dollars the government spends each year on everything from after-school programs to healthcare for children.

In promoting a kids-first agenda, money is a necessary condition for success. But money isn't enough. Unless there emerges a disciplined collaboration among the philanthropists and the interest groups, it will, as Yogi Berra famously said, be déjà vu all over again.

What's required to make the needs of children truly salient—to build a movement that might ultimately have the kind of clout that's wielded by the senior citizens' lobby—is the alignment of money, message, innovation, and a coordinated strategy.[24] Political skill, deployed in the service of changing widely held values, will be essential—not simply through reframing the issue, "unlocking" Americans' brains, but with old-fashioned leadership that can persuade the public to accept greater responsibility as citizens and taxpayers. This is the theme of the final two chapters of this book, which take us first to Great Britain and then to North Carolina and Texas, places where such a value swing can already be seen.

Whatever their particular priorities, all the child-oriented foundation and interest groups know that simply delivering a decent education to three- and four-year-olds, especially those in problematic circumstances, is unlikely to rewrite their life stories. Even if the Perry Preschool model could be cloned nationwide, that wouldn't close the gaps.

State by state, the campaigns for preschool serve as laboratories for testing which amalgam of political adroitness and powerful ideas can change Americans' minds about the entirety of children's needs. These are the stories to which we turn next.

The Politics of the Un-Dramatic

IN 1990, campaign manager James Carville advised Zell Miller, at the time a young Democratic legislator running for governor of Georgia, that preschool would make a good issue. The strategy paid off, and since then a growing number of politicians have followed suit. Miller initially planned to offer free preschool only to poor kids, but after a few years in the governor's office, he realized that including every four-year-old in the state would boost the program's popularity. From that experience, "preschool for all" emerged as a national rallying cry.[1]

Although conservative organizations have fought against any state-supported preschool, they are losing that battle. But once the politicians exit the stage—once state pre-K is up and running—the essential issue is the quality of the education that three- and four-year-olds obtain.

This is a basic point for anyone who cares about the intersection of politics and pedagogy, public rhetoric and children's lives. "Quality" sounds pedagogical, not political, and the measures used to define quality—teacher training, pupil-teacher ratios, and the like—have been constructed by experts in the field. Yet it is legislators, not pedagogues, who determine how much prekindergarten teachers are paid and how many kids can be in a classroom. Quality is also defined by how the preschool system is designed, the rules and incentives that give it shape, and those decisions are also made by public officials.

The story with which this book opens, of what has transpired in Illinois, the only state that has pledged to make pre-K available to all three-year-olds as well as four-year-olds, shows both the promise of universal preschool and the possibility of derailing prekindergarten because of lack of money and the mechanical application of the No Child Left Behind benchmarks. Thirty-nine states and the District of Columbia have state pre-K programs. Taking a close look at what has been happening in four very distinctive states—Oklahoma, Florida, Texas, and California—will help fill out the picture.[2]

This narrative of sandbox politics explores the efforts of little-known backstage advocates as well as highly visible champions. It's an account of the politics of the *un*-dramatic—a political reenactment of the story of the tortoise and the hare, where slow and steady wins the race. These reports are consequential in their own right, and they also offer a starting point for estimating the prospects for a broad kids-first initiative.

Oklahoma: Doing Good by Stealth

In the popular imagination, Oklahoma is associated with oil billionaires, football dynasties, and religious fundamentalists. The Sooner State is an unlikely candidate to be running one of the country's best preschool programs.[3] Its history is pockmarked with items that its tourism office would just as soon forget: the last stop on the Trail of Tears for the Cherokee Nation; the Tulsa race riots of 1921, in which as many as three hundred people were killed, almost all of them African American; the *Grapes of Wrath* Dust Bowl miseries of the 1930s; and the visible presence of the Ku Klux Klan through the mid-twentieth century.

A populist streak courses through this history, and the state even flirted with socialism during the 1930s. But ever since Oklahoma became a focal point of Richard Nixon's 1968 "Southern Strategy" to recruit what was called the "silent majority," its politics has veered increasingly to the right. In the 2004 senatorial campaign, GOP candidate Tom Coburn warned of lesbians lurking in high school bathrooms, supported the public's right to buy and use bazookas, urged the death penalty for abortionists—and won handily.[4] Even in eastern Oklahoma, where the populist legacy endures, abortion is "the third rail," says Democratic legislator Joe Eddins. "If people ask," he cautions any aspiring candidate who seeks his advice, "just say 'I'm pro-life' and move on, or else they'll kill you."

"Thank God for Mississippi" is the Oklahoma liberals' bittersweet joke. "At least we're not last."

The Children's Defense Fund rates the state's congressional delegation as the least child-friendly in the country. But things are very different in the state capital.[5] Largely because of the exertions of a handful of shrewd bureaucrats, unassuming politicians, and philanthropically minded business leaders, Oklahoma ranks first nationwide in the proportion of four-year-olds enrolled in prekindergarten, and those classes meet stringent standards for quality.

In 2000, when a bill establishing a public-private partnership to promote early childhood initiatives was introduced in the state legislature, political leaders predicted its easy passage. The measure had an impeccable pedigree. It was proposed by a task force chaired by a prominent power-company CEO, Pete Churchwell, an earnest Republican who had served on a commission established by the legislature to reexamine the long-ignored Tulsa race riots, and it had the backing of Governor Frank Keating, also a Republican. Besides, the legislation appeared innocuous, since the new partnership would have only the power of persuasion. But ultraconservatives hated the bill.

"When I ran for office, I thought I was Rush Limbaugh incarnate," jokes GOP state representative Ron Peters, but then he heard what some of his colleagues had to say. The *Daily Oklahoman* assailed the proposed law as promoting a "nanny state." Some legislators envisioned a "socialist plot" to take over children's lives. On the floor of the legislature one lawmaker claimed that reading makes youngsters go blind, and another, noting that the new partnership would promote preschool for three-year-olds, asked rhetorically, "Why not take them away in the hospital?" Flummoxed by the opposition, Keating ended up threatening to veto his own bill. Not until 2003, with Democrat Brad Henry installed in the governor's mansion, did the measure become law.

Yet even as the opposition fumed, universal preschool was already a widespread reality across the state. Doing good *quietly* was the winning strategy. "This was a stealth campaign," says Nele Rogers at the Oklahoma Child Care Resource and Referral Association, a statewide advocacy group. In other states the pre-K movement became identified with a highly visible politician or celebrity, but only Oklahoma insiders ever heard anything about Pete Churchwell or oil-company executive Bob Harbison or Tulsa billionaire George Kaiser.

"Oklahoma is a very small world," says Steven Dow, who runs Tulsa's Community Action Project. Dow knows how to bring that world together. "When it came to pre-K, four people sat around a table at the request of a state legislator who said he wanted to do something good—to expand preschool with high-quality providers." In 1980 few people noticed when a pilot program crafted by Ramona Paul, a midlevel bureaucrat in the state's Department of Education, was launched to serve preschoolers, regardless of family income. A decade later, few people noticed when a seemingly technical change in the school finance formula enabled local districts to be reimbursed for educating four-year-olds (the starting age for school had been five).

"The reason that early childhood education initially caught on had nothing to do with superintendents being progressive," says Bob Harbison. "The new money did the trick. They learned how to buy jockstraps for the football team by using money that was supposed to be educating four-year-olds." In 1999 another bookkeeping tweak slipped through, this one boosting the amount of state reimbursement for pre-K while closing the "jockstrap" loophole. The change made preschool even more financially appealing to chronically money-hungry school districts.

Quietly and carefully the right strings were pulled to set public preschool in motion. "Only six people in the state understand the education finance formula," jokes Harbison. One of them, the deceptively easygoing state representative Joe Eddins, shepherded the measure. "I'm a useful person, not a headliner," says Eddins, a one-time stockbroker and schoolteacher who raises cattle on his century-old family ranch.

Prekindergarten quickly proved popular. In 1992–93, just 10 percent of all four-year-olds were enrolled; in 2006, nearly 70 percent attended pre-K, more than anywhere else in the country.

A 2004 survey showed the broad appeal of the program—five out of six Oklahomans, a higher percentage than in most states, favored enlarging the state's preschool budget.[6]

Kindergarten teachers reported that youngsters who had been in pre-K classes came better prepared, and were likely to do better three years later, when they took the reading and math test mandated by the federal No Child Left Behind Act. Although this emphasis on narrowly defined academics at the expense of creativity, and at such an early age, troubles most child development experts, the teachers' reports influenced the attitudes of parents and school administrators.

"This isn't altruism," Steven Dow observes. "Superintendents know that investing at the front end is paying off educationally"—and is enhancing their schools' reputation. Administrators who were initially hostile were won over after parents began to vote with their feet. "When the program was first implemented, superintendents came to me and said, 'I'm not going to have pre-K in my school,'" recalls Ramona Paul at the Department of Education. "The next spring they said, 'I need some help with the program.' 'What changed your mind?' I asked. 'Twenty families transferred out of the district.'"

Oklahoma's standards are as tough as any in the nation. There can be no more than ten students for each teacher in a pre-K class, and every teacher must have a bachelor's degree with an early childhood–education certificate. Because the program is run by the public schools, where most of the classes are located, pre-K teachers earn as much as those who teach Shakespeare or trigonometry.[7]

The state subsidizes only half a day of preschool, but communities are increasingly dipping into their own coffers to offer full-day classes.[8] Pre-K has also been linked to child care. Oklahoma is among the top five states in the country in terms of the proportion of poor children in subsidized day care, and it is among the very few that don't have a long child care waiting list. Nationwide, rivalries between preschool and child care are deep-rooted and perennial, but efforts have been made to bring the two camps together, to give children an education that continues even after the preschool day ends. As with preschool, it helps that there are so few key players. "Everyone can come to the table," says Ramona Paul. "There are enough children for all of us." And because the state's Department of Human and Social Services gives child care centers a financial incentive to improve, the quality of care has been getting better.

The prekindergarten protocols reflect the research on what's likely to benefit kids, and there is good evidence that putting those standards in place has made a difference. A meticulously crafted study of preschool in Tulsa shows that the program boosts all children's language and cognitive test scores.[9]

Preschool has been especially valuable to children from the state's poorest communities. Several school districts in down-at-the-heels southeast Oklahoma, where 70 percent of the families live close to the poverty line, have spent scarce local dollars to provide full-day pre-K and kindergarten classes, with remarkable results. In the past, students from those districts have fared the worst on the third-grade tests called for by No Child Left Behind, but in 2005 only 17 percent of the third graders there required remedial reading. School administrators and school boards across the state are well aware of where their town sits in the pecking order, and so these reports have pushed wealthier districts with less impressive records to expand their own pre-K offerings.

"On the last day of the 2004 legislative session," Steven Dow remembers, "when I knew that the Republicans were going to take over the assembly, I tried hard to convince one of my friends there to change a single word in the funding formula—'four' to 'three.'" Had this "doing good by stealth" strategy worked yet again, school districts could have spent state dollars on preschool for three-year-olds. The lawmaker demurred, though, and when the GOP took control of the assembly in the 2004 election, the idea of expanding pre-K seemed dead.

But reports of its demise proved premature. During the past few years a number of school districts started subsidizing prekindergarten for three-year-olds with their own tax dollars. And in 2007 Democratic governor Brad Henry introduced legislation that would expand the voluntary early-childhood education program to include three- as well as four-year-olds. Meanwhile, in partnership with George Kaiser and other philanthropists, Oklahoma has adopted its own version of Early Head Start. That undertaking, while initially modest in scope, is as carefully thought through as the statewide prekindergarten. Overall, this is as impressive a track record as any state can boast of. The politics of the un-dramatic paved the way.

Florida: The Voters Propose and the Legislators Dispose

In 2002, the voters of Florida amended their state constitution to guarantee "high-quality" prekindergarten for every four-year-old. That was big news nationwide, for it made Florida one of just six states to offer universal preschool, and the only state to enshrine pre-K for all as a constitutional right.[10]

Like Oklahoma, Florida is improbably cast as a social pioneer. While the state frequently makes the news, the stories are tragic, bizarre, or both—the Terri Schiavo deathwatch turned three-ring political circus, the drama that surrounded the fate of Elián Gonzalez, and those notorious hanging chads. Florida's unofficial bard, novelist and columnist Carl Hiaasen, describes his native land as "paradise screwed."[11]

The state legislature is dominated by conservative Republicans whose agenda has been to shrink government, privatizing whatever can't be wiped out. The public schools, chronically underfunded, are a shambles. The state has the nation's worst high school graduation rate, and in 2006, 71 percent of its public schools were rated as "failing" by the criteria fixed by No Child Left Behind.[12] The only fix the lawmakers could agree on, a school voucher plan, was struck down by the Florida Supreme Court.[13] "The state's motto could be 'We're cheap, and proud of it,'" says Marilyn Brown, who covers education for the *Tampa Tribune*.

In politics, well-organized interest groups usually get to call the shots—in Florida that means the sugar industry, the anti-Castro Cubans, the Disney Empire, the good old boys from the Panhandle, and the retirees. Yet at times a determined outsider can galvanize a movement that overturns the familiar ways of doing the public's business. That's how Florida's preschool amendment came to be.

There are limits to what any private citizen can accomplish in remaking this terrain, of course. In Florida, as in most states, direct democracy has a limited function. If a reform like preschool is going to survive, it must be embedded in the political system, as it is in Oklahoma. That hasn't happened in Florida.

The persisting refusal of the legislature to give real meaning to the constitutional mandate, the disinterest of a governor whose focus was elsewhere, and the absence of a children's lobby capable of swaying lawmakers' votes—those are the reasons the pre-K movement stalled in Florida. What has transpired there is a classic example of how a diffuse majority, those who voted for the constitutional amendment, lost out to a concentrated and determined minority, the operators of private and faith-based preschools.[14]

David Lawrence, who launched the pre-K campaign, has told his own life history scores of times. It's an updated *Mr. Smith Goes to Washington*, and by repeatedly delivering it Lawrence has made his personal odyssey a backstory for the state's preschool movement. Much as Rob Reiner came to represent the prekindergarten movement in California, for Floridians Lawrence became the public face of preschool.

Throughout his entire career Lawrence had been a newspaperman—"a paid skeptic"—when, in 1996, Governor Lawton Chiles recruited him for what he calls the "mission" of school readiness. "I knew nothing about those issues," he says, "but what I learned reenergized my life." Reforming public education meant starting very early, "bringing children to formal school in far better shape than so many of them are." Lawrence stepped down as publisher of the *Miami Herald*, and then he was "off to the races." During his self-education he went to France to observe the system of *écoles maternelles*, and he came home determined to adapt Paris to the Panhandle. "I've seen the new world," he announced.

Universalism—*solidarité*—has been a bedrock principle in France since the 1789 Revolution, and it's taken for granted that the *écoles maternelles* are open to all children. Florida needed to do the same, Lawrence believed, because making preschool available to all was the only way to assure its permanency. "You'll never get to the promised land if you say it's about this or that neighborhood."

Lawrence turned to Miami mayor Alex Penelas to assume the political leadership for the preschool drive. He was the natural choice. "The idea made sense," says Penelas, who, like Illinois governor Rod Blagojevich, saw pre-K through the lens of his own family's experience. "My son William was in a fee-based prekindergarten class that the Miami school district operated. It was a great program, what every child ought to have. I could pay the tuition, but some of my neighbors couldn't." In 1999 the mayor and the ex-newspaperman organized strategy sessions and neighborhood meetings throughout Miami. When nearly 5,000 people turned out for a "Children's Summit" to determine which issues to focus on, early education topped the list.

Statewide polls showed that two-thirds of likely voters supported universal pre-K. But selling preschool to the legislators was another matter. "'You're creating an entitlement,' some of them told me," says Lawrence, "and to them, 'entitlement' is a dirty word." The notion that four-year-olds should be getting an education at public expense, rather than staying at home with mom, prompted the proverbial grousing about the nanny state.

When the politicians in Tallahassee buried one pre-K bill in 2000 and another in 2001, Lawrence and Penelas turned to the voters. They raised $1.8 million to put a constitutional amendment on the ballot, and in 2002 the electorate approved it by a three-to-two margin. The measure specified that a statewide preschool system would be up and running by 2005.

For a season, Florida was the toast of the country's preschool activists.[15] "I worked like a bunny rabbit to have no opposition," Lawrence recalls, and he succeeded. Operators of mom-and-pop for-profit preschools, fearful that they would be driven out of business, were reassured by promises that any prekindergarten, public or private, that satisfied state standards could participate. And faith-based schools, many of them Christian fundamentalist academies uneasy about state regulation, received similar reassurances. "These weren't just cheerleading sessions," says Phyllis Kalifeh, president of the Florida Children's Forum, an umbrella early education program. "There were egos to be assuaged, hands to be held, deep concerns to be allayed."[16]

The text of Florida's sixty-four-word constitutional amendment declares, twice, that prekindergarten must be "high quality." But the measure does not specify the cost of quality or how to pay for it—those judgments were left to the very lawmakers who had already made their animus plain. An advisory council appointed by the state Board of Education concluded that high quality translated into classes that ran for six hours a day, with four hours of teaching by certified teachers. But the legislators approved only a skeletal three-hour preschool day, with minimal requirements for teachers. Not until May 2005, just three months before the start of the school year, did state pre-K even have a budget. The $387 million appropriation provided $2,500 a year for each four-year-old, not the $4,320 that the advisory council had said that high-quality preschool would cost, and $1,000 below the national average. That amounts to $2.77 an hour, well below what a teenage babysitter gets paid. Not surprisingly, the National Institute for Early Education Research ranks the state's pre-K program as "poor."[17] This outcome is not just a disappointment to the state's voters, who had been led to expect much better, it is also a corrective for those who popped the Champagne corks too early.

While some of Florida's problems can be traced to growing pains, even those were of its own making. "Florida created in two months the fourth-largest voluntary universal prekindergarten program in the country," boasted Susan Pareigis, director of the Agency for Workforce Innovation, which manages the state's pre-

K. But that doesn't mean it did the job well.[18] "The rollout was a nightmare," says Paula Bender, who ran the Miami-Dade Early Learning Coalition during that topsy-turvy first year. And the Tallahassee bureaucrats sometimes made things worse. The mission of Pareigis's agency, for example, is to get mothers off welfare and into jobs, not to get their children into good preschools.

"The system is built for transparent information. It is the parents' responsibility to decide what's best," insists Gladys Wilson, who administers the preschool program. Paeans to parental choice roll off the tongue of every Florida politician and bureaucrat, but there's too little information for parents to make informed judgments. Some Head Start parents were wrongly led to believe that they couldn't enroll their youngsters in the state pre-K classes as well. Private schools, mostly run as businesses, enrolled more than three-quarters of the prekindergarten kids. These centers often operate on a shoestring, and some were forced into bankruptcy by the state's arcane bookkeeping and tardy payments, leaving parents scrambling to find another place that would accept their youngsters.

Space constraints in the public schools also constricted parents' options. At the same time that voters mandated preschool, they passed another constitutional amendment requiring a reduction in class size. But the legislature, true to form, didn't come up with the money needed to build new classrooms, so in many communities there was simply no room to house pre-K classes. Seventeen school districts, including Tampa and St. Petersburg, opted not to participate in the school-year program. Prekindergartens run by the public schools, which relied on certified teachers, were widely regarded as among the best—their waiting lists were long, and in several places children were admitted by lottery—but only 12 percent of preschoolers made it into those classes.

Even as parents queued up for the public preschools, some for-profit centers had empty seats. Overall, the pre-K enrollment was well below what had been projected. While the state had estimated that 150,000 children, 70 percent of all four-year-olds, would participate, only 92,000 showed up. Since the state collects almost no data about pre-K, there is no way to account for the "missing" children. Nor does anyone know whether the universal preschool law attracted four-year-olds who otherwise would not have had the opportunity to attend preschool, or whether, as is widely believed, the main beneficiaries have been middle-class families, who demanded a $2,500 tuition rebate from the nursery schools their children were already attending. There was some hope that poor parents would have a chance to send their children to the top preschools, but that doesn't seem to have happened—savvy, well-off parents claim those spots by signing up their babies soon after they are born.

"The idea of the law is to lower the cost to parents, who can now send their children to preschool," says Romero Moreno, who operates the REM Learning Center, a highly regarded for-profit preschool in Miami. "In fact it may be that the best schools are filled with kids of well-off parents, who are now getting a free preschool, while poorer parents must do with less or do without." Lobbyist Danny Morris, the president of the Florida Association for Child Care Management, who also operates several private preschools, is pithier. "The only thing that really changed is that the parent who was paying me $2,500 a year can now buy a new TV and the state picks up the preschool bill."

Most of Florida's preschool problems are neither transitory nor inadvertent. They represent deliberate judgments. The law contains no meaningful curricular standards, and because there is no oversight, the legislative requirement that the curriculum be "developmentally appropriate" is meaningless. There is no requirement, just a hope, that pre-K teachers will eventually be required to have even as much as an associate's degree. While the state has adopted strenuous-sounding standards for many aspects of preschool life—going so far as to require that four-year-olds be taught how to floss their teeth—enforcement is nonexistent. What's more, the legislation permits preschools to discriminate in deciding which children to enroll and which teachers to hire. That means a Baptist-run pre-K is free to say "No Catholics need apply."

Rather than assessing the caliber of prekindergartens—whether the materials on hand engage the minds of the children; whether there are real conversations, not just didactic instruction—Florida has adopted the "no child left behind" approach of high-stakes testing. The state law requires that all the youngsters entering kindergarten take a "readiness screener." Even if the test accurately reports what these children know—and there's good reason to doubt that it does—it cannot show what they learned in preschool, since they weren't assessed beforehand. Nonetheless, the legislation says that any prekindergarten program in which the children perform badly on the readiness test risks being put in receivership, and if that doesn't do the trick, being shut down.[19]

The statute doesn't take into account the youngsters' background—whether they come from homes where English isn't spoken or from families that don't have the wherewithal to give them out-of-school advantages. Because those children are likely to fare the worst on the state exam, the law gives preschools a powerful and perverse incentive to grab those kids who will predictably perform well, leaving the neediest out in the cold.

The real winners are the for-profit and faith-based preschools, which together enroll 88 percent of the state's four-year-olds. For those prekindergartens, the legislative determinations about class size, teacher qualifications, curriculum, and religion were life-and-death matters, and they got almost everything they asked for. Danny Morris, the lobbyist and private preschool operator, knows who to massage in Tallahassee. The members of his organization, the Florida Association for Child Care Management, contribute both money and sweat equity to political campaigns, and in a heartbeat they can mobilize a lot of irate parents. It was easy enough for Morris to convince lawmakers to sign laissez-faire into law. The only battle they lost was over class size, and it took David Lawrence's threat of a lawsuit to persuade the legislators that preschool classes needed to be smaller than classes for ten-year-olds.

Faith-based prekindergartens also got their way. While many states support church-run preschools, they are generally forbidden to proselytize. Not so in Florida. When the preschool law was being drafted, says Lawrence, "legislators were receiving a daily boatload of e-mails from some in the faith and private-school communities expressing terrifying prognostications about the impending invasion from the state." The state chose to stay out of the business of mandating what and how to teach, whom to hire and enroll. Those promises weren't enough for the Catholic preschools, which opted not to get involved, but other churches did sign up. "I was hesitant to join voluntary pre-K," says Anita Howard of the Little Disciples Preschool in the wealthy Miami neighborhood of Palmetto Bay, "because I was afraid of interference, standards, rules about the kind of curriculum we would be forced to use. Fortunately that didn't come to pass."

The religious preschools aren't just faith *based*—many deliver a faith-*driven* education. "If they had told us we couldn't include

Jesus in our curriculum," says Kathy Knudtson, director of Faith Lutheran Preschool in Palm Beach, "we wouldn't have participated." Linda Hopkins, who runs the preschool at First Baptist Church in West Palm Beach, estimates that "90 percent chose here for the religious component."[20] Many Christian prekindergartens use the A Beka curriculum, a rote-learning pedagogy that requires four-year-olds to memorize Bible verses as well as lists of vocabulary words. "The ministry God has given us is to assist your Christian school ministry in its effectiveness for the Lord," says the A Beka Web site. "It is our desire to help you train children in the Christian way of life."

Had the Florida Department of Education been obliged to specify curricula suitable for preschoolers, as it does for K–12 students, A Beka would not have passed muster. "The schools were afraid that we wouldn't approve it because it's not developmentally appropriate," admits Shan Goff, who heads the state's Office of Early Learning, "but there are political implications of [our] making decisions. While the A Beka materials cause me concern, Florida favors parental choice."

"The legislators use money and choice as excuses," former Miami mayor Penelas counters, "but in reality they're influenced by religious child-care providers who don't want accountability and don't want standards."

This is what "high quality" can mean in Florida. Jack and Jill, two twenty-year-olds, decide to open the Little Bo Peep Preschool. Jill has a high school degree and a child development credential, which requires about a year's worth of classes, and she has done some practice teaching. Jack is a high school dropout. Neither has been convicted of child molesting. Both are Lutherans, and they limit enrollment to children from Lutheran families; if more teachers are needed, Jack and Jill will hire only fellow Lutherans. Little Bo Peep Preschool uses the A Beka curriculum. Since the preschool day lasts only three hours, Little Bo Peep is free to operate morning, afternoon, and evening classes. If it can attract middle-class kids it probably won't run afoul of the state's testing regime, since even if those youngsters learn nothing while in nursery school, they've likely absorbed enough at home to do decently on the test.

Little Bo Peep is meant as an extreme example, but some preschools come uncomfortably close. What brought this system into being was the venerable confluence of money, ideology, and political power. While the activists won over the voters, they haven't swayed the legislators. And although the private-school lobbyists know how the insiders' game is played, the children's advocates are amateurs. When Phyllis Kalifeh, president of the Florida Children's Forum, violated the first rule of politics by going after a powerful state legislator, the lawmaker struck back by shutting down a much-lauded preschool-teacher training program run by her organization.

"The real world in Florida is that we have to push and shove to get anything," says David Lawrence. Speaking at a 2005 conference at Northwestern University, he acknowledged the difficulties. "Having a slot for every child is only one necessary step. The defining issue for me is 'high quality' because *only* high quality leads to *real* outcomes for children. That's where the real work remains."[21]

That is also the direction in which Shan Goff at the Department of Education hopes to go. She envisions ratcheting up the standards, strengthening oversight, and obliging preschools whose children fail the kindergarten test to switch to a state-approved curriculum. But Paula Bender, who ran Miami's Early Learning Coalition, doesn't see that happening. "When the state calls, all they care about is the numbers. It's a lot easier to get bigger than it is to get better."

Roy Miller used to manage political campaigns. Now he runs Florida's Children's Campaign, where he uses those skills to promote an array of kids' causes. Miller looks at the state's preschool legislation with disdain. "The law does not mandate a date for employing degreed teachers. It does not prescribe an assessment instrument appropriate for four-year-olds. It does not provide an adequate rate of reimbursement."

The advocates have considered bringing a lawsuit to enforce the constitutional guarantee of high quality. Litigation has the advantage of evening the stakes, especially where, as in Florida, the facts are so plainly on the plaintiffs' side.[22] "I want to retain the ability to litigate if we don't get high quality," Lawrence says. "That's what the people voted for."

Linda Alexionic, the chief operating officer of the Children's Campaign, puts her faith in organizing. "We have to go back to the citizens. We have a situation that we have to reverse. The elected people think they are the bosses. The legislature wants to override the people." To be effective, she adds, "we have to partner with seniors' organizations like Generations United and the AARP. Seniors will pay for preschool because of its impact on their own lifestyle—the poll data show almost 87-percent support."

Expanding the pre-K coalition has worked well elsewhere, and whatever the issue, seniors make a potent partner. But in Florida, one well-placed observer notes, the advocates behave "like crabs in a bucket," seemingly incapable of uniting. That makes it hard to reach out.

Among those who believed that the 2002 constitutional amendment marked a great victory for Florida's children, the frustration is palpable because the high quality they anticipated has proven a hoax. "Are we just training our kids to take care of other people's children at Mickey Mouse Land?" asks Linda Alexionic. "What's wrong with Florida?"

Texas: Strange Bedfellows

For supporters of universal preschool, the Texas legislative session that convened in January 2005 seemed fated to be a total loss. A redistricting plan, implemented with brute force two years earlier by then Speaker of the House of Representatives Tom DeLay, had transformed the state's political map. Not only had the scheme taken gerrymandering to a new level; it had also shifted enough voters to give Republicans control of both houses of the state legislature for the first time since Reconstruction.

Among those victorious Republicans were some truly brontosaurian conservatives.[23] "Where did this idea come from that everybody deserves free education, free medical care, free whatever?" fumed Debbie Riddle, a GOP representative from Houston. "It comes from Moscow, from Russia. It comes of out the pit of hell. It's not a tender heart. It's ripping the heart out of this country."[24] Even in Florida or Oklahoma, states that have their share of retrograde lawmakers, such rhetoric would have been eye-opening. Legislators of this species have never met a social program they didn't want to get rid of, and preschool was no exception.

As if this weren't discouraging enough, those whom the advocates might plausibly expect to rely on—the public schools, Head Start centers, and child care centers—viewed one another with disdain. Drafting a preschool measure that all of them could embrace required a level of finesse more frequently associated with

Armani-clad lobbyists than habitually feckless children's advocates.

Yet legislation adopted in that 2005 session in fact made the Texas prekindergarten program marginally bigger, with an infusion of $55 million. And it incorporates a model that may make the preschools better as well. That year, the prekindergarten bill was the only proposal that attracted support across party lines. Even though it was limited in its scope—hardly to be confused with the universal program in neighboring Oklahoma—it did give a lift to the pre-K movement. It also prefigured future expansion.

Looking at how this small victory came to pass reveals a textbook example of how to build a coalition.[25] Working in tandem, adept children's rights activists and a powerfully placed researcher with a taste for the rough-and-tumble convinced the antagonists in the preschool crowd that they would be better off joining forces. Then, with a nudge from an influential outsider, First Lady Laura Bush, they convinced the lawmakers to go along. It's a story whose ramifications reach well beyond the Rio Grande.

"Children's advocates have seldom been seen around here," says Judith Zaffirini, the most powerful Democrat in the state senate, "and they have been the least sophisticated lobby that knocked on our doors. They've never known how to leverage relationships."

A few Texas activists have rewritten that stereotype, including Karen Johnson and Jason Sabo of Texas United Way, who converted the normally staid agency into a politically progressive organization, and Kaitlin Guthrow, who breathed life into the Texas Early Childhood Education Coalition. Among them, these three know everyone who matters politically, and they have earned the trust of parties who usually don't trust one another.

They patrol the capitol's corridors in Austin, cornering lawmakers to plead their case. And Sabo, the vice president for public policy at United Way, barnstorms the state from Amarillo to Brownsville to stir up interest in children's issues. "He gets the light bulbs to go off," marvels Patti Everitt, who used to run the Texas office of the Children's Defense Fund.

"Kids are the best organizing tool," explains Sabo. "People get it."

The preschool world has more than its quota of purists. But the Austin activists are relentlessly pragmatic, a necessary approach in a state as preternaturally conservative as Texas. In July 2006, the Texas Public Policy Foundation, a right-wing think tank, drafted an op-ed piece claiming that preschool was a waste of money.[26] United Way president Karen Johnson responded, not by talking about how important pre-K was to children's lives but by stressing its economic virtues. Pre-K is "compassionate conservatism," she wrote—lifting a slogan from George Bush's 2000 campaign—a way to cut future welfare costs by training a globally competitive workforce.

As executive director of the Early Childhood Education Coalition, Kaitlin Guthrow nudged child-minding organizations into making preschool a priority, and this well-defined focus gave them a level of access they had never known. "This is a 'come to Jesus' moment," says Sabo, talking about why such clarity is so important. "From an advocacy perspective, kids' needs are so big and varied that trying to do everything means nothing gets done."

Politicians often deride academics as impractical and out of touch. But two feet-on-the-ground professors, an economist and a developmental psychologist, both with strong ties to the state's Republican establishment, helped to mold the preschool conversation.

Lori Taylor had been an economist with the Federal Reserve Bank before joining the faculty of the Bush School for Government and Public Service at Texas A&M. She became the darling of the state's GOP when her 2005 study, prepared at the legislature's behest, disparaged the economic underpinnings of a plan to aid poor school districts. Soon afterward, the Texas Early Childhood Education Coalition gave Taylor a small grant to study the economic impact of preschool. It was an intrepid move on the coalition's part, given Taylor's conservative credentials, but Taylor is much more an economist than an ideologue, and her 2006 report said everything the advocates could have hoped for.

Prekindergarten was a wise use of public funds, Taylor concluded—but only if it delivered high-caliber education.[27] "The increment is well worth spending," she says. "Invest in high quality and the return is high. You get nothing back from substandard programs." That conclusion is consistent with speeches that have been delivered around the country by Art Rolnick, the Federal Reserve economist from Minneapolis who has been a Pied Piper for preschool. Yet because it was a home-grown Texas report, drafted by someone whom Republican lawmakers regarded as a friend, it carried special weight.

Taylor also had a message for the Texas Workforce Commission. The agency has a $1 billion budget, and 92 percent of its funds come from the federal government. Child care is its largest line item, which makes it far and away the biggest public player in the state. It has also been the least responsive to children's needs. It's "the most ideologically pure conservative agency in the United States," says James Strickland, longtime head of the Head Start program in Austin.

As its name implies, the Workforce Commission sees its charge as getting as many mothers as possible into jobs. What happens to the children while their mothers are working hasn't been a priority. But Taylor's study pointed out the shortsightedness of that approach. "The benefits of providing good preschool include more people in the labor market and reduced absenteeism."

This economic-investment argument never dominated the political conversation in Texas. What counted far more was the fact that a well thought through pre-K scheme, devised by someone with long-standing ties to the Bush White House, was on the table.

The 2005 pre-K legislation built on a $15 million pilot project—the Texas Early Education Model, or TEEM—that the legislature had approved during the previous session. TEEM combines a training regime for preschool teachers, a tool for teachers to evaluate pre-K youngsters, and a pre-K curriculum that balances learning how to read with learning how to work and play well with others. The model relies heavily on technology (the teacher training is web-based, and children's progress is monitored with wireless handheld devices), which makes it possible to implement on a large scale. It also includes mentoring by experienced teachers. TEEM is meant to work anywhere three- and four-year-olds are being taught, and it's designed for prospective preschool teachers who have no more than a high school diploma.

TEEM was developed by Susan Landry, a developmental psychologist at the University of Houston Medical Center. Mention Landry's name among the country's leading preschool authorities and reactions range from the dismissive—"What does she know about preschool?"—to the grudgingly admiring—"What she is doing may be useful." That tepid reaction is partly rooted in jealousy, since Landry's ideas have acquired a life beyond child development journals. It's also attributable to the widespread belief that she is focused entirely on cognitive development. Landry objects. "The idea that cognitive stimulation will hurt social-emotional development drives me nuts," she says. "Children's capacity to manage their own emotions, to learn to wait and to share, can't be separated from their skill at figuring out how to decode the written word."

Whether all preschool teachers should have a college degree is hotly contested. And Landry's conviction that 130 hours of online instruction, coupled with the guiding hand of a mentor, can turn a high school graduate into a teacher who's as good as a college graduate strikes many experts as preposterous. Both sides cite reams of studies to support their position, but the merits may matter less than what's doable. "We are dealing with a financial reality," Landry points out. "In Texas we won't have degreed teachers five or ten years from now," because the state won't foot the bill. In a world of second-best solutions, a decent teacher training course is far better than the meager requirements in states like Florida.

The most justified criticism is that TEEM, though marketed as "evidence-based," has never had an outside evaluation. The only evidence of its effectiveness comes from evaluators handpicked by Landry, and that's fuel for skepticism. Still, the model is intriguing enough that educators in Ohio, Maryland, and Florida have tried it. Even if Susan Landry's name weren't attached, Texas might have given it a go. There her imprint makes a world of difference—when she talks, Texas lawmakers feel obliged to listen. Landry's clout stems from her close ties to First Lady Laura Bush and Education Secretary Margaret Spellings. They worked together when George Bush was governor; and in 2001, when Laura Bush was planning her maiden policy voyage, a White House conference on early education, it was Landry to whom she turned.

Those connections were instrumental in getting the pilot preschool project off the ground, and after Landry set out to expand the program, those ties once again came in handy. Lawmakers reported getting calls from the White House: "This is Laura Bush's office calling about the preschool bill." State senators also heard from their colleague Democratic senator Judith Zaffirini, a cosponsor of the preschool bill. Zaffirini knows how to do business across the aisle. Together with Robert Scott, deputy commissioner of the GOP-led Texas Education Agency and a strong supporter of preschool, she worked to line up Republican support.

"This legislation is a small gain," Zaffirini says. It's nothing like her universal preschool bill, which she has filed session after session, on which she can't even get a hearing. "But the law makes great politics because it unites the players. It institutionalizes the idea and it builds momentum."

Lois Kolkhorst, a Republican from central Texas who sponsored the bill in the assembly, is widely touted as a comer. She is that most exotic of Texas fauna, a GOP moderate. She is also a young mother, who was pregnant when she first ran for the assembly. Her opponent attacked her as a neglectful mom. "Who's going to take care of that baby?" he kept saying. "I'm voting for that baby."

It was the research on early brain development that drew her into the pre-K fold. "The Good Lord must have wanted me to get involved," Kolkhorst says. "One night, when the kids were asleep, I was flipping the channels when I saw a PBS show on the importance of zero to three. It clicked—the first three years set the course of how the brain develops. I believe in the Mozart theory [that infants become more intelligent if they listen to music]. I think of that MRI of a neglected child's brain [from a Romanian orphanage], and I can see why they turn out the way they do."

During the winter and spring of 2005, as negotiations with the early education forces and the politicians proceeded, Landry and the preschool advocates became an effective tag team. "Kaitlin and Jason, they're marvelous," Landry says, "and we worked on this together. They have a ten-year plan for universal preschool, but we have to take this step by step." Sandy Borland, the executive director of the Texas Association of School Administrators, admires how "Landry is using the lawmakers, and allowing herself to be used, to further her agenda for young kids."

Getting everyone, including the child care centers, the public schools, and Head Start, to speak with a single voice was hard work. Not only did the leaders of those groups rarely confer with one another, on occasion they had gotten into fistfights in committee hearing rooms at the capitol.

The public schools wanted to control any state preschool initiative. This desire to expand is part of any organization's neuronal structure, but in this instance it also stemmed from the belief that the public education system would do the best job of making sure that toddlers are, as the catchphrase goes, "ready to learn."

The idea that children should be ready to learn means something very different to old-school Head Start administrators. In their view, three-year-olds shouldn't be expected to acquire the skills that Susan Landry's hand-held computers are designed to measure. Learning happens mainly through play, not skill and drill, they argue, and many things, including health care and nutrition, matter more than knowing ten letters in the alphabet. Susan Landry was booed when she spoke at a national Head Start Association convention, because to that crowd she represented the prevailing infatuation with the narrowly cognitive view of early education.

If the expansionist tendencies of the public schools vexed Head

Start, which has never had enough money to serve more than half of the eligible children, they terrified the for-profit child care centers. "They are the most conservative clients I've ever had," says their former lobbyist, William Pewitt, who has been at the business of lobbying for thirty years, and they were antagonistic to an expansion of state prekindergarten because it threatened their survival.

"I've never met an angrier group," says Landry. "If those guys had rocks, I would have been bruised all over. I had to convince them we had their best interest in mind. Developing trust was the key." She did that the old-fashioned way, with pork-barrel politics. None of the communities where the leaders of the child care association were operating preschools was part of the 2003 pilot project, but Landry made sure they were all included in the 2005 plan. The lure worked. "When they testified," Landry enthuses, "they were the best!"

TEEM offers something to everyone. The public schools surrender some of their control over preschool funding, but they get more money, and their teachers still do much of the pedagogical heavy lifting. The child care centers and Head Start receive free mentoring for their teachers. The promise of certification, the state's Good Housekeeping Seal, motivates the centers to beef up their programs.

And participating in TEEM afforded the Texas Head Start Association a chance to show that it could break out of its political insulation—an important message in 2005, when the Bush administration was contemplating the elimination of this Great Society–era program. "If demonstrating literacy is what it takes to keep Washington from cutting us out, then that's what we'll do," Helen Wright, the association's president, told Landry. Money for the expanded TEEM program came from the budget of the Texas Workforce Commission, which was ready to shed its image as indifferent to the caliber of preschools available to workers' children, and the fact that the legislation didn't require the lawmakers to lay out new dollars made it much easier to garner GOP support.

Promoting coordination among agencies is a piety in public administration circles.[28] But as James Strickland at Austin's Head Start points out, "The landscape is strewn with failed attempts." Without a strong leader to fight for preschool, prospects for its expansion in Texas depend on the continuing persuasive capacities of Susan Landry and the adroitness of the advocates.

Landry's emphasis on improving teacher training and strengthening the curriculum—in contrast to measuring the square footage of classrooms or allowing anyone without a criminal record to teach preschool—along with the gradual implementation of the program, have kept the state's pre-K from turning into another Florida. For their part, the activists have used baling wire to tie together a preschool deal, and they see that achievement as just a first step.[29] As we'll see in the last chapter, in 2006 their unflashy style of politics brought them a bit closer to their goal.

California: Catch a Falling Star

The scene at San Francisco's Grace Child Development Center could have been lifted straight from a feel-good movie. On a perfect summer day in July 2005, the TV cameras rolled and reporters crowded around as actor, filmmaker, producer, and preschool activist Rob Reiner joined a table of four-year-olds. He found himself talking about movies with a precocious girl named Diamond, who has ambitions to be a movie star—both are fans of *The Cat and the Hat*—and about careers with April, a would-be doctor who could almost spell her name.

Reiner was on hand to celebrate the launch of San Francisco's universal prekindergarten program, bankrolled by the city's voters, but his aspirations were far broader. Flanked by local politicians, he turned the occasion into a pep rally for a state constitutional amendment, to be on the ballot in June 2006, that would guarantee every four-year-old in California access to a good preschool. Unlike in Florida, where voters had delivered a similar mandate only to see it denatured by the legislature, the California measure bristled with specifics that gave "quality" meaning and bite. A proposed tax on some of the state's wealthiest taxpayers was projected to generate $2.3 billion, a handsome sum with which to pay for pre-K.

"California is the future of this movement," says Karen Hill-Scott, a child development expert and UCLA professor who knows the state's preschool world inside out. "There are enough children under age five here to constitute the seventh biggest state in the country." With Reiner leading the charge, hopes ran high that the voters would approve the measure. This was more than a California moment—it was anticipated that the state's thumbs-up would become the tipping point for the nationwide prekindergarten movement.

Unlike those states where universal preschool is already up and running—improbable pioneers like Oklahoma—California is the place where new ideas often get their start. For thirty years, with one ballot proposition after another, the electorate, rather than elected officials, has made many of the most consequential policy choices. Since 1978, when the voters endorsed the tax-cutting Proposition 13 and provoked a nationwide taxpayers' revolt, conservatives have been especially adroit in turning this Progressive Era ideal of direct democracy into a tool for decimating government.[30]

If liberals were to be equally successful, they needed to persuade voters that a goal like improving early education was so imperative that it couldn't be left to the vagaries of state budgetary politics, and that they had a workable plan. "If we believed that there was a chance to do this legislatively, we'd do it in a second," Reiner insisted. "In 1999, when the state was flush, I talked to [then governor] Gray Davis. He thought preschool was a great idea, but that this wasn't the right time. For those politicians, it's *never* the right time."

But in a plot twist so unexpected that few Hollywood screen writers would have dared to script it, Reiner's visibility became a major liability to the effort. In 2006 the preschool measure, Proposition 82, which at the outset had seemed a shoo-in, was defeated. And that wasn't the final act in the drama. Barely a day after the votes were tallied, pre-K in California acquired a surprising new ally—Governor Arnold Schwarzenegger.

The push for universal prekindergarten in California was largely Rob Reiner's brainchild.[31] In 1998 he pulled together a coalition, which included the American Cancer Society and the American Heart Association, to back a first-in-the-nation First Five ballot initiative in his state. The program was designed to pay for children's services, ranging from home nurses' visits to day care. Funds would come from a new fifty-cent tax on each pack of cigarettes sold, which was anticipated to generate about $650 million a year. This tax spurred the tobacco industry into furious opposition, and it spent over $40 million, more than four times what Reiner could raise, to fight the initiative. Conservatives grumbled that Reiner was a "tiresome busybody" and that the ballot measure was "subjecting public policy to the mid-life crises of bloated Hollywood big-shots."[32] Still, the initiative passed, and two years later an industry-sponsored attempt to repeal it was crushingly rejected.

"First Five is the national model," says Jane Henderson, the first director of the First Five Commission, "and it's all because of Rob." The commission, which Reiner chaired until 2006, disburses 80 percent of the tobacco tax money to the state's fifty-eight counties. But with so many competing needs, at first the funds were just "sprinkled around," says Henderson. "Pressure groups pushed for everything from fluoridation to breast-feeding." To focus the counties' efforts, the commission made school readiness its main concern. "That's really what zero-to-five is pointing to, the start of school," said Karen Hill-Scott, who was a member of the commission in its first years. The commission provided $400 million in matching funds to counties that expanded their prekindergartens.

First Five's greatest success was its use of the electronic bully pulpit to promote pre-K. Between 2000 and 2006, it spent close to $200 million on TV public service spots—almost as much as the state lottery spends on its ads. The initial advertisements were shaped to open parents' eyes to the importance of early learning. In one, the opening image shows a parent reading a book to her child; then, fast forward to the image of those same kids, years later, reading big books themselves. The most hard-hitting ad tied crime prevention to prekindergarten. Two policemen, one an African American, tell parents there is something they can do now to keep their children out of the back of the police car later on: send them to preschool.

Across the country, popular support for preschool was growing during this period; in California the media blitz may have accelerated the process. In 2001 more than half of all parents surveyed said they believed it was better for children to stay home full-time; two years later, two-thirds of those polled thought preschool was the better option. In a 2004 poll, three out of four Californians agreed that making preschool available to all interested parents was an important priority, and by a similar margin they said that the state should underwrite universal prekindergarten.

"The people got the message," says Maryann O'Sullivan, CEO of Preschool California, a statewide advocacy group supported by the Packard Foundation. "They know that preschool is a good thing, that there are studies that say it makes a difference." To O'Sullivan, a veteran activist, this is cause to cheer. "Somewhere in California, the land of anomie, we are a cohesive society. Somewhere we care commonly about one another, not just about our own kids."

Bolstered by the poll results, in 2004 Reiner teamed up with the California Teachers Association, a potent force in statewide politics, to formulate a ballot measure that would generate $1.5 billion a year for preschool. But the initiative was written without consulting any other groups. As a result, it was widely perceived as a full-employment act for the teachers' union, and, reasonably enough, that angered other preschool operators. When the polls started to look iffy, the union, which had bigger fights on its hands, withdrew.

A year later Reiner was back, this time convening the interested parties to hammer out an initiative together. "It was like a legislative process," says O'Sullivan. Among those at the table were investor Michael Milken, who pushed for a market-based system; child care providers, who wanted assurances that they would be able to stay in business; and the teachers' union, which was eager to sign up new members.

The initiative that emerged, which became Proposition 82 on the June 2006 ballot, incorporated the research on what's needed to provide an education beneficial to young kids.[33] It specified a "developmentally appropriate" curriculum and fixed a maximum of twenty children in a classroom with two teachers. Within a decade every pre-K teacher would be required to have a bachelor's degree, as well as a credential in early learning (the measure included funds to defray the cost of tuition). Although the California Department of Education would set guidelines and county school boards would manage the program, nonprofit and for-profit preschools, religious as well as sectarian, would be included in the mix. There was no disputing that full-day preschool, open to three- and four-year-olds, would have been ideal. But that cost seemed prohibitive, and so the decision was made to stress quality over numbers: the state pre-K would be a half-day program, and would be available only to four-year-olds. Critics insisted from the outset that California, which faced a multibillion-dollar deficit, couldn't afford such a pricey venture, but the advocates relied on a Rand Corporation report that estimated that within a generation, preschool would return $2.62 for every dollar spent.[34]

Proposition 82 was budgeted at $2.3 billion. That's a very big-ticket item. It's nearly the size of the nationwide budget for Head Start, and more, by orders of magnitude, than any other state spends on early education. It was to be paid for by a new 1.7 percent income tax on individuals earning more than $450,000 a year and couples making more than $900,000. This revenue-raising strategy built on an initiative, passed in 2004, that requires millionaires to pay a similar tax for mental health programs.

Despite the public drumbeat for preschool, private polling showed that only a bare majority supported the combination of state-funded preschool and a new tax. Those in the know understood that the fight would be tough. "The conventional wisdom is that you don't put a measure on the ballot unless you're polling in the high 60s, and we weren't there," Maryann O'Sullivan says.

"But as an advocate, you pray for someone like Rob to come along and take on an issue. It's not like an institution, where you can put it on the calendar—this was the moment when he was there." Reiner appreciated the odds but he decided to go ahead. "If you don't try," he contended, "you don't accomplish much."

Ben Austin, a former staffer in the Clinton White House who initially ran the Prop. 82 campaign, is blunt in his assessment of what happened next. "With the low poll numbers, we had to run a perfect campaign. But the campaign was a god-awful disaster, from our decision to put the measure on the June primary ballot, when the Democratic turnout was low, to the weak messaging."

"The plan was to create the perfect storm," says Austin, "to write a proposition that got labor to agree to concessions over competition and accountability, that brought the private pre-school providers aboard, that got business to endorse a big tax increase. We got nine chambers of commerce, including Los Angeles and San Francisco, to sign on, and we went to the state chamber of commerce, hoping for a love fest. Instead we got massive opposition."

Soon afterward, Austin himself was sidelined—and so was Reiner. In a front-page *Los Angeles Times* story that ran on February 20, 2006, just as the campaign was getting under way, both were attacked for misusing public funds from the First Five Commission to improve the initiative's prospects.[35] The next day, a *Times* editorial asserted that the commission had become "an unelected government agency controlled by Rob Reiner," that had spent "millions, against the spirit if not the letter of the law, on campaign propaganda aimed at influencing their votes." Even though this "propaganda" had touted the overall benefits of pre-school, not Prop. 82, the editorial insinuated that the conflict-of-interest allegations tainted the ballot measure. "Voters may want to take a more skeptical look at the First 5 program before they decide whether to give their approval to Reiner's latest brainchild."[36]

The ads were "legal and entirely proper," insisted Reiner's attorney, a position that state officials confirmed months after the election. But what followed the *Los Angeles Times* story was a vintage example of political piling-on, and six weeks after the story broke Reiner quit the commission.

"When it's all about you and you run into some problems, it tends to carry over," says Rick Claussen, who ran the No on Prop. 82 campaign, dissecting his opponents' failures. No more photo ops with perky four-year-olds. As veteran GOP strategist Dan Schnur noted, "The conflict-of-interest story put Reiner on the sidelines, and they lost all of the positive media."[37]

Campaigns in California are a sport that only the wealthy can play—this was Wal-Mart versus Hollywood star power, the Gap versus the teachers' unions, Indian tribes versus the chamber of commerce. Most of the "no" money came from Silicon Valley venture capitalists. They had slept through the mental health initiative, but this time they got organized. "They thought they were being taxed into oblivion," says Austin, "and when they went on TV, reinforcing people's cynicism about any government program, our numbers tanked. It was all over." Even though the Yes on 82 side spent more than $20 million, twice as much as the opposition, it never got its vision across.

The measure's proponents had a costly and unwieldy initiative to promote, twenty-eight fine-print pages.[38] The other side framed the issue simply, to capitalize on voters' big objection: hostility to big government. That argument resonated with editorial writers, and all of the major papers in the state came out against the proposition. The *Los Angeles Times* declared that Prop. 82 would "set up a cumbersome bureaucracy and place it under the state Department of Education, which has done a disappointing job with K–12 schools."[39]

"You come away from the 'No on 82' ads and what do you remember? It's the word 'bureaucracy,'" says Susanna Cooper, the communications director at Preschool California. "It would have been a pretty efficient system, but the facts really didn't matter."

Once the contention that the proposition would create a bloated new agency had been driven home, the opponents broadened their attack. "Why would we turn over our very successful system to a failed system?" asked Pamela Zell Rigg, president of an organization called the California Montessori Council, and her question was repeatedly recycled in the press.[40] Rigg actually represented just 80 of the state's more than 500 Montessori schools, but that went unmentioned, as did the fact that most of the 40,000 private preschool operators were supporters of the measure. The No on Prop. 82 advertisements confused things further. One ad featured a teacher and a principal who were fearful that the preschool measure would harm the public schools. The message was that teachers opposed Prop. 82, while in fact the teachers' unions were major backers. The characters in the ad were just actors: the casting call had been for someone to play a teacher who was "female/Asian, Caucasian, 40–45, professional manner" and a principal who was "male/multi-ethnic/50–52, gentle with authority."[41]

Claims that were purportedly premised on research also played a prominent part in the anti-82 campaign. The libertarian Reason Foundation's report that attacked the Rand study, questioning whether prekindergarten really was a good long-term investment, got considerable attention from a media habitually drawn to controversy. "We depend on an 'earned media' strategy," says Lisa Snell, who directs the Reason Foundation's education program. This means placing op-ed pieces and contacting bookers for radio talk shows. Snell also relied on a shoe-leather strategy. She made about 150 appearances statewide—speaking to groups ranging from the GOP club in Bakersfield and the chamber of commerce in Ontario to an undergraduate political science class at Berkeley.

Bruce Fuller became the major voice from the world of academe on the "no" side, relying to good effect on his status as an education professor at the University of California at Berkeley.[42] Fuller was everywhere—offering sound bites on the research findings, writing opinion pieces, giving interviews to reporters, stirring up fears among preschool operators that the measure would wipe them out. Despite abundant evidence to the contrary, he kept insisting that the measure represented a giveaway to well-off parents who could easily afford to pay the preschool tuition, and that it imposed a lock-step curriculum that discouraged creativity.

Preschool enrollment wouldn't increase much, Fuller contended, since most parents were already sending their children to some kind of program, and so it would be wiser to concentrate the money on poor children. That argument ignored the abysmal quality of many of those programs. "Middle-class families are [already] benefiting," he told a *San Francisco Chronicle* reporter, "but if we move toward universal preschool, it's not clear that universal preschool would close gaps in early learning, because the gain experienced by low-income kids may not ever be enough to catch up with the gain by middle-class kids."[43] By this logic, the only way to help poor children would be to deny opportunities to the middle class.

"Fuller was a huge factor," says *Sacramento Bee* editorial writer

Pia Lopez. "He demonstrated incredible energy about communicating with opinion-makers on editorial boards, talking to legislators." Most professors don't relish the advocate's role, and although many social scientists disagreed with him, until the final weeks of the campaign Fuller had the field entirely to himself.

Conservative economists chimed in. "Nothing is more ill-conceived than creating a new government bureaucracy to hand out subsidies to middle-income and rich people to pay for services they already are getting—and financing the whole scheme with huge tax increases on small businesses and successful entrepreneurs," wrote Michael Boskin, a senior fellow at Stanford's Hoover Institution, in a *Los Angeles Times* opinion piece.[44] That argument went national when, four days before the election, *New York Times* columnist David Brooks, relying on Bruce Fuller's analyses, jeered that the initiative "seems to have been devised under the supposition that it takes a bureaucratic megalopolis to raise a child."[45]

This miscellany of denigration had the desired effect of planting doubts in the voters' minds, and when it comes to ballot measures, doubts are all it takes. In the June 2006 election, only 39 percent of the voters endorsed Prop. 82.

Eleven months after Rob Reiner was in San Francisco to tout universal prekindergarten, California luminaries gathered at a Los Angeles preschool for a photo op. It was June 7, the day after Proposition 82 was defeated. The big change was the cast of characters. Reiner was gone, and in his place stood Arnold Schwarzenegger. The Republican governor had opposed the ballot measure, citing his objection to the proposed tax. Now he appeared on the preschool stage, Fortinbras come to Denmark to save the day. "While the people have voted against Proposition 82 they did not vote against preschool," he said. "The people of California love preschool. So we want to do it right, in a fiscally responsible way that will help the kids who need it most, the students who live near our most struggling schools."[46]

The governor made a modest proposal. The ballot measure had prescribed preschool for all four-year-olds, at a cost of $2.3 billion. Schwarzenegger pledged less than a tenth as much, a $50-million-a-year increase for each of the following three years.[47] That money would be used to expand state prekindergarten where the educational need was greatest, the neighborhoods where students' scores on the state achievement test ranked in the lowest 30 percent. "It's a good start," said assembly member Wilma Chan, who had earlier tried and failed to extract such a commitment.

Passage of the bill was swift and easy, and Schwarzenegger turned the ceremonial signing into another media event. As the cameras rolled at a Los Angeles preschool, he bent down and asked a four-year-old to help him sign the bill into law. His remarks could have been delivered by Rob Reiner: "By investing in our preschoolers, reaching out to the parents, we can give our kids a really strong foundation for education and a strong foundation for their life."

Even though the preschool initiative was clobbered at the polls, the campaign had succeeded in altering the political dynamic. "Prop. 82 gave us a platform," notes Susanna Cooper at Preschool California. "One of the nice things that came out of the experience was that the governor realized he could not afford to ignore this issue anymore."

Schwarzenegger was elected in 2003, and in his first years in office he had positioned himself as the outsider, eager to change the way California did its political business. But in a special election called by the governor himself in October 2005, the voters rejected his sweeping plans, and polls showed that his popularity had plummeted. Schwarzenegger publicly acknowledged his mistakes, a rarity in political life, and moved swiftly to seize the center. Pre-K is now part of his revised agenda, along with such traditionally liberal concerns as combating global warming and increasing the minimum wage.

It is easy enough for preschool advocates to imagine how the governor's plan might be expanded over time. In a few years, if the state's coffers permit, children growing up in communities where the plight of students isn't quite so desperate might be entitled to attend a publicly funded prekindergarten; down the road, if the economy continues to grow, those preschools might be opened to all, as Prop. 82 envisioned. Maria Shriver, Schwarzenegger's wife and political soul mate, is the daughter of Sargent Shriver, a luminary in the Great Society era, and she wants children's issues to be part of her husband's legacy. Preschool dovetails nicely with that aspiration.

Campaigning in Poetry, Governing in Prose

If success is measured by the sums that states are spending on early education, then the prekindergarten campaign has done remarkably well. Between 2004 and 2006, states poured more than $1.2 billion into new funding for preschool, despite the pressure to cut taxes, build prisons, and underwrite health care without running a deficit.

At the start of the new century the issue of preschool was nearly invisible, but this too has changed. In 2005 there were more than 5,000 media clips on pre-K policy; in 2006 the Democratic response to the State of the Union address included a preschool proposal, and the idea has become a darling of many Republicans as well. The prekindergarten movement has reached clear to Kansas, where self-reliance is the best-known verse in the policymakers' bible. As Kansas goes, so goes Idaho?

Slowly but steadily, preschool has acquired a raft of champions. For some, it has personal resonance—the memory of Sargent Shriver, for Arnold Schwarzenegger; the conviction, on the part of Illinois governor Rod Blagojevich and former Miami mayor Alex Penelas, that every child in their home state ought to have the kind of education that their own children received. Others have found their inspiration elsewhere.

Passion matters in politics, but passion is often insufficient to carry the day. Preschool is just one of the many ideas competing for politicians' consideration. Peer beneath the surface in any state that invests heavily in prekindergarten, and you will find someone who knows how to interest a public leader.

Successful preschool politics, like politics generally, isn't a one-person show. It demands an active network to get the details right and carry out the gritty long-term work. In Oklahoma, well-placed bureaucrats and laconic legislators, as well as bankers and oil men turned policy wonks and philanthropists, have carried the day. In Texas the pre-K coalition includes the United Way, the one powerful Democrat in the state legislature, and an academic entrepreneur with White House ties. When the season is right—whether it's because of a budget windfall, a state lottery surplus, a new "sin" tax, or a blue-ribbon commission report on why preschool offers children a better future—these advocates have learned how to move in. And activists can't afford to be ideological purists—they need to deliver their message to whoever will listen. During the 2006 gubernatorial campaigns in Ohio and Pennsylvania, pre-K promoters made a point of being assiduously nonpartisan. They worked to win over the Republican and the Democratic candidates so that whoever was elected, preschool would emerge as a winner.[48]

Once preschool legislation is adopted, the issue takes on a life of its own. While a pre-K measure may start small, the constituency expands naturally. Good programs are embraced by parents eager for their children to do well on the omnipresent tests of literacy and numeracy, as well as by teachers and school administrators who see firsthand the difference they make. These new waves of support motivate more politicians to leap aboard the bandwagon.

Increased enrollment plays well with public officials. But because quality is less tangible, it is a harder sell. Even as the numbers of children enrolled in pre-K grew by 20 percent between 2004 and 2006, the amount of money spent on each child was cut by nearly 10 percent, to $3,500; that's less than half of what the average state expends on students in primary and secondary schools. While New Jersey spends $9,305 per pre-K youngster, other states spend less than a fourth as much.

Four-year-olds make for great publicity photos, but few elected officials have the time or desire to parse the details of putting prekindergarten in place. As they move on to other causes, the politics of the un-dramatic emerges.

One battleground is the budget. Where, as in Florida and California, the goal has been to launch a big new program overnight, the result has been defeat. Elsewhere, though, the strategy has been to aim lower—to secure the kind of small, steady victories evident in Texas. "The budget is a powerful index of a society's values," economist Joseph Schumpeter observed long ago, "not merely in its language and numbers but in the lived experience of its impact on people, families, workers, businesses and organizations."[49]

The measure of the preschool movement's success cannot be calibrated simply by the numbers. Success is also a matter of making prekindergartens better, by adopting new standards—for class size, for example—or by offering incentives to improve quality, such as giving preschools more money if they hire better-trained teachers.

These issues have received far less public attention than the head counts or budget figures—and here conservatives have done quite well. They may have lost the fight over whether the state will educate three- and four-year-olds, but in many states they have enshrined the market as the mechanism that defines the character of prekindergarten.

Embracing the "one best system" approach that has long been in place for K–12 education is both implicit in the Pew Charitable Trusts' strategy for its universal preschool initiative, devised in 2001, and consistent with the studies that Steven Barnett has subsequently conducted at the National Institute for Early Education Research. The goal is to expand the public schools downward in age, into preschool, thus guaranteeing decent salaries for teachers and good educational standards. That's the Oklahoma model, and it has worked well there. Elsewhere, however, politicians have made market sovereignty and parental choice the policy bywords.[50]

Competition can strengthen quality, as many economists contend, but only if parents have good information and government sets sensible standards. That is the version of the preschool market that Art Rolnick, at the Minneapolis Federal Reserve, has been talking about.[51] But when a preschool market is unregulated and usable information isn't available, quality is likely to suffer. Florida is the textbook example. What has happened there is Bre'er Rabbit politics—for-profit preschools, which initially resisted state involvement, wound up the winners, as did church-run prekindergartens, which receive no-strings pubic money to promote the Gospel among four-year-olds. That outcome pleases social conservatives, but it upsets those who believe that taxpayers shouldn't be subsidizing religion.

The relatively slow expansion of prekindergarten nationwide doesn't sit well with advocates—understandably enough, since they see the futures of today's children as being on the line. The constitutional amendment adopted by Florida's voters, like the failed proposition in California, was supposed to be an end run around a drawn-out process, a way of achieving through direct democracy what lawmakers were unwilling to do voluntarily. But since legislators pass the budget, they get the last word, which is how Florida's constitutional standard of high quality for all turned into a flawed $2,500 voucher for some.

Bringing a lawsuit is another time-honored way to trump unresponsive politicians. Advocates have tried this tactic in several places, claiming a state constitutional right to preschool. The New Jersey Supreme Court bought the argument (embedded in a school finance case that has stretched out over more than thirty years), and the result was the introduction of high-caliber prekindergarten in poor school districts. While judges elsewhere have rejected the contention, filing a lawsuit can reshape the political map, in a manner akin to the public conversation provoked by Proposition 82 in California. A lawsuit in Georgia, which claimed to be offering preschool to all, embarrassed lawmakers into spending enough money to back up the bragging. Litigation in North Carolina gave Governor Michael Easley added ammunition for his pre-K plan.[52] A lawsuit seems the only way to secure high-quality preschools in Florida.

When Arnold Schwarzenegger announced his $150 million preschool proposal in 2006, he summoned up the memory of his father-in-law, Sargent Shriver. "He started many different programs, but one of the programs that he was most proud of was Head Start. He said that those kids, it's almost like they're starting at the starting line—kind of like ten, twenty, or thirty feet behind that starting line—and how we have to make sure to give the kids the opportunity to start equally with everyone else at the starting line, to start equally. That is the most important thing."[53]

While this homage was a gracious gesture, it underscores the profound difference between the 1960s and the present. Head Start was a nationwide venture with grandiose hopes of transforming society. Three-quarters of a million children enrolled in Head Start nationwide in a matter of months; Schwarzenegger's three-year plan is designed to serve only 43,000 youngsters in a single state. Yet rather than complain that Schwarzenegger was offering a half measure, the activists did what good politics dictates and praised his good deed. They appreciated that he had taken the sting out of the defeat at the ballot box—that he had changed the subject, away from dissecting a political failure, toward a focus on good preschool. This would not have satisfied Great Society–era big dreamers like Sargent Shriver, but those days are long gone. Modest steps are the essence of the politics of the un-dramatic.

Might a *giant* step become possible? Could the concerns of children—not just what happens to them for half a day, at the age of four, but writ large—become a political priority?

That was the vision of the Pew Charitable Trusts in the early

1990s, when, seeking to capitalize on a moment when the byword was children, the foundation set out to reinvent the array of child-centered state programs. And Pew's decision to pull out once it appreciated the enormity of the task had its political counterpart in Congress's failure to seize the day. One significant piece of legislation did emerge during this period—the 1997 Children's Health Insurance Program, a federal-state partnership that enrolls more than four million children. Since then, aside from the problematic No Child Left Behind Act, there has been silence from Washington.

A hundred years of frustrated hopes, from the confident pronouncement at the dawn of the twentieth century that it would be "the century of the child" to the 1997 White House Conference on Child Care that led nowhere, give children's advocates good cause for pessimism. But history isn't always destiny, and counterexamples do exist.

As recently as the late 1990s, Great Britain, whose market-driven social policies were largely borrowed from the United States, was even less mindful of children's needs. But that situation was reversed after Prime Minister Tony Blair's startling pledge to end child poverty won popular raves. What's more, here in this country some astute and committed political leaders in several states have persuaded the citizenry to shoulder more responsibility for the well-being of children. These developments, and their far-reaching implications, are the focus of the final two chapters.

English Lessons

IT IS notoriously difficult to persuade American policymakers to consider any idea not made in the USA. This parochialism frustrates children's advocates, who look enviously at what Western European nations generally, and France in particular, have accomplished—the crèches open to all infants, the preschools where teachers have graduate degrees and those whose calling takes them to the most troubled neighborhoods are the best paid. They marvel at a country where every three- and four-year-old gets the same high-quality education, and where evaluation isn't fetishized because the value of early learning looks so obvious.[1] Why, the advocates wonder, can't what we see in France be replicated here?[2]

But the United States is unlikely ever to open standardized French-style nurseries or adopt a uniform regime for its preschoolers. Despite his tactlessness, former Defense Secretary Donald Rumsfeld got one thing right when he dismissed France as part of "old Europe": in their appreciation of the importance of personal choice, the two nations are so far apart they might as well occupy different planets.

While far less has been said in praise of Britain's approach to children's policy, it is the British track record from which the United States can learn the most.[3] These days the vaunted "special relationship" between the two countries isn't only about affairs of state. When Tony Blair's restyled Labour Party—New Labour, as it is called—swept the Tories out of office in 1997, it borrowed wholesale from the playbook of the Clinton White House, and so its domestic policies have a decidedly American cast.[4]

Gone is the Labour Party's instinctive belief that decisions are best made in Whitehall. There has been less faith in command-and-control, more of a stress on local knowledge as well as a mixed public-private market; in this respect, the Labour and Conservative parties have moved closer together. Talking with members of Parliament or those who run British think tanks is surprisingly like speaking with their American—more particularly, their liberal-centrist American—counterparts; it's as if the Democratic Leadership Council had gathered in the House of Commons, the Brookings Institute relocated on the Thames.

That's why Britain's experience is pertinent to the backers of a kids-first strategy on this side of the Atlantic. While America has been moving slowly toward making prekindergarten available to every four-year-old, in Britain almost all three- and four-year-olds currently attend preschool—a marked change in recent years. "I want the U.S. to be Tony Blair's England," says NYU psychologist Lawrence Aber. "It's an 'existence proof' that this can happen—that it is possible to arrive at overarching goals, and to link beliefs, values, and marketing strategies to get there."

In 1999, to the astonishment of all, Tony Blair pledged to end child poverty in a generation. Might something similar happen in America? It's a long shot, as economists Jared Bernstein and

Mark Greenberg pointed out in a 2006 *Washington Post* op-ed, because "it's hard to imagine that anyone in high office in this country would get near an idea like this right now." But this is exactly the kind of vision that could help to revive faith in government by giving meaning to the notion of the common good. Could it be one of those "big ideas" progressives have been dreaming about?[5]

As the prime minister's limousine pulled out of the unprepossessing precincts of Downing Street, Tony Blair was reviewing the text of his speech. The date was March 18, 1999, and the occasion was the Beveridge Lecture, an annual event to honor the man credited with having created the British welfare state.

Prime ministers, like presidents, are forever giving speeches, but this one mattered more than most. The Labour Party's left flank—academics, policy dreamers, union leaders—would be out in force, and this was the constituency that, two years after Blair's election, was feeling betrayed. To his critics, New Labour looked suspiciously like "Margaret Thatcher Lite," with its pledge not to increase taxes and its cuts in benefits for single parents. The view from the left, says Ed Balls, economic secretary to the Treasury, is that "Labour always betrays its progressive heritage."

What Tony Blair told the audience that day stunned everyone, including his closest advisers. "Our historic aim will be for ours to be the first generation to end child poverty forever. It will be a twenty-year mission, but I believe that it can be done."[6]

That speech marked the start of an era. During its years in power the Conservative Party had devised a child care voucher scheme, but it was underfunded and used mainly by middle-class families. Otherwise, the business of child rearing had been left entirely to parents. For its part, the Labour Party didn't talk about child poverty during the 1997 campaign. Although "education, education, education" was a rallying cry, this meant reducing class size in primary schools, not responding to the array of younger children's needs. And while the Labour platform declared that every three- and four-year-old had a right to attend free preschools (nurseries, in British parlance), that commitment went unnoticed.

Soon after taking office, Tony Blair visited the Aylesbury Plus Estates, a dilapidated if grandiosely named housing project barely a mile from Parliament. "Cheers went up from those hanging out of tower-block windows," Polly Toynbee reported in the *Guardian*, "when Blair promised that, under Labour, there would be 'no forgotten people and no "no-hope" areas.'"[7] But leaders often make such promises—how many American presidents have visited the South Bronx?—and then the motorcade passes.

"Why did Blair make that pledge?" a puzzled Secretary of the Treasury Gordon Brown asked Ed Balls. After all, reducing inequality was Brown's obsession, not Blair's. It was Brown, the perpetual heir apparent to the prime minister's post, who had brought down the house when he described child poverty as "a scar on the soul of Britain."[8]

"Who gives a toss?" replied Balls. "This is just what we wanted, a galvanizing objective"—and that's just what it has been. In less than a decade, Mach speed in government, the country has doubled its spending on children.

During the Conservative Party's eighteen-year rule, the rate of child poverty in Britain tripled. The nation had the highest proportion of children living in poverty among Western European countries, and the level of income inequality also rose to rival that of the United States.[9] That's one reason why the voters tossed out the Tories: a 1997 poll showed that three Britons in four favored expanding social services, even if that meant higher taxes.[10]

Labour was committed to reducing child poverty—but how? "This was policy-free territory," says Norman Glass, then a deputy director at the Treasury assigned to frame the government's program.

Well before Blair made his pledge, the Treasury had started hunting for new ideas, and it had looked first to Bill Clinton's America. "We began with the American research and our own political concern," says Beverly Hughes, Minister of State for Children, Young People and Families, a one-time probation officer and university lecturer. The Treasury led the way because it regarded spending for children as a sound investment. "End welfare as we know it," Bill Clinton's slogan, resonated with Gordon Brown, who borrowed Clinton's line about "making work pay." Among British politicians Brown is "almost unique," writes widely read blogger Tony Rudd, "in still being fundamentally socialist but having America as his lodestar pointing the way forward."[11]

Child-centered policy held the dual promise of drawing mothers into the labor force and bettering the lives of the young, and so preparing the next generation for knowledge work. "Tackling childhood poverty is not about providing either more money or better public services," Brown said. "It is of necessity about both."[12] Putting money directly into the pockets of the poor was one favored approach. For the first time in the country's history, a minimum wage was set—nearly ten dollars an hour, about twice as high as in the United States. When Conservatives prophesied that companies would have to fire low-wage workers, the government relied on research by maverick American economists in asserting—correctly, as things turned out—that this oft-recited prediction was wrong.[13]

The American Earned Income Tax Credit was adopted in Britain as the Working Tax Credit; and a Child Tax Credit, an idea also borrowed from the U.S., pays for up to 70 percent of poor families' costs.[14] While the tax credits have done their job of redistributing income, this has been policymaking by stealth. In Britain, as in the United States, politicians worry that taxpayers will object to paying the working poor out of tax dollars, and so the reform goes unpublicized. Paid maternity leave—about $200 a week in 2006—is provided for six months, and there are plans to extend it to a full year. Ingeniously, Britain now guarantees every newborn a tax credit worth nearly $400—the guarantee rises to $1,000 for poor children—and, because of compound interest, by the time these youngsters can cash in, that account, invested in stocks and bonds, will have mushroomed in value.[15]

"No child shall be left behind," avowed Gordon Brown, expanding the American rhetoric to cover life chances broadly. By 2006 the number of children living in poverty in Great Britain had fallen by 700,000—a 17-percent drop, within shouting distance of the government's short-term goal.[16]

When it comes to children, the jewel in Labour's crown has been an initiative called Sure Start. As its name suggests, America's Head Start program provided the template. "I was so naïve," says Norman Glass, who developed the concept while at the Treasury, "that I assumed that Head Start was a casualty of the Reagan era." Glass was a quick learner. He was impressed by the Head Start studies and considerably more impressed by the long-term impact of Perry Preschool and the Abecedarian Project. But the initiative that Glass sold to Gordon Brown looked a lot more like a 1960s-style community action agency than Head Start or Perry Preschool. Sure Start, launched in 2000 with a budget of

$450 million over the first three years, was supposed to benefit two generations, poor children as well as their parents.

From the outset, all the Sure Start centers had the same targets, including lowering the number of low-birth-weight babies and increasing breast-feeding. They also offered certain core services, such as mentoring for young parents. But initially there was little guidance from the central government about how the centers should be run; instead, parents were invited to figure out which priorities matched local preferences.

"Families without social supports start badly, and things go downhill from there," Norman Glass argues. Sure Start was meant to break that cycle. Some of the centers hired top-notch professionals to respond to the particular needs of those who lived in the area. But leaving parents to run the show could also mean aromatherapy and head massages, coffee bars and trips to the seaside for the parents.

Glass is unapologetic. "Is the question 'What's most efficient' or 'What gets people into the system'?"

From the outset, Sure Start was wildly popular. "That's partly because mothers have such a big say," says Polly Toynbee at the *Guardian.* All families living in a neighborhood where there's a center are welcome to use it, and the resulting diversity of participants, including the families of some members of Parliament, has boosted the initiative's appeal. There is a historical logic behind this "targeted universalism." Until Labour came to power, the government took no notice of young children unless they were being neglected or abused. "It was the 'here comes the beadle' era," says University of Bristol economist Paul Gregg, who advises the Treasury on child poverty. "The idea now is to make sure no stigma attaches to being a 'Sure Start kid.'"

Toynbee waxes poetic when she describes the best of the Sure

Start centers. "Every child from birth finds here everything necessary to thrive, especially for those who never see a book at home or learn to count, and barely talk. Here speech therapists, social workers, health visitors and high-calibre nursery teachers help all children reach primary school ready to learn. Here working mothers are guaranteed affordable childcare, in a place where parents of all classes create a hub for the local community. That's the dream and in some places it's all there."[17]

In a survey of parents involved in one Sure Start center, an astonishing 99 percent reported that it was satisfactory or very satisfactory.[18] Members of Parliament take notice of such statistics. There is no way to have your picture taken alongside a tax credit, but an appearance at the local Sure Start center now makes a favorite photo op for Conservative and Labour politicians alike. "It's a great brand name," says Phil Collins, Tony Blair's speechwriter.

The program grew quickly. In 2001 the number of centers doubled, to 500. Yet with this rapid expansion came a blurring of mission. Sure Start became the policy equivalent of a Rorschach ink blot, with various factions, both inside and outside government, defining it as whatever they wished it to be. Was it supposed to help new parents do a better job of child rearing—or, very differently, to deliver child care as a way of motivating mothers to get a job, and so reduce child poverty? Was it meant to concentrate on the least well-off or to help all comers—to "lift all boats on a rising tide," as Blair suggested in off-the-cuff comments?[19]

Two widely publicized reports, a 2005 study conducted by academics from the University of London and Oxford, and a 2006 paper prepared by the National Audit Office, the government's watchdog for spending, highlighted Sure Start's dilemma.[20] Reinforcing the earlier findings, these studies showed that parents who used the centers regarded them very highly. But both inquiries underscored a problem well known to poverty warriors across the Atlantic—the immense difficulty of reaching families that most need help. Fewer than a third of the centers had been able to connect with the single-parent families and teen mothers who stood to gain the most from parenting training, medical attention, and good child care. And because neither study undertook the kind of cost-benefit analysis that has often been conducted in appraising American preschools, no one could confidently say that Sure Start "worked."

In the United States, such a mixed report card would have been read by conservatives as yet another example of the failure of the nanny state; in a policy environment impatient for results, the initiative might have been scuttled.[21] Not so in Britain. There, the research has generally been treated as simply a progress report and a spur to improvement.

After the release of the 2005 study, reforms were quickly instituted. The new model for Sure Start is the American Early Head Start program. The emphasis has shifted away from doing what parents want and toward delivering what, on the basis of solid evidence, the government has determined that children require. "Parent satisfaction doesn't necessarily mean good outcomes for kids," says Naomi Eisenstadt, an American expatriate who ran Sure Start until 2006. Eisenstadt was a well-regarded community activist before going to work for the British government, and her viewpoint represents something of a change of heart. "If services aren't building on something parents want, they won't work," she says. "But the fact that parents like what's happening doesn't necessarily mean there are benefits for kids."

Along with the switch in objectives has come a new blueprint for management. No longer do the centers stand alone. Instead, local governments run the show, coordinating a host of children's services, private and public, including Sure Start. And what had initially been seen as a ten-year experiment was enshrined in statute in 2006, so that, as Minister of State for Children, Young People and Families Beverly Hughes points out, "it will be much harder now for the Tories to get rid of it, even if they wanted to." The number of centers keeps growing, mainly in response to widespread pressure from parents who want a center in their own neighborhood. The one thousandth Sure Start center opened in October 2006; by 2010, if things go according to plan, every child in the nation will be able to attend one of 3,500 centers.

The British government has poured money into an array of children's initiatives, not just Sure Start. Between 1997 and 2003, financial support for zero-to-five initiatives nearly doubled, to about $40 billion—that's nearly 1 percent of the gross national product.[22] More than 800,000 youngsters are involved in Sure Start. There are also more than half a million new child care places, an 80 percent increase since Labour came into office.[23] By 2010, all public schools will be required to keep their doors open until 6:00 p.m., offering everything from care for infants and toddlers to sports and homework clubs for teens.[24]

A report from the Organization for Economic Cooperation and Development concludes that "the United Kingdom stands out as investing more than any other country per child at the pre-primary level," almost twice the European average.[25] Since 1999 Britain really has gone from worst to first.

After the 2005 study on Sure Start was published, the Conservatives flirted with the idea of entirely privatizing, if not burying, the program, only quickly to retreat in the face of its broad and bipartisan appeal. In a May 2006 press conference, Tony Blair acknowledged that "there is a group of people who have been shut out against society's mainstream and we have not yet found a way of bringing them properly in." But that didn't mean he regarded Sure Start as a failure. Five months later, on a visit to another Sure Start center, the prime minister hailed the venture as one of the Labour government's greatest achievements. "This is what a modern welfare state should do. Be on the side of people, when they need it—allowing them greater freedom, greater choice and greater power over the things that they want to do. Not a nanny state, but an enabling one."[26]

Meanwhile, and entirely without controversy, preschool has become nearly universal in Britain. Expanding preschool was premised on neuroscience, which was seen as confirming the importance of early learning; developmental psychology, which suggested what kind of early learning was most effective; and the Perry Preschool and Abecedarian evaluations from the United States, which showed the potential long-term gains of early education.[27] A 2005 study of preschool, says one of its authors, Oxford professor Kathy Sylva, "has been used by ministers as the 'evidential base' for expanding universal service."[28] Free prekindergarten became available to all four-year-olds in 1998, and a year later it was expanded to include all three-year-olds. By 2003, 98 percent of four-year-olds and 88 percent of three-year-olds were enrolled.

The government hasn't imposed a common pre-K curriculum—Great Britain isn't France—but it has devised a detailed framework for educating children from birth to age five.[29] Pedagogy has sometimes been politicized, Beverly Hughes acknowledges, and the very use of the word "taught" in early childhood legislation incited a fearsome debate. To some professionals this statutory language signaled a letters-and-numbers, "no pre-schooler left behind" approach to the education of three-year-olds, but that's not the case. Even though the goal of school readiness is the same in Britain and the United States, policy-makers in the two countries hold opposing views about how children learn best. While Washington has been pushing a narrow-gauge, cognitively focused approach, in Britain the framework specifies a "play-based" practice, with little if any repeat-after-me direct instruction.

An ongoing nationwide study shows that prekindergarten, especially high-quality prekindergarten, affects children's attitudes and behavior, as well as how well they can think for themselves.[30] Youngsters who attended preschool arrive in kindergarten an average of four to six months ahead in their reading and math skills, compared with those who stayed at home. If they went to pre-K for two years and were taught by a trained teacher, the gains were twice as big. More university-trained nursery school teachers were needed, the researchers concluded.

The British study breaks new ground by specifying the importance of the social background of a four-year-old's classmates. Poor children who went to preschool with middle-class kids performed better in school than those educated in social-class isolation. That's intuitively right and consistent with American research showing that the background of a child's classmates exerted a powerful effect on K–12 scholastic achievement. The British research offers a powerful argument for making prekindergarten open to all, rather than treating it as the twenty-first-century version of the old paupers' schools.[31]

The biggest question mark is entirely familiar to American observers. Will there be enough money to meet all the commitments to children that Labour has made—expanding programs and making them better while continuing to lower the rate of child poverty? As the rate of economic growth slowed after 2003, there has been less new tax revenue on which to draw, and no official has dared to push for a tax hike. Champagne tastes on a beer budget—Britain, says the *Guardian*'s Toynbee, has a "Swedish dream but American tax phobia." The country's other problems also have a well-known ring. The National Health Service is hemorrhaging money, and so is the government-run pension plan.

When he ran the Social Market Foundation, a centrist think tank, speechwriter Phil Collins carried out an extended thought experiment. "What would it mean," Collins wondered, "to take seriously [economist] Jim Heckman's argument, cutting programs for later life and expanding programs for earlier life? What would happen if 'skill begets skill' became the benchmark of policy?" But when he invited politicians to join the conversation, he found that "while everyone liked the idea in general, no liked it in the particular."[32]

The Labour government, like its American counterparts at both the state and national levels, is committed to a mixed market. And in Britain, as in the United States, sharp questions have been raised about how good the privately run programs really are. "There is a gap," says Beverly Hughes, "between what we know in the Education Department and what's actually happening on the ground."

The situation of British preschools brings home the problem. Because they aren't obliged to hire trained teachers, most private prekindergartens make do with young women just out of high school, who are paid the minimum wage. Some of these nursery schools are glorified play groups, and the government's inspectors rank barely a quarter of them as good.[33] "Public nurseries are overwhelmingly the best, the beacons where nursery teachers train," says Polly Toynbee. "A new profession is being created—the early-years professional—that could be a brilliant combination of nursery teacher, social worker and health visitor, steeped in child development, with graduate [bachelor's degree] status and teachers' pay. Without money, they risk becoming cheap sub-teachers."[34]

Politicians are always tempted to go for numbers at the expense of quality, but that makes children the losers. With Sure Start, says Oxford professor Kathy Sylva, the government-run children's centers that combine day care and education, rather than private nurseries, have the biggest impact; and the best preschools are run by the public sector. They are also far more costly than their private-sector counterparts.

The rhetoric surrounding Sure Start treats the program as if it were "an inoculation," argues Collins, the prime minister's speechwriter, "but if it's going to meet its potential, then more needs to be done, not just for young children but also in primary school. British initiatives in early childhood have reached a point at which expectations have been excited. There's a sense that the field is taking off, at just the moment when money is running out. If the government really means it when it says that money spent early is critical, there would have to be a change in priorities."

Actually, a near-revolution has occurred during the past decade. "The speed of change has been extraordinary," says Oxford don Kathy Sylva, "the early childhood landscape has been transformed."[35] Without the prime minister's epochal speech, and the creation of Sure Start and the expansion of state preschool that immediately followed, Britain's record would be much less impressive.

Might such a transformation be possible in the United States? That's the question posed in the final chapter, which presents an assessment of little-noticed, but potentially seismic, political shifts in several unlikely places.

Kids-First Politics

DESPITE the best efforts of the lobbying groups and the over-whelming support registered in the polls, children's needs aren't high on the American political agenda. Social solidarity, a phrase that, in Europe, trips easily off the tongue, isn't in the lexicon. The deep love that parents feel for their offspring is seen as something intensely private and personal. The idea that other people's children might merit the public equivalent of love, through policies that provide for them, remains nascent. Is there reason, then, to contemplate the emergence of a kids-first politics—a version of what has happened in Britain—in the United States?

The drive for preschool can be seen as a prelude to such an effort—a jumping-off point for elected officials in search of a way to do well, politically, by doing good; a training camp for advocates to hone their skills; and a chance to inform the public about the life-shaping impact not just of preschool but of the early years more generally.

Much of the argument for preschool has been evidence-based. But the fundamental political choices, which go beyond the rhetoric to reveal who we are as a nation, are rooted in values rather than analytics. An artful leader knows how to talk about values in a language that doesn't come off as preachy or hypocritical, how to translate theories about how the world ought to be working into commonsense concepts of what government ought to be doing.

This is the smart politics of the heart, and it can change people's minds. Dispatches from North Carolina and, once again, from Texas exemplify how this kind of leadership can transform the public's commitment to children. If the pragmatic dreamers, the un-starry-eyed activists, have their way, these won't be rarities but exemplars for the future.

"Force of Nature"

"What started it was a walk in the woods," says ex–North Carolina governor James Hunt. It was a bone-chilling day in the winter of 1992. Hunt, who had already served two terms as governor, from 1977 to 1985, was home on his farm and contemplating another run for office. "At a turn in the road there's a little shack with a very poor family. I noticed a little baby coming out, trying to suck a bottle long-since empty. This is the child we need to be helping, I realized. If we don't do something for that child *right now* he will never be successful." That was the moment, says Hunt, when he began to think about how the state of North Carolina might help.

The best way to describe Jim Hunt, the longest-serving governor in North Carolina's history, is to imagine Bill Clinton without the zipper problem. Hunt, who ran and won in 1992 and again in 1996, can dive deep into policy minutiae. He also possesses the gravitational pull of the truly gifted politician who knows how to give someone in a packed room the sense that he is speaking to her alone. "What kind of situation do you want your children in?" he challenged those who came to town meetings during his 1992 campaign. "Are you satisfied with sitting your kid in front of a damn TV? Let's talk about stimulating brain development, not just food, water, oxygen. That's what gives kids a sense of self-confidence, integrity, a conception of their own worth, their creativity—that's what's critical."

When Jim Hunt first ran for governor, in 1976, he was the conservative Democrat in the primary, an opponent of gun control and a supporter of the death penalty, and those views have remained consistent over the years.[1] Yet what drives him—obsesses him—is the welfare of children. In his 1972 campaign for lieutenant governor, he had pushed for universal kindergarten at a time when the state wasn't contributing a dime, and the needs of the young have been his calling ever since. "My heart was right," he says, sounding a little like a pastor, "to talk about little children."

"The governor didn't just come up with child care purely out of beneficence," observes Dick Clifford, a senior scientist at the University of North Carolina's Frank Porter Graham Child Development Institute. "It was also good politics. Focus groups identified child care as a top priority for the state." The state's demographics help to explain why. This is *Norma Rae* country: because furniture and textile mills, which rely heavily on women workers, are located there, North Carolina has long had the nation's highest percentage of working mothers. As early as the 1970s, half of the mothers of infants were working, and there was often no one at home who could take care of their children.

No American politician has done as well as Jim Hunt at transforming his passion for children into an effective strategy, turning a political triumph into an enduring change in how government does business.[2] "Every child will arrive in school healthy and prepared for success" was the pledge Hunt made in his successful 1992 race. Then he faced another test: getting the legislators to embrace the zero-to-five program he called Smart Start.

At the time Hunt was pushing Smart Start, resistance to the state's meddlesomeness was as potent in North Carolina as it was anywhere in the country. To complicate matters, Hunt wasn't talking about four-year-olds, just a year shy of going to school and so a straightforward political sell; he was talking about newborns and infants. And the governor wasn't proposing to reform education, a time-tested refrain, but rather to do whatever it took to give all children a decent shot at success.

"There was no map for this," says Karen Ponder, the executive director of the North Carolina Partnership for Children, which is responsible for Smart Start statewide. "No one had said 'every child must be prepared for school.' We're writing the book."

"I became a zealot. I ran the issue like a campaign," Hunt says, recalling what it took to get Smart Start on the books. There were daily strategy meetings with his "kitchen cabinet," half a dozen of the state's top child development researchers and advocates, all of whom had been working together for years. He worked to sell business leaders on the fact that it was smart economics to contribute to the well-being of young children. Walter McDowell, president of North Carolina banking for Wachovia, committed $2 million to pay for messages aimed at young families, and the bank also drafted a report, *Wachovia Invests in Smart Start*, which McDowell hand-delivered to every state lawmaker.[3]

Conservative church leaders were initially among Hunt's staunchest opponents. "This program is government at its worst," they preached. "It will set children straight on the road to hell." After every one of those sermons Hunt received hundreds of phone calls from parishioners, echoing their pastor's sentiments.

Soon after being elected, Hunt invited a group of influential pastors to the governor's mansion. Hunt saw the meeting as an obvious move, since he had grown up in the church and counted on the support of the state's Bible Belt, but it was the first time in memory that a Democratic governor had reached out to church leaders this way. "I come from a religious background," he told them, "so I know how important churches are to our communities. I want to help families who aren't coming to your church, who don't have support. We want their children to be ready for school too. And it's really up to families to decide, not the government. They should have the very best. If they're sending their children to church, then that is the best place."

To Karen Ponder, whose father was a minister, it was a familiar moment. "I felt like I was back in church," she says. The ministers were impressed as well. They started talking up Smart Start to their congregations.

Because Smart Start was so closely identified with Hunt, he had to rely almost entirely on Democratic lawmakers to get the bill passed. And even though the Democrats controlled both houses of the General Assembly, winning their votes wasn't easy. Finally, in the waning days of the 1993 session, the General Assembly appropriated $20 million for a trial run of Smart Start.

"This was my top priority for the entire time I was in office," Hunt says. "We are on a mission for little children." By 2000, Smart Start's budget had increased more than tenfold, to $204 million, and the state was spending nearly a billion federal and state dollars on children.[4]

If Jim Hunt's project was to have a prayer of surviving beyond his tenure as governor, it had to be embedded locally, and Smart Start was designed with that in mind. Instead of a top-down, eat-your-spinach model of the type that liberals often favor, determinations about which children get what services were left to public-private partnerships in each county.

Handing over control to the local powers-that-be effectively co-opted them, and over time Smart Start was able to attract Republican as well as Democratic support. "The beauty of Smart Start," says Democratic legislator Jennifer Weiss, "is that it's tailored to county needs." To receive state funds, everyone with a stake in children's welfare, from Head Start administrators to the proprietors of for-profit nurseries, as well as local government officials and ambassadors from the world of business, had to come to the table and shape the county's proposal. While that often made for a messy and anguished process, it eased habitual suspicions of secret deals and special-interest politics.[5]

"When I was a county commissioner I was conscripted to work on the Smart Start plan," says GOP state senator John Garwood, whose heavily Republican district is tucked into Appalachia. "When I went to the capitol to lobby on behalf of Smart Start, the senators from my district called me a turncoat, but I didn't see this as something the Republicans necessarily should oppose. Lots of kids in my rural counties don't even know how to hold a fork. And when a program starts affecting those kids, you give it a chance. You don't say, 'We don't need it.'"

Still, as Jennifer Weiss points out, there is always a battle over the size of the Smart Start budget. Some lawmakers want to spend money on bread-and-butter items like tax breaks to encourage companies like BMW to settle in the state. "It's like planting seeds for a crop that doesn't bloom for a long time," says Weiss. "If ever there were an example of bang for the buck—but people see only a bulging budget, not the need for a highly educated workforce."

"We want you to do cutting-edge work. We welcome failure." That's what Robin Britt, named by Governor Hunt to run the Department of Human Resources, told the county directors during the first days of Smart Start. But the upside of localism, the emphasis on variation and experimentation, is also its potential downside, and with each county going its own way, missteps were inevitable. A 2003 state auditor's report identified a handful of questionable expenditures, such as money spent on "playground equipment despite legislative restrictions."[6] State lawmakers also asked pointed questions about some of the other things Smart Start money was being used for, such as pony rides for disabled three-year-olds, symphony visits to preschools, and trips to faraway conferences for Smart Start staffers. Although the amounts involved were small, these revelations made for embarrassing reading.

Over time, Robin Britt's belief in total decentralization gave way to a more tightly focused approach. The legislators ratcheted up the requirements, limiting the counties' degree of freedom. There are no more ponies, and, more troubling, fewer home visits; 70 percent of all Smart Start funds must go to child care centers.

Unlike such states as Illinois, where the number of children who receive *any* care is what matters most to public officials and advocates alike, in North Carolina an emphasis on quality drives the system. "Politicians always reach for expanding the system because that's what gets them reelected," asserts Phil Sparks at the Communications Consortium Research Center in Washington, DC. Not Hunt, however. "From the beginning," says Dick Clifford at the Frank Porter Graham Institute, "quality was the governor's mantra. 'Do it right, then expand. Put money in a small number of counties to make a difference.'"

Smart Start nudges child care centers into improving themselves—the better a center's ranking on a nationally used assessment instrument, the more state money it's entitled to. Parents have also become a force for improving the centers. When parents sign up for Smart Start, they learn to be knowledgeable consumers; they find out why differences in quality really matter, and then they are more likely to opt for something good. "Seventy percent of Smart Start youngsters are in the [good to excellent] centers, as compared with 20 percent when the program began," says Sue Russell, a member of Governor Hunt's original kitchen cabinet and founder of a nationwide program called TEACH, which focuses on strengthening the skills and raising the salaries of preschool teachers. "Compare that to what's happening in Illinois, where more than two-thirds of the kids aren't in any kind of center—that drives me crazy."

It's no coincidence that the instrument used to assess the centers is homegrown, developed by Clifford and his colleagues at Frank Porter Graham. Every professional in the child care trade knows about FPG, as it's called; and for more than thirty years the evaluation of the Abecedarian Project—among the most famous of the long-running early education experiments—has been conducted there.[7] "We have been a big player in the state since the 1980s," says FPG associate director Donna Bryant. The institute's aspiration to make early education much more than babysitting—to create what might be called a "culture of quality" for child care and preschool—has been percolating in North Carolina for a long time.

It was only natural, then, for Jim Hunt to rely on FPG for help in designing Smart Start. The governor knew Clifford and

Bryant from his earlier efforts to expand and upgrade kindergarten. Both were members of his kitchen cabinet, and when the initial Smart Start legislation passed, the governor chose Clifford to be the state's first director of child development. "It was a nonstop job," Clifford recalls. "This was Hunt's top priority."

Michael Easley, who succeeded Jim Hunt as governor in 2001, also emphasized early education in his campaign. But elected officials need their own distinctive calling cards, initiatives that bear their imprimatur. For Easley, a Democrat elected at a moment when the pre-K movement was taking off nationwide, preschool, rather than child care, was an obvious focus.

Easley's More at Four initiative picks up where Smart Start leaves off, when child care segues into prekindergarten. Like Smart Start, it's a public-private program (half the children are enrolled in pre-Ks run by the public schools; most of the others are in for-profit preschools), and the culture of quality is similarly prevalent. The maximum class size is eighteen, which meets the national standards. All preschool teachers must be licensed, and regardless of where they teach they are paid public-school salaries.[8] Each pre-K must choose from a list of research-based curricula, such as High/Scope, the program developed at Perry Preschool. "There's a real framework for what's expected of children, not a 'recognize five letters of the alphabet' framework," says Carolyn Cobb, the executive director of the state's Office of School Readiness, which runs More at Four, taking a jab at the federal Head Start rules.

More at Four is offered only to children from poor families, those who are learning more slowly than most of their age group, and those who don't speak English at home. That restriction won't be lifted any time soon. Governor Easley pushed through a state lottery in 2005, with most of the proceeds earmarked for education, but it won't raise enough to secure places for all four-year-olds in More at Four classrooms. "The next challenge," says Cobb, "is linking More at Four with what happens *next* in these children's education. It's not just preparing all kids to be ready for school, it's also creating schools that are ready for all kids."

When Jim Hunt left office, GOP legislator Jeff Barnhardt recalls, "there were people who were saying, 'Smart Start is Hunt's baby. Let's take it down.'" But the program has survived because of its popularity. Polls show that it is supported by 70 percent of the state's voters, Republicans and Democrats alike. Participants in the county-based Smart Start partnerships, thousands of stakeholders, banded together to save it.

"With Governor Hunt, the Smart Start door was opened and we went there," says Sue Russell at TEACH. "Initiatives like More at Four mean there's more money. Add them up and it is a gain for early childhood—more kids are better off. You go wherever the door is open at the time."

Jim Hunt didn't retire to the farm when he left office in 2001. State legislators report that he has been more of a presence at the capitol than the incumbent. "A Force of Nature"—that was the headline of a front-page story about Hunt that ran in the *Raleigh News and Observer* five years after he stepped down.[9]

Nor is Hunt's influence confined to his home state. The politician who was regarded as the likely choice of both Al Gore and John Kerry to be secretary of education started his own institute, which runs symposia on education policy issues for politicians nationwide. His theme is promoting kids' creativity. "We've got to go beyond No Child Left Behind. Encouraging kids to think for themselves is the only way we'll survive in the global economy," he says. His reputation for policy innovation and political success has been a potent convincer. "I had fifteen governors come to last year's meeting, and earlier I had sixteen lieutenant governors," he notes. Soon after she was elected governor of Arizona, Janet Napolitano spent three days visiting Smart Start centers, and Hunt has the pride of a political parent when he reports that "this is now her focus—early childhood education." A number of states, including Iowa, Oklahoma, and West Virginia, are picking up the "theme" of Smart Start, he says, and using "bits and pieces."

After attending one of Hunt's symposia, Iowa governor Tom Vilsack was won over. "He plays on my Catholic guilt," says Vilsack. That pleases Hunt, who is prepared to use whatever it takes to convince leaders across the country to embrace the Smart Start model. "I am giving my total life to children, and I'm not being shy."

When Republicans Become Democrats for a Day

"The country is most barbarously large and final," writes Billy Lee Brammer in *The Gay Place,* a ballad to Texas and one of the finest novels about American politics. "It is too much country—boondock country—alternately drab and dazzling, spectral and remote. It is so wrongfully muddled and various that it is difficult to conceive of it as all of a piece."[10]

Brammer might well have been writing about the Seventeenth Congressional District. The district is among the most lopsidedly Republican in the nation. More than 60 percent of the voters are registered Republicans; 64 percent call themselves conservatives and just 12 percent describe themselves as liberals. In 2004 President Bush carried the district with nearly 70 percent of the vote—not an unexpected outcome, especially since Crawford, where the president has his ranch, is located there. But in the race for a seat in the U.S. House of Representatives that same year, a Democrat named Chet Edwards bucked long odds and won, running 37 percent ahead of the national Democratic ticket.

The Seventeenth District is a sliver of land, 180 miles long from north to south and barely 20 miles across at its widest point. It was carved out in 2003 when Tom DeLay, at the time the majority leader in the House of Representatives, and his friends in the Texas legislature redrew the state's electoral map—revising it sixty-three times, defying geography and a sense of place—to secure additional Republican seats in Congress and the legislature.

The outermost suburbs south of Fort Worth and Dallas form the district's northern border, and Waco lies at its heart. A century ago, when cotton was a big cash crop, Waco was larger than Dallas, and the Amicable Life Insurance Company's twenty-two-story headquarters, built in 1911, was the tallest skyscraper south of the Mason-Dixon Line. Waco was a wide-open city then, the only place outside Nevada where prostitution was legal, but as it lost its hold on cotton it found religion. Now local wags call it Jerusalem in the Brazos. Baylor University, the country's foremost Baptist institution of higher learning, is located there; this is also where, in 1993, the religious sect called the Branch Davidians made their fateful stand. South of Waco the cotton fields give way to cattle ranches. Highway 35, which forms the spine of the district, is dotted with small towns like Marlin and Reagan, Box Church and Irene. At the southern end of the district is College Station, home of Texas A&M University. George H. W. Bush's presidential library and the Bush School of Government and Public Service are on the campus; there, visitors are confronted by a mammoth sculpture, *The Day the Wall Came Down*, which depicts the trademark horses of Texas smashing down the Berlin Wall.

Chet Edwards was among the Democrats who saw his district

disappear when the redrawn map took away two-thirds of his constituents. Edwards, first elected to Congress in 1990, was high on Tom DeLay's enemies list. He had earned the enmity of the majority leader by voting against President Bush's tax cuts, and DeLay wasn't the only one who badly wanted him out of office. Edwards was a prime target for the National Rifle Association because he had voted in favor of a ban on assault weapons; his criticisms of efforts to breach the wall between church and state had won him no friends on the religious right; and right-to-life organizations hated him because he opposed the ban on late-term abortions. "If we don't get Edwards [and two other Democrats]," said DeLay's aide Jim Ellis, "then the redistricting wasn't worth it."

Edwards's opponent, Texas state legislator Arlene Wohlgemuth, looked like just the candidate to unseat him, and the conservative establishment went all out to get her elected. Three million dollars from the Club for Growth, a GOP fund-raising behemoth, went for attack ads in the three weeks before the election, more than Edwards spent on his entire campaign. Vice President Dick Cheney and Republican strategist Karl Rove came calling. The district was plastered with posters showing Wohlgemuth together with President Bush, standing on the steps of Air Force One and waving to an imaginary crowd.

Wohlgemuth ran a vintage Karl Rove campaign. She went after Edwards as being more liberal than Ted Kennedy, insisting that he wanted to keep schoolchildren from praying for the safe return of American soldiers and, more implausibly yet, that he had voted to spend tax dollars to promote gay adoption.[11] "Arlene preached the Ten Commandments," says Edwards, "but she forgot the one about bearing false witness against thy neighbor."

Wohlgemuth's big selling point was her diehard fiscal conservatism. Her crowning achievement was the 2003 revamping of the state's health and human services agencies, which saved Texas taxpayers $1 billion. Edwards used political jujitsu to turn this supposed strength into her biggest vulnerability. What undid her were the cuts she'd inflicted on the budget of the Children's Health Insurance Program, generally known as CHIP—150,000 youngsters removed from the rolls, half a million denied any dental and eye care, all in the name of lean government. "Children were never my primary concern," she said. It was a remark she grew to regret.[12]

Edwards's dedication to children's well-being sprung from his personal history. "My son, JT, was sick as an infant," he recalls, "and I felt helpless. Did he need a cool towel on his forehead or did he have a life-threatening disease? I'll never forget feeling, 'What if I couldn't afford to call a doctor?'" In 2004 he was ready to pack it in, though, after seeing the boundaries of his new district; because he'd never represented two-thirds of the voters who lived there, his chances of winning seemed remote. Wohlgemuth's decision to run changed his mind. "If I beat Arlene and never accomplished another thing," he says, "I would have justified the space I take up in this world by being a catalyst for increasing CHIP funding in Texas."

As expected, Wohlgemuth had the early lead in the polls. But Chet Edwards's first TV ad changed everything, because it powerfully illustrated how real people were being hurt by the CHIP cuts. Staring straight into the camera, in a black and white image that's as evocative as a Walker Evans photo, a woman named Jamie Jones held her daughter Bailey in her lap while she told her story. Jamie was a hardworking woman, widowed when her husband died in a house fire, who worked every day to support her child, but now the state had cut off her daughter's health care coverage. "I love my daughter more than anything in the world," she said, "and if she gets sick I don't know what I'll do." The commercial didn't mention Arlene Wohlgemuth by name. There was no need. "One TV ad, and twenty-five years of Republican talk about how 'less government is better' went out the window," says Edwards.[13]

"CHIP was the issue that set the table," Edwards believes. "It defined everything that came later. I never would have won without it." The Jamie Jones ad damaged Wohlgemuth's credibility and stirred criticism from the press. Wohlgemuth was forced to go on the defensive—instead of bragging about the budget cuts, she tried to minimize their effects—but to no avail. "She's an ice cold lady who took a little too much joy in breaking someone's jaw," says an aide to one senior GOP state legislator. "She walked the Republican line, and walked right over the edge of a cliff."

According to the exit polls, 11 percent of the voters—enough to swing the election—said that Wohlgemuth's record on children had made up their minds. A quarter of those who supported Edwards said they were thinking foremost of children. "Wohlgemuth had to justify her vote to cut CHIP, but she couldn't," the *Dallas Morning News* editorialized. "The lesson here: heartlessness doesn't sell."[14]

Barely a week after the election, state senator Kip Averitt, whose district is part of the Seventeenth Congressional District, filed a bill to restore the cuts from CHIP's budget.

It isn't easy to appeal to the social conscience of right-wing Texas Republicans. But to Averitt, the lesson from Arlene Wohlgemuth's defeat was that embracing CHIP was a matter of political survival, not ideology. "I think it is one of the most important programs the state has," said Averitt, "and with the economy looking up again, it's certainly one of the first programs that should be put back."[15]

In the 2005 session of the Texas legislature, with Democrats fuming over having been mauled by DeLay and Republicans out to score more victories, disputatiousness was the order of the day. When GOP lawmakers proposed naming a stretch of road after George Bush, Democrats countered by suggesting that it be called the Ronald Reagan Highway instead, obliging their opponents to vote against a GOP icon.

The restoration of CHIP funding was one of the few measures that received bipartisan support. The Republicans were interested in political cover, not children's well-being, says Democratic state senator Judith Zaffirini, who was also influential in getting the state's preschool legislation passed that year. But even with the vote, it wasn't evident that the Republicans had bought themselves more than a reprieve. The lawmakers only partly restored the CHIP budget—Jamie Jones still had no health insurance for her daughter Bailey, and thousands of families were in the same situation. The issue wasn't going to go away.

Good-Bye to "Teddy-Bear Politics"

Political activist Mike Petit has made it his life's work to keep issues like CHIP from going away. To satisfy the requirements of federal election law, Petit runs two organizations that are housed in the same cramped quarters in Washington—a political operation, Vote Kids, and a project to educate voters, Every Child Matters. In the summer of 2004 he met with Chet Edwards, and in the months that followed, Vote Kids worked in tandem with the Edwards campaign. Petit sent out 35,000 brochures detailing Wohlgemuth's record on children's health insurance, early education, and child abuse prevention. "A Is for Abandoned," the message read. "Arlene Wohlgemuth abandoned our children."

Registered GOP women as well as independents were the targeted audience, because focus groups had shown that they were most likely to be swayed when they heard about the impact of the CHIP cuts. "When you tell a grandmother who has always voted Republican that a Republican candidate is hurting children," Petit explains, "she votes the other way."

Mike Petit is a rough-hewn guy with French-Canadian roots, who grew up dirt poor in rural Maine. "I knew about hunting and fishing," he says. "Sailing was for people who came from 'away.'" He went to Bowdoin College—"I must have been an affirmative action admit; there weren't many French-Canadians there"—and then to Boston College to study social policy. He spent many years as a social worker and eventually became Maine's commissioner of social services.

Petit then headed to Washington, where he practiced the lobbyist's art of gentle persuasion, but he tired of "going to congressmen's offices with detailed memos and getting shunted off to summer interns." He also became impatient with the "teddy-bear politics," the feckless enterprise of making nice that has long been practiced by children's advocates. Petit wants to get public officials' attention—not necessarily by convincing them that supporting children is the right thing to do, but by making them fearful of what might happen if they were perceived as heartless.

"I'm not interested in a organizing a 'kumbaya' campaign," Petit says. "Power rules."

The Edwards-Wohlgemuth race marked Mike Petit's first foray into electoral politics, and it was a stunning success. In an overwhelmingly Republican district, 88 percent of the voters agreed with the proposition that "it is our moral responsibility to make sure all children have the opportunity to succeed and it is important for government to invest in children's programs proven to reduce child abuse, improve child health, and better educate our children."[16] The public square had been expanded to make room for all kids.

The Chet Edwards victory makes a great political story. But it's too soon to know whether it represents a harbinger or a one-off. The significance for children's politics of the 2004 election in the Seventeenth Congressional District is, in a sense, analogous to the relevance of the Perry Preschool study for widely implemented prekindergarten. Each is an experiment that has had a remarkable outcome—lifelong benefits for the Perry preschoolers, and a Democratic victory, pivoting on a kids' issue, in George Bush's home district. It remains to be seen, though, whether it's possible to build on either result, to turn these elegant experiments into projects of national scope—high-quality universal preschool, in the one instance, and a kids-first politics in the other.

In the run-up to the 2006 election, Every Child Matters, the nonpolitical arm of Mike Petit's operation, commissioned polls in five swing states, including Pennsylvania and Iowa. As in Texas, those surveyed were overwhelmingly inclined to spend more on children's health care and education. Two-thirds said that Congress doesn't do enough to help working families with children. Nearly 90 percent said children's issues are important to them when voting.

Petit wants to turn these pro-child sentiments into votes. To do that, he is forming a network of children's agencies, everything from clinics to child care centers.[17] His office walls are festooned with state maps that pinpoint thousands of these agencies, as a way of illustrating the movement's potential. Hillary Clinton took one look at those maps and agreed to speak at a fund-raiser for Every Child Matters.

"We need a couple of big election wins to reach a tipping point, so that we can project strength," says Petit. "The public hasn't yet associated the federal tax cuts and budget cuts with why schools don't have money and why kids are waiting in line at health clinics. We will make the connection visible by coming at the politicians on the issue they're not anticipating—children." Those candidates will "learn the hard way," says the Vote Kids Web site.

In the 2006 elections Vote Kids targeted Pennsylvania senator Rick Santorum, author of *It Takes a Family*.[18] The Children's Defense Fund's 2006 analysis of congressional votes on measures that benefited children ranked Santorum near the bottom, and Petit cast him in the mold of Arlene Wohlgemuth—a hypocrite when it came to kids.[19]

"We set out to 'Swift boat' Santorum on family values," he says, "to come after him from a direction that he never expected."

"Family Values? Rick Santorum Says One Thing but Votes Another," read a Vote Kids flyer featuring a photo of a distraught girl—the same haunting image that had been used to great success in Chet Edwards's race—and the message was reiterated in radio ads and a voter registration drive. Santorum lost the election, but Petit claims no credit because "so many factors were at play." Petit will be back for the 2008 campaign, hoping to pick off another Arlene Wohlgemuth. "It doesn't take many victories like that to get politicians to pay attention."

Mike Petit is one half of the odd couple of the kids-first political campaign. Rob Dugger is the other. While their political opinions are similar and their strategies complementary, on the surface the two men couldn't be more different. Dugger, an economist and Beltway insider, has the effortless charm and polish that come from generations of Virginia wealth (his family owns the Oshkosh clothing company). He has worked for decades in Washington, first as a staffer with both the House and Senate banking committees as well as the Federal Reserve Bank, and later as chief economist for the bankers' lobbying group.

While he has been managing director of a private investment firm since the mid-1990s, Dugger has stayed very much involved in the policy world, and has taken up the banner for children. "Wandering through the public sector has led me to these conclusions about what it takes, in terms of investing in kids, to make this society competitive," Dugger explains. As he sees things, sophisticated economic research and Petit-style political roughhousing go hand in hand. Dugger lined up an impressive network of social scientists and business leaders to form the Invest in Kids Working Group, which has a ten-year vision to make children the country's top economic priority.

The first step toward that goal is doing the analysis needed to make the dollars-and-cents case for kids. In 2006 Invest in Kids teamed up with the Pew Charitable Trusts on a project called the Partnership for America's Success; the partnership is directed by Sara Watson, who also is responsible for Pew's nationwide preschool project. With more than $3 million in the bank, including $1 million from Pew and Dugger's own six-figure contribution, Invest in Kids is now carrying out research on the efficacy of different public investments in children. Dugger is convinced that these studies, coupled with on-the-ground politics of the Mike Petit variety, can change the direction of American policy.[20]

Rod Dugger spins an audacious scenario for kids-first politics with the fervor of a pitchman who truly believes in his product. In constructing that scenario he relies on research from across the social sciences—economics, psychology, and political science—as well as his own Beltway smarts.

Promoting economic growth is Dugger's goal. Like many economists, he focuses less on eliminating inequality ("the rich will always figure out what's good for their kids first," he says) than on generating opportunities for individuals and wealth for the society. His analysis starts with the research that shows the economic payoff generated by investments in prekindergarten, prenatal care, Early Head Start, and home nursing visits. "The message is that high-quality pre-K delivers a 15-percent return forever," he says, but the nation has slipped into a "structural trap," as pressure from interest groups has led to public investments that favor housing and consumerism over human capital, and seniors over children. The consequences are disastrous, Dugger argues. A generation from now countries like China, which are spending heavily on early education, will have a skilled workforce that will leave Americans in the dust.[21]

The only way out of this trap, says Dugger, is to alter the spending priorities of the United States, making children's success the top concern. To do so requires tapping into what he calls the "visceral pull" exerted by youngsters, identifying those in the "youth human capital sector"—everyone from pediatricians to preschool teachers, child care workers to parents—and showing them that, like bankers and retailers and those in other capital sectors, they share important interests. That's precisely what Mike Petit is trying to accomplish with his densely speckled state maps. As the common values become more apparent, Dugger anticipates that these fragmented groups will come together, registering to vote in greater numbers and endorsing candidates who view every issue, from education to Iraq, through the lens of children's needs.

The elderly represent the classic example of such a movement.

They are superbly organized, and the short list of what they expect from government is well known: Social Security, Medicare, and prescription drug insurance. Dugger wants candidates to see the wisdom, both for the economy and for their own political future, of giving similar respect to children.[22] "If candidates can be convinced to become 'kids-first' and voters perceive candidates that way," says Dugger, "then the dynamic of kids-first politics really begins to unfold."

"My hope is that when the *real* budget crisis arrives, we will have the power to go to Congress and say, 'We know, Mister Congressman or Mister Senator, that this Gucci-shod SOB wants you to rewrite the tax code so that the CEO can deduct the depreciation on his Gulfstream 7. But there are a thousand sites that serve kids in your district, and those people are registered. If you go with that SOB, we will knock you out of office.'"

"We have to drive the discussion," Dugger insists, "so that we can change the budget priorities."

Geoff Garin, a highly regarded Democratic pollster, doesn't buy into the entire Rob Dugger scenario, but he does believe that kids-first is a plausible strategy. "It's like the League of Conservation Voters' 'Dirty Dozen,' but it has the potential to work better," he says. "Married moms and grandmas are a natural constituency."

Over the years, hopes for a genuine children's movement have often surfaced. Decade after decade, in language variously goody-goody and pragmatic, White House conferences have discoursed about the needs of the young. A library's worth of papers have been written, a decade's worth of three-day conferences held, entire disciplines built on the unmet needs of the young.

"If we could have but one generation of properly born, trained, educated, and healthy children, a thousand other problems of government would vanish," one public official argued. "We would assure ourselves of healthier minds in more vigorous bodies, to direct the energies of our nation to yet greater heights of achievement. Moreover, one good community nurse will save a dozen future policemen." This statement could have been issued today, but it's taken from Herbert Hoover's address to a 1930 White House Conference on Children.[23]

What distinguishes Mike Petit and Rob Dugger from their predecessors isn't their agenda—today's children would be better off if the "Children's Charter" formulated at the 1930 conference had been adopted—but their sophisticated understanding of how to use power. Instead of relying on teddy-bear politics, they talk about how best to target their message. Mike Petit's decision, in the Texas congressional race, to concentrate on women registered as Republican or independent is a primitive example of such targeting. Since the mid-1990s, Dugger notes, a company called Target Point has been giving the GOP detailed demographic information about every likely voter. If a candidate has a message for Republican women over fifty, Target Point can provide lists of millions of such women, and specify which of them are gun owners or nurses or Nordstrom's shoppers. That's the capacity that Dugger and Petit aspire to develop, but it's an expensive undertaking.

The emphasis on targeting and voter registration may oblige the kids-first advocates to ally with the Democratic Party, which has been playing database catch-up. However, as the polling data and the results in the Seventeenth Congressional District in Texas show, the appeal of children's welfare transcends party lines. Even in a highly politicized environment, Republicans can be drawn to the cause. Moreover, in many states Democrats are a semi-permanent minority, and so GOP support is essential.

With the right issue at the right time, it is possible to revive the endangered idea of bipartisanship, expanding public responsibility for the welfare of children. That's the message of the final episode, which brings us back to Texas.

What Other Heroes?

On April 17, 2006, Texas governor Rick Perry summoned the state legislature into special session to restructure the state's tax system. The lawmakers had to fill a $10 billion hole in the budget created by cuts in the property tax.

While this wasn't a likely moment to entice the representatives into underwriting a new entitlement for children, the preschool lobbyists saw an opening. In 2005, as we've seen, they had secured bipartisan backing for an expanded, state-funded preschool program.[24] Then, the political lever was the involvement of an academic entrepreneur with close ties to the Bush White House. One year later, the motivating factor was the Iraq war.

Eligibility for state-supported preschool in Texas had been restricted to poor children and youngsters who don't speak English at home. In the 2006 special session, the move was to add all three- and four-year-old children of active-duty military parents and reservists, together with the offspring of those who had been injured or killed in action.

Libby Doggett, the executive director of Pre-K Now, proposed the idea to Jason Sabo at Texas United Way, who had previously pushed for expanding and strengthening the state's preschools. "That's brilliant," said Sabo. "We can do it."

A universal preschool bill would never have made it out of committee in 2006, for there was neither the money nor the political backing to sustain it. But this measure encountered no opposition. Not a single lawmaker complained about prekindergarten as a waste of public money—rather, it was praised as an opportunity that the state owed the children of its soldiers. Just as in Chet Edwards's campaign against Arlene Wohlgemuth, the issue was given a human face—for this occasion the advocates recounted the story of the widow of a soldier killed in Afghanistan, who, because of the new program, could afford to keep her four-year-old in prekindergarten.

At a time when tax dollars were especially scarce, it helped that the cost of the initiative was just $8 million (a figure that would increase as Army personnel were reassigned to Texas from bases in Europe). For the preschool advocates, the modesty of the proposal was a key asset, for while the plan started small, it cleared a path for adding other categories of children to the rolls in the future.

"The trick," says Sabo, "is to take this enthusiasm and roll it over into the next legislation. What other Texas heroes do we want to help?" What about the children of police officers and fire fighters, prison guards and public school teachers? Doesn't the state also owe their kids a decent education? At the end of the day, would anybody be left out? In conservative Texas, preschool had completed the transformation from being a plot hatched in Moscow to a mainstream program.

"We have a crack," says Sabo. "Let's put a wedge into the crack and start hammering." And not just in Texas—the same approach would likely prevail everywhere.

It has been more than forty years since Perry Preschool opened. The idea of running a prekindergarten for poor children was almost unknown then. Those children were not only poor, they also had below-average IQs—and it's worth a reminder that some experts believed it was risky to expose such youngsters to the rigors of problem solving and a regime of words, words, and more words.

What has happened in the years since has transformed our understanding not just of preschool but of childhood more generally. Research showing why early learning matters so much has been harnessed to a political approach intended to make preschool available to all three- and four-year-olds.

The value of Perry Preschool, the Abecedarian Project, and the Child-Parent Centers in Chicago—to the children who attended and to society as well—is now widely appreciated. By showing that preschool is a wise investment, economists have drawn the support of business leaders and politicians. Research in brain science has revealed both the incredible plasticity of the brain and the importance of its earliest stages of development. All these findings have been put to good use by advocates who have cultivated improbable supporters, such as DAs and police chiefs, and who have eschewed teddy-bear politics in favor of opportunistic strategies.

Today the prekindergarten movement has arrived at a crossroads. Even as more states are offering preschool, more children are enrolling, and more public dollars are being spent, the quality of instruction remains mixed and the amount of money being spent on each child has declined.

Pre-K isn't simply about enrollment—the particulars make all the difference. Good preschools can rewrite the scripts of children's lives, but a four-year-old doesn't gain anything from attending a prekindergarten where untrained instructors, obliged to manage large classes, driven by the narrow objectives of No Child Left Behind, substitute skill-and-drill for thinking. Since advocates of high-quality preschool can't monitor every prekindergarten, the challenge is to design a system that will sustain a culture of quality—one that gives parents usable information, lays out the best practices, and offers inducements to preschools that improve themselves.

This is a tall order, and it's only the beginning, since the wish list—better, the *needs* list—for kids reaches well beyond pre-K. Illinois, where this account began, has taken the lead, with preschool for three- and four-year-olds, money set aside for infants and toddlers, and guaranteed health insurance for children. But Illinois merits only two cheers. Even though the governor made children his priority, the caliber of kids' programs in his state remains uneven.

Universal health care for children is the item on the needs list most likely to be widely adopted during the next few years. It is popular with voters, and its cost isn't prohibitive since, over the past decade, the Children's Health Insurance Program has substantially whittled down the number of uninsured youngsters.

What comes next? The kids-first agenda includes high-quality care and education for infants and toddlers, especially for those from poor families, along the lines of that provided in the Educare and Early Head Start programs, available at hours that match the frenetic working lives of parents; paid leave for parents, so they can stay home to care for their newborns; and home nurses' visits for new mothers. And for kids beyond the age of five, decent public schools and after-school opportunities are necessary to build on the gains recorded in preschool.

There is already solid evidence that Early Head Start and home nurses' visits pay off, and though the cost-benefit studies haven't been done, there's ample reason to surmise from experience elsewhere that such a kids-first agenda makes sense generally. The big question mark, of course, is money. At present, the share of the public budget spent on children before they go to school is so small as to be virtually a rounding error. Still, the example of Great Britain shows how budgetary priorities can suddenly shift, and polls report that American voters are ahead of the politicians on these issues, willing to spend more on kids even if it means paying a bigger tax bill.

Preschool for an ever-expanding part of the population, and for three- as well as four-year-olds; health insurance for children in families with an income up to 250 percent above the poverty line, which would mean that virtually every child was covered—even as Mike Petit and Rob Dugger are planning the grand theoretical and political strategy, and the leading-edge foundations like Pew and Gates broaden the scope of their activities, advocates like Jason Sabo and Libby Doggett are building the house of children's entitlements, brick by brick. Getting beyond this point will require the smart politics of the heart epitomized by Tony Blair and, closer to home, Texas congressman Chet Edwards and North Carolina governor Jim Hunt.

Since the 2000 election, tax cuts and deficits, domestic security, and an endless, pointless war have been our public preoccupations. It isn't pie-in-the-sky, though, to imagine that over the course of a generation, and as the result of deliberate political and policy choices, the United States will become a far better place to grow up.

NOTES

ACKNOWLEDGMENTS

INDEX

NOTES

Research for the chapters in this volume included personal interviews conducted with many experts and leading public figures as well as practitioners in the field of early education. Quotations that are not attributed to other published sources are taken from those interviews.

Introduction: Before School

1. Timothy Noah, "Whopper of the Week: 92nd Street Y," *http://www.slate.com/id/2074070/;* "Is Your School as Good as the 92nd Street Y?" November 15, 2002, *http://www.educationworld.com/a_issues/issues363.shtml.* The Grubman story was broken, fittingly, by the *Wall Street Journal.*

    The financial relationships among the players were complicated, involving key votes by members of the Citigroup board. Soon after his daughters were admitted to the preschool, Grubman lowered his appraisal of AT&T; "Armstrong [AT&T chairman and Citigroup director C. Michael Armstrong] never knew that we both [Sandy and I] played him like a fiddle." A spokesman for the school insisted that "the implication that a large donation—and it is by no means one of our largest—can grease the wheels is just not true." Noah, ibid. In 2002 Grubman, under investigation for manipulating "buy" and "sell" recommendations, accepted a $15 million fine and a lifetime ban from the securities industry.

2. Barbara Beatty, *Preschool Education in America* (New Haven: Yale University Press, 1995).

3. The description of Crème de la Crème is drawn from Betsy Hart, "Welcome to Harvard Preschool," *http://www.jewishworldreview.com/cols/hart110199.asp.* The preschool chain's website features glowing articles from major newspapers across the country.

4. Edward Zigler and Susan Muenchow, *Head Start: The Inside Story of America's Most Successful Educational Experiment* (New York: Basic Books, 1992).

5. Throughout the book, the terms *preschool, prekindergarten,* and *pre-K* are used interchangeably.

6. See *http://www.answers.com/topic/childcare;* Mark Schmitt, "Kids Aren't

Us," *American Prospect,* June 29, 2004; *www.census.gov/prod/2003pubs/ c2kbr-26.pdf.*

7. See *www.4president.org/speeches/bush2000announcement.htm.*

8. New York's guarantee of preschool for all has not been fully funded; indeed, advocates there had to fight a proposal to eliminate the program that was put forward by Governor George Pataki.

9. The National Institute for Early Education Research issues regular reports on trends in preschool enrollment and state funding; *http:// nieer.org/yearbook.*

10. David Kirp, "You're Doing Fine, Oklahoma!" *American Prospect,* November 2, 2004. In July 2006 Jim Holt, the GOP candidate for lieutenant governor in Arkansas, described prekindergartens as "Soviet-style socialism." The Democrats turned this into a major campaign issue, labeling him an extremist. The state's largest newspapers were similarly blunt in dismissing Holt's characterization as bizarre. See *www.ardemgaz.com/ShowStoryTemplate.asp?Path=ArDemocrat/2006/06/ 17&ID=Ar02002&Section=Editorial-10k-Jul 5, 2006.*

11. The American belief in self-reliance when it comes to raising children is demonstrated by the lack of universal child health care, the inadequate supply of early child care, and the resistance to a family-leave policy, all of which are common in postindustrialized democracies. Sheila Kamerman, "Early Childhood Intervention Policies: An International Perspective," in Jack Shonkoff and Samuel Meisels, eds., *Handbook of Early Childhood Intervention,* 2nd ed. (New York: Cambridge, 2000), 613–629.

12. Early Head Start, which serves children from birth to age three, is another example. While new social programs have been developed at the state and local level, they don't have comparable national scope.

   The Earned Income Tax Credit, on the books since Ronald Reagan was in the White House, has put billions of dollars in the pockets of the working poor. That's an impressive accomplishment, but the EITC is a tax transfer, not an on-the-ground program. What's more, it has been managed by stealth; the fear is that publicity would anger taxpayers. As a result, millions of eligible taxpayers don't know about the program. The program could be expanded to include a child care and preschool credit, as is the case in Great Britain. Max Sawicki, "It Takes a Tax Credit to Raise a Child," *American Prospect,* January 1, 2001.

13. See Chapter 2 for a discussion of the preschool research literature.

14. W. Steven Barnett et al., "The State of Preschool: 2005 State Preschool Yearbook," *http://nieer.org/yearbook/.*

15. Research does in fact show that preschoolers who have better letter

naming and recognition skills tend to become better readers later on, but that these skills are best developed through "natural literacy activities," not drill and memorization. "Research showing that letter recognition predicts reading success is based on assessing children who learned letters through natural literacy activities, like having stories read to them or playing with picture books. There is no evidence that memorizing alphabet letters out of context predicts later reading skill. But the test will lead teachers to spend more time on alphabet drills and less on reading—just the opposite of what Head Start needs." Richard Rothstein, "Too Young to Test," *American Prospect*, November 2, 2004, *http://www .prospect.org/web/page.ww?section=root&name=ViewPrint&articleId= 8774*. See also Cybele Raver and Edward Zigler, "Another Step Back? Assessing Readiness in Head Start," *Young Children*, January 2004, *http://www.journal.naeyc.org/btj/200401/raver.asp*.

16. See generally Deborah Stipek, *Motivation to Learn* (Boston: Allyn & Bacon, 1993).

17. See Gene Maeroff, *Building Blocks: Making Children Successful in the Early Years of School* (New York: Palgrave Macmillan, 2006).

18. But see Judith Rich Harris, *The Nurture Assumption: Why Children Turn Out the Way They Do* (New York: Free Press, 1998), arguing that neighborhood effects are most important.

19. Ellen Key, *The Century of the Child* (New York and London: G. P. Putnam's Sons, 1900); Judith Sealander, *The Failed Century of the Child: Governing America's Young in the Twentieth Century* (New York: Cambridge University Press, 2003). National Commission on Children, *Beyond Rhetoric: A New American Agenda for Children and Families* (Washington, DC: National Commission on Children, 1991). The report was the result of years of work by a panel drawn from both ends of the political spectrum.

20. Martha Minow and Richard Weissbourd, "Social Movements for Children," *Daedalus* 22, no. 1 (1993): 10.

21. Richard Brandon, "Financing Access to Early Education for Children Age Four and Below: Concepts and Costs," unpublished paper, Brookings Institution, 2004, *http://www.brookings.edu/es/research/ projects/wrb/200411brandon.htm;* Isabel Sawhill and Jens Ludvig, "Success before Ten," unpublished paper, Brookings Institution, 2006.

1. Small Miracles

1. John Dewey, *Democracy and Education* (New York: Macmillan, 1916), 117. Vivian Paley, *A Child's Work: The Importance of Fantasy Play* (Chicago: University of Chicago Press, 2004). On the Lab School's history,

see William Harms and Ida DePencier, *Experiencing Education: 100 Years of Learning at the University of Chicago Laboratory Schools* (Chicago: Laboratory School, 1996).

2. Carl Sandburg, "Chicago"; E. M. Forster, *www.brainyquote.com/quotes/quotes/e/emforste141583.html.*

3. Anthony Bryk, *Charting Chicago School Reform* (Boulder, CO: Westview Press, 1999). See, generally, "A Big Change in Chicago," *Economist,* October 20, 2005.

4. David Brooks, "Page One's Missing Characters," *New York Times,* July 6, 2006.

5. Peter Huttenlocher, *Neural Plasticity: The Effects of Environment on the Development of the Cerebral Cortex* (Cambridge, MA: Harvard University Press, 2002).

6. James Heckman and Alan Krueger, *Inequality in America: What Role for Human Capital Policies?* (Cambridge, MA: MIT Press, 2003).

7. See, e.g., Greg Duncan and Katherine Magnuson, "Promoting the Healthy Development of Young Children," in Isabel Sawhill, ed., *One Percent for the Kids* (Washington, DC: Brookings Institution, 2003); Greg Duncan and Katherine Magnuson, "Costs and Benefits to Promote Human Capital and Positive Behavior," in Norman Watt et al., eds., *The Crisis in Youth Mental Health,* vol. 4 (Westport, CT: Praeger, 2005).

8. It is estimated that 200,000 three- and four-year-olds remain "unserved" in Illinois, but this figure is an overstatement. Many wealthy parents choose to send their children to preschools that opt not to participate in the state program because of the legal requirements.

9. See, generally, Annette Lareau, *Unequal Childhoods: Class, Race, and American Life* (Berkeley: University of California Press, 2002).

10. See, generally, Alison Gopnik, Andrew N. Meltzoff, and Patricia K. Kuhl, *The Scientist in the Crib* (New York: Harpers, 1999). Gopnik writes about infants and toddlers, but the "child as scientist" metaphor also applies to three- and four-year-olds.

11. Diane Early et al., "Pre-Kindergarten in Eleven States: NCEDL's Multi-State Study of Pre-Kindergarten and Study of State-Wide Early Education Programs (SWEEP)," *www.fpg.unc.edu/~ncedl/pdfs/SWEEP_MS_summary_final.pdf.*

12. There are professionally developed criteria by which good and bad preschools are measured, including those developed by the Frank Porter Graham Child Development Institute at the University of North Carolina, *http://www.fpg.unc.edu/~ecers/,* and the National Association for the Education of Young Children, *http://www.naeyc.org/.*

13. James Bryce, *The American Commonwealth* (1888; repr. Washington, DC: Liberty Fund, 1996).

14. David Tyack, *The One Best System* (Cambridge, MA: Harvard University Press, 1974).

15. The names of children, as well as some of the preschool teachers, have been changed.

16. Robert Kominski, Amie Jamison, and Gladys Martinez, Population Division, U.S. Bureau of the Census, *At-Risk Conditions of U.S. School-Age Children* (Washington, DC: 2001), *www.census.gov/population/www/documentation/twps0052.html.*

17. Although methodologists prefer random-assignment experiments to natural experiments because in the former the similarity of the two groups can be assured, the comparison group in this study does appear to resemble closely the group of children who went to a Child-Parent Center.

18. Arthur J. Reynolds, *Success in Early Intervention: The Chicago Child-Parent Centers* (Lincoln: University of Nebraska Press, 2000).

19. Arthur Reynolds et al., "Effects of a School-Based, Early Childhood Intervention on Adult Health and Well Being: A 20-Year Follow Up of Low-Income Families," unpublished manuscript, 2006. Steven Barnett at NIEER is critical of the Child-Parent Center teacher follow-up in which teachers were asked to recall the pedagogical approach they took, twenty years after the fact. Barnett argues that teachers cannot reliably remember how they taught a generation earlier.

20. Despite the preference for diversity, there is some evidence that publicly run preschools do a better job. See Gary Henry et al., *The Georgia Early Childhood Study, 2001–2004*, Domestic Programs, Andrew Young School of Policy Studies, Georgia State University, 2005, *http://aysps.gsu.edu/publications/2005/EarlyChildhoodReport.pdf.*

21. On the Reggio Emilia approach, see Carolyn Edwards et al., eds., *The Hundred Languages of Children* (Norwood, NJ: Ablex Publishing, 1993); Joanne Hendrick, *Next Steps toward Teaching the Reggio Way* (Columbus, OH: Pearson Education, 2003); Diane Dunne, "Pre-K–3 Educators Learn from the Reggio Emilia Approach," *Education World*, January 3, 2006, *http://www.education-world.com/a_curr/curr256.shtml;* Amy Klein, "Different Approaches to Teaching: Comparing Three Preschool Programs," *Earlychildhood*, January 5, 2006, *http://www.earlychildhood.com/Articles/index.cfm?A=367&FuseAction=Article.*

22. Barbara Kantrowitz and Pat Wingert, "The Ten Best Schools in the World," *Newsweek*, December 2, 1991.

23. One of the Chicago Commons schools is also a zero-to-five school.

24. Quoted in "Pre-K Education in the States," *Early Development*, 9, no. 1 (2005): 18.

25. The Child-Parent Centers are funded through the No Child Left Be-

hind Act, not by the state's prekindergarten program; that makes it easier for the public schools to cut their budget and spend the money on
other, nonpreschool programs.

26. The school district may well be right in anticipating that public preschools encourage parents to keep their children in the public
schools. That has been Denver's experience. Nancy Mitchell, "DPS
Preschools Likely to Boost City Enrollment, Study Shows," July
20, 2006, *http://www.rockymountainnews.com/drmn/education/article/
0,1299,DRMN_957_4856667,00.html*.

27. Alison Gopnik, "How We Learn," *New York Times Education Supplement*, January 16, 2005.

2. Life Way After Preschool

1. Lawrence J. Schweinhart et al., *Lifetime Effects: The High/Scope Perry
Preschool Study through Age 40* (Ypsilanti, MI: High/Scope Press, 2004).
Other monographs on Perry Preschool were published by High/Scope
in 1970, 1978, 1980, 1984, and 1993.

2. There are few truly novel ideas, as historians like to remind us; it's all
about "standing on the shoulders of giants," and preschool is no exception. In this country, Head Start is widely regarded as revolutionizing
the education of three- and four-year-olds, a project that the universal
preschool movement is carrying forward. In fact, however, as early as
the 1820s many children of preschool age were being educated, and by
1840 about 40 percent of all three-year-olds in Massachusetts were attending infants' school.

Like their present-day counterparts, reformers then regarded early
education as a way to eradicate child poverty and lower welfare costs, to
free poor mothers to work outside the home and enable poor children to
do better in school. And then as now, there was disagreement about
what was to be taught. Some teachers stressed play, while others prod-
ded children as young as two years old to learn their ABC's.

Soon enough, middle-class women became fearful that their own
children might lose out in the education competition and started clam-
oring for their own infants' schools. "It is now in contemplation to open
a school for the infants beside the poor," *Ladies' Magazine* reported in
1829. "If such a course be not soon adopted, at the age for entering primary schools those poor children will assuredly be the richest scholars.
And why should a plan which promises so many advantages be confined
to children of the indigent?"

Within a generation, though, this movement had run its course.
Experts spoke out against the alleged dangers of intellectual over-
stimulation. "Many physicians of great experience are of the opinion,

that efforts to develop the minds of young children are very frequently injurious," wrote one influential doctor. "In attempting to call forth and cultivate the intellectual faculties of children before they are six or seven years of age, serious and lasting injury has been done." The public heeded those warnings, and the infants' schools were forced to shut their doors. When the kindergarten movement surfaced at the end of the nineteenth century, this history was deliberately ignored for fear of reigniting old fears. See Maris Vinovskis, "Early Childhood Education: Then and Now," *Daedalus* 122, no. 1 (1993), which describes infant schools for poor children established as early as the 1820s.

3. David P. Weikart, *How High/Scope Grew: A Memoir* (Ypsilanti, MI: High/Scope Press, 2004), 49.

4. Shortly after he arrived in Ypsilanti, Weikart confronted the school district's principals with statistics about racial disparities in elementary school performance. "The reaction was electric; several went to the window to have a smoke, several left the room . . . 'What could you expect? [said those who made any comment]. Their ability was what they were born with.'" Ibid., 48.

5. In contrast, the Chicago Child-Parent Center Study is a natural experiment: it compares children who attended one of the centers with others, presumably the same in all relevant respects, who did not. This research design does not make it possible to factor out all the reasons underlying the choice to go the Child-Parent Center—to say with certainty that there isn't, say, an important difference in those families themselves. The Perry Preschool study is a randomized clinical trial: one random group received, and a virtually identical group did not receive, a particular intervention. Planned-variation studies systematically implement different programs with carefully designed control groups, and so allow the researchers to point to the effects of particular kinds of interventions. The Early Head Start evaluation is a good example of this research strategy. See Mathematica Policy Research, Early Head Start Research and Evaluation Project, *Final Technical Report* (Princeton, NJ: Mathematica, 2005), *http://www.mathematica-mpr.com/earlycare/ehstoc.asp;* Early Head Start Research and Evaluation Project, "Preliminary Findings from the Early Head Start Prekindergarten Follow-up," unpublished manuscript, 2006.

6. The names of the participants in the Perry Preschool study have been changed to protect the integrity of the study.

7. David Weikart et al., "The Ypsilanti Perry Preschool Project: Preschool Years and Longitudinal Results through Fourth Grade," *Monographs of the High/Scope Educational Research Foundation* 3 (1978).

8. "Significantly" is used here in its technical statistical sense.

9. Steven Barnett of the National Institute for Early Education Research, who got involved in the study in the 1980s, reports that the difference in effect between those who participated in the program for two years and those who were in it for just one is about 50 percent. If so (and his claim is based on differences that don't meet the conventional measure of statistical significance), that's a strong argument for beginning preschool at age three.

10. Lawrence Schweinhart and David Weikart, *Lasting Differences: The High/Scope Preschool Curriculum Comparison Study through Age 23* (Ypsilanti, MI: High/Scope Press, 1997). Keen to test its model, High/Scope ran an experiment that compared the long-term impact of three curricula: its own "plan, do, review" model; a play-based nursery school approach; and a teacher-directed, skill-and-drill method called Direct Instruction. At the age of fifteen, the youngsters who had been in the High/Scope class fared better than those from the Direct Instruction prekindergarten on measures ranging from placement in special education classes to juvenile arrest records. Those who had been in the nursery school class also did better, though on fewer measures than those exposed to the High/Scope curriculum.

    The High/Scope curriculum was on the market when the study was conducted, competing with Direct Instruction for the favor of preschool teachers. Though the study was scrupulously designed, critics—including, naturally enough, the developer of Direct Instruction—questioned the value of an evaluation carried out by researchers who had an economic stake in its outcome. Yet when the Head Start Family and Child Experiences Survey (FACES, as it is called), looked at several widely used curricula, children in classes whose teachers reported using High/Scope or a similar curriculum did better in elementary school than those who'd been in classrooms where other curricula, including a more proscriptive, "direct instruction" pedagogy, were used. None of this surprises Schweinhart: "Students who are given Direct Instruction are good at taking directions, but they aren't good at making their own decisions. In terms of their futures, the big question is who is giving those directions."

11. Frances Campbell et al., "Early Childhood Education: Young Adult Outcomes from the Abecedarian Project," *Applied Developmental Science* 6, no. 1 (2002). Abecedarian is the only one of the model program studies to record lasting IQ gains.

12. Lyndon B. Johnson, *Public Papers of the Presidents of the United States*, vol. 2, entry 301 (Washington, DC: Government Printing Office, 1966), 635.

13. Quoted in Edward Zigler and Susan Muenchow, *Head Start: The Inside Story of America's Most Successful Educational Experiment* (New York: Basic Books, 1992), 27.

14. See Steven Gould, *The Mismeasure of Man* (New York: Norton, 1982). The nature/nurture issue is discussed at length in Chapter 4.

15. Sheldon White and Deborah Phillips, "Designing Head Start: Roles Played by Developmental Psychologists," in David Featherman and Maris Vinovskis, eds., *Social Science and Policy-Making: A Search for Relevance in the Twentieth Century* (Ann Arbor: University of Michigan Press, 2001), 83; Dorothy Ross, "Changing Contours of the Social Science Disciplines," in Theodore Porter and Dorothy Ross, eds., *The Cambridge History of Science*, vol. 7: *The Modern Social Sciences* (New York: Cambridge University Press, 2003), 83.

16. Konrad Lorenz, *Evolution and the Modification of Behavior* (Chicago: University of Chicago Press, 1967).

17. Benjamin Bloom, *Stability and Change in Human Characteristics* (New York: John Wiley, 1984); J. McVicker Hunt, *Intelligence and Experience* (New York: Ronald, 1961).

18. Edward Zigler and Sally Styfco, "Epilogue," in Norman Watt et al., eds., *Early Intervention Programs and Politics* (Westport, CT: Praeger, 2005).

19. Sigfried Engelmann and Theresa Engelmann, *Give Your Child a Superior Mind* (New York: Simon and Schuster, 1966). The book was translated into seventeen languages.

20. Martin Deutsch et al., "The IDS Program: An Experiment in Early and Sustained Enrichment," in Consortium for Longitudinal Studies, ed., *As the Twig Is Bent: Lasting Effects of Preschool Programs* (Hillsdale, NJ: Lawrence Erlbaum, 1983), 377; Susan Gray et al., "The Early Training Project: 1962–1980," in ibid., 33.

21. Featherman and Vinovskis, *Social Science and Policy-Making*, 205.

22. Zigler and Muenchow, *Head Start*, 26.

23. Ibid.

24. Westinghouse Learning Corporation, *Impact of Head Start: Evaluation of the Effects of Head Start on Children's Cognitive and Affective Development* (Washington, DC: Clearinghouse for Federal, Scientific, and Technical Information, 1969).

25. Maris Vinovskis, "Do Federal Compensatory Education Programs Really Work? A Brief Historical Analysis of Title I and Head Start," *American Journal of Education* 107, no. 3 (May 1999). The school-year program survived until 1970, largely because it provided summer jobs for teachers, a powerful lobbying group. Timothy Hacsi, *Children as Pawns: The*

Politics of Educational Reform (Cambridge, MA: Harvard University Press, 2002), 33.

26. Scott Stossel, *Sarge: The Life and Times of Sargent Shriver* (Washington, DC: Smithsonian Books, 2004).

27. Lyndon Johnson, *Public Papers of the Presidents of the United States,* vol. 1, entry 3 (Washington, DC: Government Printing Office, 1968), 2.

28. James Coleman et al., *Equality of Educational Opportunity Survey* (Washington, DC: U.S. Department of Health, Education, and Welfare, Office of Education, 1966).

29. Zigler and Muenchow, *Head Start,* 60.

30. Arthur Jensen, "How Much Can We Boost IQ and Scholastic Achievement?" *Harvard Educational Review* 39, no. 1 (1969).

31. Lois-Ellin Datta, "The Impact of the Westinghouse/Ohio Evaluation on the Development of Project Head Start," in Clark Abt, ed., *Evaluation of Social Programs* (Beverly Hills, CA: Sage, 1976), 129.

32. Consortium for Longitudinal Studies, ed., *As the Twig Is Bent: Lasting Effects of Preschool Programs* (Hillsdale, NJ: Lawrence Erlbaum, 1983).

33. Steven Barnett argues that the fadeout effect is likely exaggerated because many of the studies, including Westinghouse, compare children from the experimental and control groups who remained in regular classes. But the fact that a smaller percentage of preschool students have been left back or assigned to special education classes means that the comparison understates the IQ differences, because it excludes the very students whose lower IQs would reduce the average of the nonpreschool group. W. Steven Barnett, "Does Head Start Have Lasting Cognitive Effects? The Myth of Fade-out," in Zigler and Styfco, "Epilogue," 221.

34. Spencer Rich, "Lasting Gains Provided by Preschool Programs," *Washington Post,* November 30, 1979; "Federal Study Finds Poor Children Helped by Preschool Classes," *New York Times,* December 1, 1979.

35. Zigler and Muenchow, *Head Start,* 192.

36. Editorial, "Changed Lives," *Washington Post,* September 17, 1984; "Head Start on Head Start," *New York Times,* January 13, 1987; Connie Leslie et al., "Everybody Likes Head Start," *Newsweek,* February 20, 1989; "For Head Start, Two Steps Back," *New York Times,* June 30, 1992. The confusion continues. A November 2004 *New York Times Magazine* article describing the "Perry at Age 40" study was headlined "Life *Waay* after Head Start."

37. 20 USC §§ S811 and S812 (1994).

38. John Hood, "Caveat Emptor: The Head Start Scam," *Policy Analysis* 187 (December 18, 2002).

39. "Is Early Childhood Education Working? It Depends on Which Study

You Read," *Education Vital Signs 2006* (a supplement to *American School Board Journal*, 2006): 8–9.

40. The Florida political story is recounted in Chapter 7.

41. Senta Raizen and Sue Bobrow, *Design for a National Evaluation of Social Competence in Head Start Children* (Santa Monica, CA: Rand, 1974).

42. Nicholas Zill et al., *Head Start FACES 2000: A Whole-Child Perspective on Program Performance* (Washington, DC: U.S. Department of Health and Human Services, 2003). This most analytically rigorous of the large-scale national studies compares how a random sample of children have fared in different kinds of early-education programs— home-based, center-based, or a combination of the two—but because it assesses Early Head Start, the infants and toddlers program, it has gotten essentially no attention in the Head Start debates. Administration on Children, Youth, and Families, *Pathways to Quality and Full Implementation in Early Head Start* (Washington, DC: U.S. Department of Health and Human Services, 2003). Students' race and ethnicity also affect how well they do in preschool, though the research seldom picks this up. Russell Rumberger and Loan Tran, "Preschool Participation and the Cognitive and Social Development of Language in Minority Students," Technical Report, Center for the Study of Evaluation, UCLA, 2006, *//mri.ucsb.edu/publications/2006_rumberger-tran.pdf.*

43. Walter Gilliam and Edward Zigler, "State Efforts to Evaluate the Effects of Prekindergarten, 1997–2003," unpublished manuscript, 2004. This paper does not incorporate the most recent and methodologically sophisticated state prekindergarten research.

44. Valerie Lee and Susanna Loeb, "Where Do Head Start Attendees End Up? One Reason that Preschool Effects Fade Out," *Educational Evaluation and Policy Analysis* 17, no. 1 (1995): 62.

45. Zill et al., *Head Start FACES 2000.*

46. NICHD Early Child Care Research Network, "Early Child Care and Children's Development in the Primary Grades: Follow-Up Results from the NICHD Study of Early Child Care," *American Educational Research Journal* 42, no. 3 (2005): 537.

47. Mathematica Policy Research, *Early Head Start Research and Evaluation Project: Final Report* (Princeton, NJ: Mathematica, 2005); Mathematica Policy Research, Early Head Start Research and Evaluation Project, "Preliminary Findings from the Early Head Start Prekindergarten Follow-up," unpublished manuscript, 2006.

48. Susanna Loeb et al., "How Much Is Too Much? The Influence of Preschool Centers on Children's Development Nationwide," *Economics of Education Review* (forthcoming). This study analyzes data from the

Early Childhood Longitudinal Survey—Kindergarten. But in ECLS-K, everything that's known about children's prekindergarten experiences comes from parents' reports, and parents' memories turn out to be unreliable. That means it's hard to attribute how children turn out in third grade to what they learned before entering kindergarten.

49. Richard J. Herrnstein and Charles Murray, *The Bell Curve: Intelligence and Class Structure in American Life* (New York: Free Press, 1994).

50. Eliana Garces, Duncan Thomas, and Janet Currie, "Longer-Term Effects of Head Start," *American Economic Review* 92, no. 4 (2002): 999–1012. White children who attended Head Start are significantly more likely to complete high school, attend college, and possibly have higher earnings. A study conducted by High/Scope found modest evidence that Head Start had a positive effect on girls' later school performance and criminal behavior, and almost no evidence of an effect on boys. Sherri Oden et al., *Into Adulthood: A Study of the Effects of Head Start* (Ypsilanti, MI: High/Scope Press, 2000).

51. W. Steven Barnett, "Long-term Effects of Early Childhood Programs on Cognitive and School Outcomes," *The Future of Children* 5, no. 1 (1995): 3.

52. There are more studies, but not necessarily better ones, on early childhood education. One national survey of a cross section of children enrolled in early-childhood programs doesn't distinguish preschool from child minding. It defines "child care" so broadly that child minding by fathers in the family home is included in the mix. Another relies on parents' recollections of their children's preschool experiences. See NICHD Early Child Care Research Network, "Characteristics and Quality of Child Care for Toddlers and Preschoolers," *Applied Developmental Science* 4 (2000): 116–135; NICHD Early Child Care Research Network, "Does Amount of Time Spent in Child Care Predict Socioemotional Adjustment during the Transition to Kindergarten?" *Child Development* 74 (2003): 976–1005; John Love et al., "Child Care Quality Matters: How Conclusions May Vary with Context," *Child Development* 74 (2003): 1021–1033; Katherine Magnuson et al., "Inequality in Preschool Education and School Readiness," *American Educational Research Journal* 41 (2004): 115–157; National Center for Education Statistics, *America's Kindergartners*, NCES 2000-070 (Washington, DC: U.S. Department of Education, 2000).

53. Ron Haskins, "Putting Education into Preschools," in Paul Peterson, ed., *Generational Change: Closing the Test Score Gap*, (Lanham, MD: Rowman & Littlefield, 2006).

54. Douglas Besharov, "Head Start's Broken Promise," *On the Issues* (American Enterprise Institute, October 2005).

55. Michelle Davis, "Head Start Has 'Modest' Impact, Study Says," *Education Week,* June 15, 2005.

56. Besharov, "Head Start's Broken Promise."

57. A review of early studies of state prekindergarten programs found little evidence of enduring benefits. Walter Gilliam, "What Can Be Learned from State-Funded Prekindergarten Initiatives: A Data-Based Approach to the Head Start Devolution Debate," in Zigler and Styfco, "Epilogue," 477.

58. Barnett argues that he didn't have to use only kids whose age differences were close to the cutoff date to make the method work; Gormley reports using several samples at different distances from the age cutoff to see how much of a difference that made.

59. W. Steven Barnett, Cynthia Lamy, and Kwanghee Jung, *The Effects of State Prekindergarten Programs on Young Children's School Readiness in Five States,* The National Institute for Early Education Research, December 2005.

60. William T. Gormley, Jr., et al., "The Effects of Universal Pre-K on Cognitive Development," *Developmental Psychology* 41, no. 6 (2005): 872–884.

3. The Futures Market

1. Robert Lynch, *Exceptional Returns: Economic, Fiscal, and Social Benefits of Investment in Early Childhood Development* (Washington, DC: Economic Policy Institute, 2004); Dana Feldman, "The New Economics of Preschool," report prepared for the Early Childhood Funders' Collaborative, October 2004, *www.earlychildhoodfinance.org/handouts/FriedmanArticle.doc.*

2. Business Roundtable and Corporate Voices for America's Families, "ECE: A Call to Action from the Business Community" (2003), *www.businessroundtable.org.* Corporations such as Verizon, Kaiser Health Foundation, and Entergy, an energy company, have also endorsed the campaign. See Jerrold Oppenheim and Theo MacGregor, "The Economics of Education: Public Benefits of High-Quality Preschool Education for Low-Income Children" (Entergy, 2003).

3. Seniors are often regarded as focused only on their own narrow interests, and the record of the AARP gives credence to that view. But when a proposal to amend the Florida constitution to guarantee that high-quality preschool was on the ballot, seniors voted for it by a ratio of three to two, the same margin by which it passed.

4. Theodore Schultz, "Investment in Human Capital," *American Economic Review* 51, no. 1 (1961): 1–17, at p. 2.

5. Gary Becker, *Human Capital* (Chicago: University of Chicago Press, 1964).

6. The Earned Income Tax Credit (EITC) transferred $31 billion a year in 2001 to lower-income families. Alan Krueger calculates that investing in education and training would have a substantially larger return. James Heckman and Alan Krueger, *Inequality in America: What Role for Human Capital Policies?* (Cambridge, MA: MIT Press, 2002), 62.

7. Peter Rossi and Katharine Lyall, *Reforming Public Welfare: A Critique of the Negative Income Tax Experiment* (New York: Russell Sage, 1976).

8. Alan Krueger, "Reassessing the View That American Schools Are Broken," FRBNY Economic Policy Review (March 1998), 29–43.

9. Steven Levitt and Steven Dubner, *Freakonomics: A Rogue Economist Explores the Hidden Side of Everything,* rev. and expanded ed. (New York: William Morrow, 2006).

10. The best of these economists, such as Greg Duncan at Northwestern University, have absorbed the relevant literature in psychology. See, e.g., Greg Duncan and Jeanne Brooks-Gunn, eds., *Consequences of Growing Up Poor* (New York: Russell Sage, 1999); Jeanne Brooks-Gunn et al., "The Black-White Test Score Gap in Young Children: Contributions of Test and Family Characteristics" *Applied Developmental Science,* 7 (2003): 239–252. In his discussions of early education, the economist James Heckman, whose work is discussed later in the chapter, draws heavily, to considerable intellectual advantage, on a wide range of social and natural science research.

11. Barnett was also influenced by the 1930s Iowa orphanage study, which is discussed in Chapter 4.

12. Arthur Reynolds and Judy Temple, "Economic Returns of Investments in Preschool Education," in Edward Zigler et al., eds., *A Vision for Universal Preschool* (New York: Cambridge University Press, 2006), 37–69, quotation on 41.

13. W. Steven Barnett, *Lives in the Balance: Age-27 Benefit-Cost Analysis of the High/Scope Perry Preschool Program* (Ypsilanti, MI: High/Scope Educational Research Foundation, 1996), 12.

14. Kai Erikson, *Everything in Its Path* (New York: Simon and Schuster, 1977).

15. None of this is news to Barnett, who acknowledges the limitations of the data. Barnett, *Lives in the Balance.*

16. Barnett makes this point in the 1983 analysis, noting "the inability to adequately value nonpecuniary benefits." W. Steven Barnett, *The*

Perry Preschool Program and Its Long-Term Effects: A Benefit-Cost Analysis (Ypsilanti, MI: High/Scope Educational Research Foundation, 1983), 93.

17. See, e.g., Sar Levitan and Stephen Mangum, *Programs in Aid of the Poor* (Baltimore: Johns Hopkins Press, 1973).

18. Barnett, *The Perry Preschool Program and Its Long-Term Effects*, 83.

19. Barnett, *Lives in the Balance*, 100.

20. Lawrence Schweinhart et al., *Lifetime Effects: The High/Scope Perry Preschool Study through Age 40* (Ypsilanti, MI: High/Scope Press, 2004).

21. Clive Belfield, *Early Childhood Education: How Important Are the Cost-Savings to the School System?* Center for Early Care and Education, Columbia University, 2004, *www.winningbeginningny.org/databank/documents/belfield_report_000.pdf;* Clive Belfield, "The Fiscal Impacts of Universal Pre-K: Case Study Analysis for Three States," Working Paper 4 (Washington, DC: Invest in Kids, 2005), *www.ced.org/projects/ids.shtml.*

22. John Donohue and Peter Siegelman, "Allocating Resources among Prisons and Social Programs in the Battle against Crime," *Journal of Legal Studies* 27, no. 1 (1998): 1–43.

23. Rob Grunewald and Art Rolnick, "Early Childhood Development: Economic Development with a High Public Return," *Fedgazette* (Minneapolis: Federal Reserve Bank, March 2003), *http://www.mpls.frb.org/pubs/fedgaz/03–03/earlychild.cfm?js=0.*

24. Interview with James J. Heckman in *The Region* (Minneapolis: Federal Reserve Bank of Minneapolis, June 2005), *minneapolisfed.org/pubs/region/05–06/heckman.cfm.*

25. James Heckman et al., "The Economics and Econometrics of Active Labor Market Programs," *Handbook of Labor Economics,* vol. 3A, Orly Ashenfelter and David Card, eds. (Amsterdam: Elsevier, 1999). Other economists disagree, however. See Alan Krueger, "Inequality, Too Much of a Good Thing," in Heckman and Krueger, *Inequality in America.*

26. In 2005 Heckman organized the Consortium on Early Childhood Development, with the intention of pulling together the relevant evaluation studies. Some researchers were prepared to share their data, he reports, but others were suspicious. He is also a founding member of the Scientific Council on the Developing Child, which is headed by Jack Shonkoff, coeditor of *From Neurons to Neighborhoods,* the benchmark book in the field.

27. Flavio Cunha et al., *Interpreting the Evidence on Life Cycle Skill Formation* (Cambridge, MA: National Bureau of Economic Research, 2005), *www.nber.org/papers/w11331.*

28. James Heckman, "The Technology and Neuroscience of Skill Formation," Invest in Kids Working Group, Center for Economic Development: Partnership for America's Economic Success, July 17, 2006, *www.ced.org/docs/ivk/iikmeeting_slides200607heckman.pdf*. There is a high payoff to private job training for educated workers, Heckman notes. James Heckman, Lance Lochner, and Christopher Taber, "Explaining Rising Wage Inequality," *Review of Economic Dynamics* 1, no. 1 (1998): 1–58.

29. Interview with Heckman, *minneapolisfed.org/pubs/region/05–06/heckman.cfm*.

30. James Heckman and Yona Rubenstein, "The Importance of Noncognitive Skills: Lessons from the GED Testing Program," *American Economic Review* 91, no. 2 (2001): 145–149.

31. Walter Gilliam, "Pre-Kindergarteners Left Behind: Expulsion Rates in State Prekindergarten Systems," unpublished manuscript, Yale University, 2005.

32. James Heckman, Jora Stixrud, and Sergio Urzua, "The Effects of Cognitive and Noncognitive Abilities on Labor Market Outcomes and Social Behavior," *Journal of Labor Economics* 24, no. 3 (2006): 411–482.

33. Ibid.

34. See, e.g., Vivian Paley, *Boys and Girls: Superheroes in the Doll Corner* (Chicago: University of Chicago Press, 1984); *You Can't Say You Can't Play* (Cambridge, MA: Harvard University Press, 1992).

35. Robert Sternberg, *Beyond IQ: A Triarchic Theory of Human Intelligence* (New York: Cambridge University Press, 1985).

36. James Heckman, "Catch 'Em Young," *Wall Street Journal*, January 13, 2006.

37. Ibid.

38. See Edward Zigler, Walter Gilliam, and Stephanie Jones, *A Vision for Universal Preschool* (New York: Cambridge University Press, 2006), for a careful distillation of the arguments. In 1985, after completing the first Perry Preschool study, Barnett had argued against universal preschool on standard economic grounds: the social return was likely to be small, and well-off parents were already investing in their children's education. What he has learned since then, about both social benefits and politics, has led him to change his mind. See Barnett, *The Perry Preschool Program and Its Long-Term Effects*, 102.

39. Jonah Gelbach and Lant Pritchett, "Is More for the Poor Less for the Poor? The Politics of Means-Tested Targeting," *Topics in Economic Analysis and Policy* 2, no. 1 (Berkeley Electronic Press, 2004): 1–28.

40. Compare W. Steven Barnett and Clive Belfield, "Early Childhood

Development and Social Mobility," *Future of Children* 16, no. 2 (2006): 1–22.

41. Jens Ludwig and Isabel Sawhill, *Success by Ten: Intervening Early, Often and Effectively in the Education of Young Children* (Washington, DC: Hamilton Project, Brookings Institution, 2007).

42. James Coleman et al., *Equal Educational Opportunity Survey* (Washington, DC: Government Printing Office, 1966).

43. This study is discussed in Chapter 8.

44. Kathy Sylva et al., *Findings from the Effective Provision of Preschool Education Project, 1999–2005*, www.ioe.ac.uk/cdl/eppe/pdfs/eppe_brief2503 .pdf; Gary Henry et al., *An Evaluation of the Implementation of Georgia's Pre-K Program* (Atlanta: Andrew Young School of Policy Studies, Georgia State University, 2004), aysps.gsu.edu/publications/2005/ GAPreK2004.pdf. See also Edward Zigler et al., eds., *A Vision for Universal Preschool* (New York: Cambridge University Press, 2006), 99–101.

    This research is far from the last word; because universal pre-K isn't an experiment like Perry Preschool, skeptics can argue that what's really important isn't the fact of integration but the initial differences between those poor kids who go to economically isolated schools and those in economically integrated ones. Still, for the policymaker, integration is a better bet than class-based segregation—what's known about preschoolers, from their own experience directly as well by analogy, from the landmark 1966 *Equal Education Opportunity Survey*, points in that direction.

45. Alexis de Tocqueville, *Democracy in America* (1835; Chicago: University of Chicago Press, 2000), 647.

46. Theda Skocpol, "Targeting within Universalism: Politically Viable Policies to Combat Poverty in the United States," in Paul Peterson and Christopher Jencks, eds., *The Urban Underclass* (Washington, DC: Brookings Institution, 1991).

47. William Dickens, Isabel Sawhill, and Jeffrey Tebbs, *The Effects of Investing in Early Education on Economic Growth*, Policy Brief 153 (Washington, DC: Brookings Institution 2006).

48. Karen Schulman and W. Steven Barnett, *The Benefits of Prekindergarten for Middle-Income Children* (New Brunswick, NJ: National Institute for Early Education Research, March 2005), nieer.org/resources/policyreports/ report3.pdf.

49. That doesn't mean that everyone has to be treated exactly the same way; since individuals have different needs, targeting within a framework of universalism makes sense. See Richard Titmuss, *Commitment to Welfare* (London: Allen and Unwin, 1968). These issues are canvassed in Nanna

Kildal and Stein Kuhnie, "The Principle of Universalism: Tracing a Key Idea in the Scandinavian Welfare Model" (2002), *www.etes.ucl.ac.be/bien/Files/Papers/2002KildalKuhnle.pdf.*

50. Richard Titmuss, *Commitment to Welfare* (London: Allen and Unwin, 1968), 129.

4. The Imprimatur of Science

1. See Ross A. Thompson and Charles A. Nelson, "Developmental Science and the Media," *American Psychologist* 56, no. 1 (2001): 5–15. Campaign journalism "begins not with the findings of relevant research but rather with the goals of an advocacy effort that has been initiated by concerned interest groups, political officials, influential celebrities, and other nonscientists" (6).

2. Jack Shonkoff and Deborah Phillips, eds., *From Neurons to Neighborhoods: The Science of Early Childhood Development* (Washington, DC: National Academy Press, 2000).

3. Matt Ridley, the author of *Genome* and other popular science books, makes a passionate plea for "nature via nurture" in his book *The Agile Gene.* Matt Ridley, *The Agile Gene: How Nature Turns on Nurture* (New York: Harper Perennial, 2004). On the concept of "paradigm shift," see Thomas Kuhn, *The Structure of Scientific Revolutions,* 3rd ed. (Chicago: University of Chicago Press, 1996).

4. Preschool California later revised its message box to be less specific; instead of saying 90 percent of brain growth occurs before age five, the new message was that most brain growth takes place before children enter kindergarten. "But it is basically the same message," says Susanna Cooper, the director of communications, "and it does make an impression on people."

5. In a few states, zero-to-five (education and care for children from birth to age five) is a reality: in Illinois, for instance, 11 percent of every early education dollar is spent on children from birth to age three (see Chapter 1). But this unequal division confirms the dominance of preschool in much present policy thinking. For an important exception, see North Carolina's Smart Start program for zero to five (examined in Chapter 9). The role of the Gates and Buffett foundations in refocusing attention on zero-to-five child care and education is discussed in Chapter 6.

6. George H. W. Bush had earlier declared the 1990s to be the "decade of the brain," but at that time the focus was on finding effective treatments for diseases ranging from Alzheimer's and Huntington's disease to depression and AIDS. Children didn't rate a mention in the 1990 presidential proclamation, which highlights how much had changed, in terms

of public attention, over the course of a few years. Presidential Proclamation 6158, July 17, 1990, *http://www.loc.gov/loc/brain/proclaim.html*.

7. Susan Begley, "Your Child's Brain," *Newsweek*, February 19, 1996.

8. J. Madeleine Nash, "How a Child's Brain Develops," *Time*, February 3, 1997.

9. In addition to the classical music CD, Zell Miller also sent home a children's storybook, which is more likely to be beneficial since it exposes a child to language.

10. The account of the White House conference is drawn from numerous sources, including the transcript of the meeting, *http://clinton3 .nara.gov/WH/New/ECDC/Remarks.html*; Malcolm Gladwell, "Baby Steps," *New Yorker*, January 10, 2000, *http://www.gladwell.com/2000/ 2000_01_10_a_baby.htm*.

11. *Starting Points: Meeting the Needs of Our Youngest Children* (New York: Carnegie Corporation, 1994)

12. The scientists knew that the first lady's time frame was considerably foreshortened—that much of what was being heralded as new had long been common knowledge among scientists—but this wasn't their day. See, e.g., Susan Chipman, "Integrating Three Perspectives on Learning," in Sarah L. Friedman et al., eds., *The Brain, Cognition, and Education* (Orlando, FL: Academic Press, 1986), 226.

13. For the text, see *http://clinton3.nara.gov/WH/New/ECDC/Remarks.html*.

14. Quoted in Marcia Baringa, "Neuroscience: A Critical Issue for the Brain," *Science*, 288:5 June 23, 2000, pages 2116–2119.

15. See *http://www.parentsaction.org/about/history/*. Chapter 7 includes a discussion of Reiner's role in promoting a California ballot initiative, rejected by the voters in 2006, which would have mandated quality universal preschool.

16. Quoted in John Bruer, *The Myth of the First Three Years* (New York: Free Press, 1999), 60.

17. E. Bruce Goldstein, *Sensation and Perception* (London: Wadsworth, 2001).

18. Michael Rutter et al., "Are There Biological Programming Effects for Psychological Development? Findings from a Study of Romanian Adoptees," *Developmental Psychology* 4, no. 1 (2004): 81–94; Alison Fries et al., "Early Experience in Humans Is Associated with Changes in Neuropeptides Critical for Regulating Social Behavior," *Proceedings of the National Academy of Science* 102, no. 47 (November 22, 2005): 17237–17240; Thomas Eluvathingal et al., "Abnormal Brain Activity in Children after Severe Socioemotional Deprivation: A Diffusion Tensor Imaging Study, *Pediatrics* 117 (2006): 2093–2100.

19. William Greenough et al., "Effects of Rearing Complexity on Den-

dritic Branching in Frontolateral and Temporal Cortex of the Rat," *Experimental Neurology* 41, no. 2 (1973): 371–378; Anita M. Turner and William Greenough, "Differential Rearing Effects on Rat Visual Cortex Synapses, I: Synaptic and Neuronal Density and Synapses per Neuron," *Brain Research* 329, nos. 1–2 (1985): 195–203.

20. Ann Hulbert, *Raising America* (New York: Knopf, 2003).

21. Eric Kandel and Larry Squire, "Neuroscience: Breaking Down Scientific Barriers in the Study of Brain and Mind," *Science* 290, no. 5494 (2000): 1113–1120 at 1113. See also Thomas Albright et al., "Neural Science: A Century of Progress and the Mysteries that Remain," *Neuron* 100 (February 2000): 51–55. For developments in neuroscience through the 1960s, see Stanley Finger, *Minds behind the Brain: A History of the Pioneers and Their Discoveries* (New York: Oxford University Press, 2000).

    Neuroscience—a 1960s synthesis of neuroanatomy, neurophysiology, neuropharmacology, neurochemistry, and behavior—incorporated "the biological study of the brain . . . into a common framework with cell and molecular biology on the one side and psychology on the other." Gordon Shepherd, *Foundations of the Neuron Doctrine* (New York: Oxford, 1991), 4. During the 1980s, occasional articles on brain science appeared in popular outlets such as *Parents* magazine. See Jane Healy, "Brainpower: You Can Make Smarter Babies," *Parents* (December 1986): 100; Jane Healy, *Your Child's Growing Mind* (Garden City, NY: Doubleday, 1987).

22. See Shepherd, *Foundations of the Neuron Doctrine*, 136–137.

23. On imaging, see Bettyann Kevles, *Naked to the Bone: Medical Imaging in the Twentieth Century* (New Brunswick, NJ: Rutgers University Press, 1997); Steve Webb, *From the Watching of Shadows* (New York: A. Hilger, 1990); Marcus Raichle, "A Brief History of Human Functional Brain Mapping," in *Brain Mapping: The Systems,* ed. Arthur W. Toga and John C. Mazziota (San Diego: Academic Press, 2000), 33–77.

24. David K. Bilkey, "Neuroscience: In the Place Space," *Science,* 305, no. 5688 (August 2004): 1245–1246.

    Actually, fMRI measures blood oxygenation in the brain rather than neural impulses. While this isn't a direct measure of neural activity, that is not a significant drawback because experimental research has shown that there is increased oxygenation of the blood in areas of neuronal activation. For more details, see Raichle, "A Brief History of Human Functional Brain Mapping."

    The pharmaceutical industry has also glamorized the brain. By the late 1980s, the life-altering, and profit-generating, benefits of neuroscience were no longer the speculations of researchers pleading for funding. Eli Lilly's development and marketing of fluoxetine hydrochloride—a previously little-known drug branded as Prozac in 1987 after the FDA approved its use—led to its becoming the second highest selling prescription drug in the United States. See *http://www.prozac.com/how_prozac/prozac_history.jsp?reqNavId=2.1*; see also *http://sulcus.berkeley.edu/mcb/165_001/papers/manuscripts/_175.html.*

25. Benedict Carey, "Searching for the Person in the Brain," *New York Times,* February 5, 2006.

26. Alissa Quart, "Extreme Parenting: Does the Baby Genius Entertainment Complex Enrich Your Child's Mind—Or Stifle It?" *Atlantic Monthly,* July/August 2006.

27. Richard Herrnstein and Charles Murray, *The Bell Curve* (New York: Free Press, 1994).

28. Jerome Kagan, *Three Seductive Ideas* (New York: Oxford University Press, 1999). Infant determinism, pushed to its logical conclusion, suggests the need for fetal brain-stimulation activities. Gary F. Marcus, *The Birth of the Mind* (New York: Basic Books, 2005).

29. Bruer, *The Myth of the First Three Years,* 9.

30. There is no scientific basis for the so-called Mozart effect. See Christopher F. Chabris, "Prelude or Requiem for the 'Mozart Effect'?" *Nature* 400, no. 6747 (1999): 826–827; Ron Kotulak, *Inside the Brain* (Kansas City: Andrew and McNeel, 1996).

31. Greenough et al., "Effects of Rearing Complexity"; Turner and Greenough, "Differential Rearing Effects on Rat Visual Cortex Synapses."

32. Eric Knudsen, "Sensitive Periods in the Development of the Brain and Behavior," *Journal of Cognitive Neuroscience* 16, no. 8 (2004): 1412–1425. "The term 'sensitive period' is a broad term that applies whenever the effects of experience on the brain are unusually strong during a limited period in development . . Critical periods are a special class of sensitive periods that result in irreversible changes in brain function" (1412). See also Eric Knudsen, "Multiple Sites of Adaptive Plasticity in the Owl's Auditory Localization Pathway," *Journal of Neuroscience* 24, no. 31 (2004): 6853–6861.

33. William Greenough et al., "Experience and Brain Development," *Child Development* 58, no. 3 (1987): 539–559. "We propose that mammalian brain development relies upon two different categories of plasticity for the storage of environmentally originating information. The first of these probably underlies many sensitive- or critical-period phenomena. This process, which we term experience expectant, is designed to utilize the sort of environmental information that is ubiquitous and has been

so throughout much of the evolutionary history of the species . . . The second type of plasticity, which we call experience dependent, is involved in the storage of information that is unique to the individual," 540. On brain plasticity generally, see Peter Huttenlocher, *Neural Plasticity: The Effects of Environment on the Development of the Cerebral Cortex* (Cambridge, MA: Harvard University Press, 2002).

34. David H. Hubel and Torsten N. Wiesel, "Functional Architecture of Macaque Monkey Visual Cortex," *Proceedings of the Royal Society of London B* 198 (1977): 1–59. Human visual development has multiple sensitive periods during which experience can influence visual development, and there are different sensitive periods for different aspects of vision. Terri Lewis and Daphne Maurer, "Multiple Sensitive Periods in Human Visual Development: Evidence from Visually Deprived Children," *Developmental Psychobiology* 46, no. 1 (2005): 163–183.

35. Susan Parker and Charles Nelson, "The Impact of Early Institutional Rearing on the Ability to Discriminate Facial Expressions of Emotion: An Event-Related Potential Study," *Child Development* 76, no. 1 (2005): 54–72; Michael Rutter and the Romanian Adoptees (ER) Study Team, "Developmental Catch-Up, and Deficit, Following Adoption after Severe Global Early Privation," *Journal of Child Psychology and Psychiatry and Allied Disciplines* 39 (1998): 465–476. In their study, Rutter and his team found that the circumference of the Romanian adoptees' heads, a rough proxy for brain development, was smaller than normal, and ongoing research is unearthing evidence of their neurological impairment.

36. John Bruer, "Avoiding the Pediatrician's Error: How Neuroscientists Can Help Educators (and Themselves), *Nature Neuroscience* 5 (November 2002): 1031–1033.

37. See Ross A. Thompson and Charles A. Nelson, "Developmental Science and the Media," *American Psychologist* 56, no. 1 (2001): 5–15.

38. Ross Thompson emphasized this point.

39. Brain development is likely to be curvilinear, not linear, as Charles Nelson pointed out. Then again, the creation of a work of art is not likely to be a linear process either.

40. James Lord, *A Giacometti Portrait* (New York: Farrar, Straus and Giroux, 1980), describes the seemingly endless process of vision and revision that went into the artist's portrait of the author.

41. Resilience is a useful concept for understanding the considerable variability in children's responses to interventions like the Abecedarian Project and Perry Preschool. It is likely that sometime earlier, or later, the children reacted differently to similar stresses, or were exposed to different stresses, that weren't measured in the studies.

42. See, e.g., National Scientific Council on the Developing Child, *Excessive Stress Disrupts the Architecture of the Developing Brain*, Working Paper No. 3 (2005), *http://www.developingchild.net/reports.shtml;* National Scientific Council on the Developing Child, *Early Exposure to Toxic Substances Damages Brain Architecture*, Working Paper No. 4 (2006), *http://www.developingchild.net/reports.shtml.*

43. See, e.g., Geraldine Dawson et al., "Infants of Depressed Mothers Exhibit Atypical Frontal Electrical Brain Activity during Interactions with Mother and with a Familiar, Nondepressed Adult," *Child Development* 70, no. 5 (1999): 1058.

44. See Elizabeth Gould and Charles C. Gross, "Neurogenesis in Adult Mammals: Some Progress and Problems," *Journal of Neuroscience* 22 (2002): 619–623; Elizabeth Gould et al., "Learning Enhances Adult Neurogenesis in the Hippocampal Formation," *Nature Neuroscience* 2 (1999): 260–265.

45. See Eric Knudsen and Brie Linkenhoker, "Incremental Training Increases the Plasticity of the Auditory Space Map in Adult Barn Owls," *Nature* 419 (September 19, 2002): 293–296.

46. The London taxi driver study, while very clever, is not without its possible flaws. Since the study doesn't use a baseline for comparison, as Charles Nelson points out, it cannot rule out the possibility that "there is something special about those who drive cabs. Perhaps they seek out this occupation because they already have a bigger or more plastic hippocampus."

47. These studies are described in Nelson et al., ibid.

48. Stan Colcombe et al., "Cardiovascular Fitness, Cortical Plasticity, and Aging," *Proceedings of the National Academy of Sciences* 101 (2004): 3316–3321. On adult learning, see also, e.g., Lisa D. Sanders et al., "Speech Segmentation by Native and Non-native Speakers: The Use of Lexical, Syntactic, and Stress-Pattern Cues," *Journal of Speech, Language, and Hearing Research* 45, no. 3 (2002): 519–530; Helen Neville and Daphne Bavelier, "Variability of Developmental Plasticity," in James McClelland and Robert S. Siegler, eds., *Mechanisms of Cognitive Development: Behavioral and Neural Perspectives (Mahwah*, NJ: Lawrence Erlbaum, 2001). Alison Gopnik, Andrew N. Meltzoff, and Patricia K. Kuhl, *The Scientist in the Crib: What Early Learning Tells Us about the Mind* (New York: Morrow, 1999.)

49. Shonkoff and Phillips, *From Neurons to Neighborhoods*, 90.

50. A nationwide program called the Clemente Course, created by Earl Shorris, offers an education to adults, many of them mothers on welfare or prisoners, that emphasizes the classics. Anecdotal reports are positive,

but no evaluation of the long-term impact of the course has been conducted; Michelle Gaps, "Expanding Horizons for Low-Income Students, *Washington Post,* April 11, 2002; Jeanne M. Connell, "Can Those Who Live in Poverty Find Liberation through the Humanities?" *Educational Studies* 39, no. 1 (2006): 15–26. Bruer relies heavily on Thomas Sticht, *Cast-Off Youth: Policy and Training Methods from the Military Experience* (New York: Praeger, 1987), a study that, as he acknowledges, is flawed.

51. Shonkoff and Phillips, *From Neurons to Neighborhoods,* 159. Chuansheng Chen et al., "Long-term Prediction of Academic Achievement of American, Chinese, and Japanese Adolescents," *Journal of Educational Psychology* 88, no. 4 (1996): 750–759; Jeanne Brooks-Gunn et al., "Who Drops Out of and Who Continues beyond High School? A 20-Year Follow-up of Black Urban Youth," *Journal of Research on Adolescence* 3, no. 3 (1993): 271–294. Ross Thompson, "New Directions for Child Development in the Twenty-First Century: The Legacy of Early Attachments," *Child Development* 71, no. 1 (2000): 145–152.

52. Gerald Edelman, *Bright Air, Brilliant Fire: On the Matter of the Mind* (New York: Basic Books, 1992), 17.

53. Matt McGue and Thomas Bouchard, "Genetic and Environmental Influences on Human Behavioral Difference," *Annual Review of Neuroscience* 21, no. 1 (1998): 1; Richard Arvey et al., "Mainstream Science on Intelligence," *Wall Street Journal,* December 13, 1994.

54. IQ, or intelligence quotient, is a familiar but problematic concept. Geneticists remain divided on the question of whether intelligence is a unified trait ("general intelligence," or "g," as it is called) or whether it is more appropriate to think of multiple types of intelligence (verbal, spatial, emotional, and so on) that we draw from to solve particular problems in specific domains. Still, many educators and psychologists rely on IQ as an important measure of mental ability.

55. Arthur Jensen, "How Much Can We Boost IQ and Scholastic Achievement," *Harvard Education Review* 39, no. 1 (1969): 1. Evolutionary biologist Richard Lewontin wryly points out that "according to [Jensen], it is not that his science and its practitioners have failed utterly to understand human motivation, behavior and development, but simply that the damn kids are ineducable." Richard Lewontin, "There Is No Evidence That IQ Differences between Races Are Genetic," in Tamara Roleff, ed., *Genetics and Intelligence* (San Diego: Greenhaven, 1996), 55.

56. Herrnstein and Murray, *The Bell Curve;* Deborah Toler, "The Right's 'Race Desk,'" *Fairness and Accuracy in Reporting* March/April 1999, *http://www.fair.org/index.php?page=1449.*

57. Claude Fischer et al., *Inequality by Design: Cracking the Bell Curve* (Princeton, NJ: Princeton University Press, 1995).

58. See Diane Paul, *Controlling Human Heredity* (Highlands, NJ: Humanities Press, 1995).

59. Richard Lerner, *Final Solution: Biology, Prejudice, and Genocide* (College Park: Pennsylvania State University Press, 1992).

60. On Binet and Terman, see Raymond Fancher, *The Intelligence Men: The Making of the IQ Controversy* (New York: Norton, 1987). Terman's approach reflects the earlier thinking of Francis Galton; see Galton, *Hereditary Genius* (London: Macmillan, 1869).

61. In an earlier study, children from orphanages had been placed in a preschool, and substantial IQ gains in the experimental group were reported. Helen Koch and Helen Barrett, "Some Effects of Nursery School Training upon Orphanage Children," *Journal of Home Economics* 21, no. 2 (1929): 365–367.

62. Harold M. Skeels et al., "A Study of Environmental Stimulation: An Orphanage Preschool Project," *Iowa Studies in Child Welfare* 15, no. 4 (1938); Harold M. Skeels, "Adult Status of Children with Contrasting Early Life Experiences: A Follow-up Study," *Monographs of the Society for Research in Child Development* 31, no. 4, serial 105 (1966). See also Beth L. Wellman and Edna Lee Pegram, "Binet IQ Changes of Orphanage Pre-school Children: A Re-analysis," *Journal of Genetic Psychology* 65, no. 2 (1944).

The methodology of the Iowa research was strongly criticized at the time. See Quentin McNemar, "A Critical Examination of the University of Iowa Studies of Environmental Influence upon IQ," *Psychological Bulletin* 37, no. 2 (1940): 63. McNemar combined personal attack with methodological critique; the Iowa researchers responded in kind. A 1948 report from the Berkeley Growth study largely confirmed the Iowa findings and "seems to have changed the thinking of many psychologists on the fixity of IQ." M. P. Honzick et al. "The Stability of Mental Test Performance between Two and Eighteen Years," *Journal of Experimental Education* 17, no. 2 (1948): 309–329; Joseph Hawes, "The Great IQ Wars," October 25, 1999, *http://www.connectforkids.org/node/ 137.* See, generally, Robert Sears, *Your Ancients Revisited: A History of Child Development* (Chicago: University of Chicago Press, 1975).

63. On infant intelligence testing, see Jeanne Brooks-Gunn and Stanley Weintraub, "Origins of Infant Intelligence Testing," in Michael Lewis, ed., *Origins of Intelligence: Infancy and Early Childhood* (New York: John Wiley, 1983), 25–66.

64. "Feeble-Minded Love," *Time*, May 13, 1939.

65. The single orphanage success story—the boy who went to college, got married, and became a typesetter—turned out to be the proverbial exception that confirmed the rule. Soon after the study began he was identified as deaf and was transferred to a residential school for the deaf. A short time later he was adopted.

66. Hamilton Cravens, *Before Head Start: The Iowa Station and America's Children* (Chapel Hill: University Press of North Carolina, 1993).

67. See, e.g., Michael Rutter and the English and Romanian Adoptees (ER) Study Team, "Developmental Catch-up, and Deficit, Following Adoption after Severe Global Early Deprivation," *Journal of Child Psychology and Psychiatry* 39, no. 4 (1998): 465; Samantha Wilson, "Post-Institutionalization: The Effects of Early Deprivation on Development of Romanian Adoptees," *Child and Adolescent Social Work Journal* 20, no. 6 (2003): 473. Charles Nelson, "Neural Plasticity and Human Development: The Role of Early Experience in Sculpting Memory Systems," *Developmental Science* 3, no. 2 (2000): 115.

68. The phrase "stalking the wild taboo" comes from *Intelligence: Knowns and Unknowns*. Report of a Task Force established by the Board of Scientific Affairs of the American Psychological Association, August 7, 1995, *http://lrainc.com/swtaboo/index.html*.

69. Christiane Capron and Michel Duyme, "Assessment of Effects of Socio-Economic Status on IQ," *Nature* 340 (1988): 6234.

70. Michel Duyme, "Discontinuity and Stability of IQs: The French Adoption Studies," in P. Lindsay Chase-Lansdale et al., eds., *Human Development across Lives and Generations: The Potential for Change* (New York: Cambridge University Press, 2004).

71. Sandra Scarr, "Developmental Theories for the 1990s: Development and Individual Differences," *Child Development* 63, no. 1 (1992): 1; this is a reprint of Scarr's presidential address to the Society for Research in Child Development, the main professional organization in the field. With the publication of Judith Harris, *The Nature Assumption: Why Children Turn Out the Way They Do* (New York: Free Press, 1998), the significance of the parents' role in child rearing was called into question. Genetic inheritance was the parents' real contribution, Harris asserted; children were said to learn more from their peers than their parents. But see W. Andrew Collins et al., "Contemporary Research on Parenting: The Case for Nature and Nurture," *American Psychologist* 55, no. 2 (2000): 218.

72. Eric Turkheimer et al., "Socioeconomic Status Modifies Hereditability of IQ in Young Children," *Psychological Science* 14, no. 6 (November 2003): 623.

73. William Kremen et al., "Hereditability of Word Recognition in Middle-Aged Men Varies as a Function of Parental Education," *Behavioral Genetics* 35, no. 4 (2005): 417.

74. Paige Harden, Eric Turkheimer, and John Loehlin, "Genotype by Environment Interaction in Adolescents' Cognitive Aptitude," *Behavioral Genetics*, forthcoming.

75. See Kimberly Noble et al., "Brain-Behavior Relationships in Reading Acquisition Are Modulated by Socioeconomic Factors," *Developmental Science* 9, no. 6 (2006): 642–654, at 642, 652.

76. Betty Hart and Todd Risley, *Meaningful Differences in the Everyday Experience of Young American Children* (Baltimore: Brookes, 1995).

77. James Flynn, "Searching for Justice: The Discovery of IQ Gains over Time," *American Psychologist* 34:1 (1999).

78. William Dickens and James Flynn, "Heritability Estimates versus Large Environmental Effects: The IQ Paradox Resolved," *Psychological Review* 108, no. 2 (2001): 346. Dickens uses basketball as an example: "Take those born with genes that make them a bit taller and quicker than average. When they start school, they are likely to be a bit better at basketball. The advantage may be modest but then reciprocal causation between the talent advantage and environment kicks in" (349).

   In a 2006 paper, Flynn and Dickens review a raft of data on the racial IQ gap. They find that between 1972 and 2002 blacks narrowed the gap by four to seven points. William T. Dickens and James R. Flynn, "Black Americans Reduce the Racial Gap: Evidence from Standardization Samples," *Psychological Science* 17, no. 10 (2006): 913–920.

79. See, generally, Lee Cronbach, "The Two Disciplines of Scientific Psychology," *American Psychologist* 12, no. 2 (1957): 671. On the research procedures in molecular genetics, see Robert Plomin and Michael Rutter, "Child Development, Molecular Genetics, and What to Do with Genes Once They Are Found," *Child Development* 69, no. 4 (1998): 1223–1242.

80. Miron Baron et al., "Diminished Support for Linkage between Manic Depressive Illness and X-Chromosome Markers," *Nature Genetics* 3 (1993): 49; Stephen Hodgkinson et al., "Molecular Genetic Evidence for Heterogeneity in Manic Depression," *Nature* 325 (February 2002): 805.

81. Michael Rutter, *Genes and Behavior* (Malden, MA: Blackwell, 2006), 174–175.

82. Significant earlier work using clinical diagnoses rather than genetic markers reached the same conclusion about gene-environment interaction. P. Tienari et al., "The Finnish Adoptive Family Study of Schizophrenia: Implications for Family Research," *British Journal of Psychiatry*

Supplementary Volume 23 (April 1994): 20. Much of the pioneering work on nature-nurture interaction was done by Michel Cadoret, a psychologist whose interests and influence spanned the field. See, e.g., Michel Cadoret et al., "Genetic-Environmental Interaction in the Genesis of Aggressivity and Conduct Disorders," *Archives of General Psychiatry* 52 (1995): 916–924; Michel Cadoret et al., "Adoption Study Demonstrating Two Genetic Pathways to Drug Abuse," *Archives of General Psychiatry* 52 (1995): 42–52.

83. Avshalom Caspi et al., "Role of Genotype in the Cycle of Violence in Maltreated Children," *Science* 297, August 2, 2002, 851; Avshalom Caspi et al., "Influence of Life Stress on Depression: Moderation by a Polymorphism in the 5-HTT Gene," *Science* 301 (July 18, 2003), 386. L. Keltikangas-Jarvinen et al., "Nature and Nurture in Novelty Seeking," *Molecular Psychiatry* 9 (2004): 208.

84. Michael Meaney, "Maternal Care, Gene Expression, and the Transmission of Individual Differences in Stress Reactivity across Generations," *Annual Review: Neuroscience* 24 (2001): 1161–1192. Meany is summarizing the work of L. G. Rusak and G. E. Schwartz, "Feelings of Parental Care Predict Health Status in Midlife: A 35-Year Follow-up of the Harvard Mastery of Stress Study," *Journal of Behavioral Medicine* 20, no. 1 (1997): 1, and Michael Rutter, "Protective Factors in Children's Responses to Stress and Disadvantage," *Primary Prevention and Psychopathology* 3, no. 49 (1979): 74.

85. Amy Hardon, "That Wild Streak? Maybe It Runs in the Family," *New York Times,* June 15, 2006, notes that daredevils are starting to credit, or blame, their genes for their reckless behavior, and parents are wondering whether it's their parenting skills or their genes that really matter. The answer is surely both.

86. See Steven Rose, "The Rise of Neurogenetic Determinism," *Nature* 373 (1995): 280. But compare Michael Rutter, "Nature, Nurture, and Development: From Evangelism through Science toward Policy and Practice," *Child Development* 73, no. 1 (January/February 2002): 1.

87. Plomin has been quoted as saying that he has unpublished data inconsistent with Eric Turkheimer's findings. It is unusual in science to attempt to rebut a colleague's argument without submitting one's own work to peer review. Rick Weiss, "Genes' Sway over IQ May Vary with Class; Study: Poor More Affected by Environment," *Washington Post,* September 2, 2003.

88. Rutter, "Nature, Nurture, and Development," 6.

89. Etienne Benson, "Breaking New Ground," *Monitor on Psychology* 34, no. 2 (February 2003): 52.

90. For an example of a study that reports finding a modest correlation between gene identification and intelligence, see Daniel Postdruma et al., "A Genome-wide Scan for Intelligence Identifies Quantifiable Trait Loci on 2q and 6," *American Journal of Human Genetics* 77 (2005): 318–326. For a review of the literature, see Ian Craig and Robert Plomin, "Quantitative Trait Loci for IQ and Other Complex Traits: Single-Nucleotide Polymorphism Genotyping Using Pooled DNA and Microarrays," *Genes, Brain, and Behavior* 5, Supplement 1 (2006): 32.

In one study, mice whose genetic makeup had been altered had better-than-average performance scores on memory tests, which are regarded as markers of mouse intelligence. But researchers later learned that this gain in intelligence had a cost: the extra-bright "Doogie" mice were more sensitive to chronic pain than ordinary mice. Deborah Stull, "Better Mouse Memory Comes at a Price," *Scientist* 15, no. 7 (April 2, 2001): 21.

91. Plomin, Turkheimer, and Garlick quoted in "The First Gene Marker for IQ?" *Science* 20 (May 1, 1998): 5364.

92. Rutter, *Genes and Behavior.*

93. Jeremy Gray and Paul Thompson, "Neurobiology of Intelligence: Science and Ethics," *Nature Reviews Neuroscience* 5 (June 2004): 471–482. On cognitive psychology, see Gopnik, Meltzoff, and Kuhl, *The Scientist in the Crib.* David Reiss et al., *The Relationship Code* (Cambridge, MA: Harvard University Press, 2000).

94. See the overview in Maxwell Cowan, Donald Harter, and Eric Kandel, "The Emergence of Modern Neuroscience: Some Implications for Neurology and Psychiatry," *Annual Review of Neuroscience* 23 (2000): 343–391.

95. Edward O. Wilson, *Consilience: The Unity of Knowledge* (New York: Alfred A. Knopf, 1998), 11.

5. Who Cares for the Children?

1. Sally Cohen, *Championing Child Care* (New York: Columbia University, 2001); Geraldine Youcha, *Minding the Children: Child Care in America from Colonial Times to the Present* (Cambridge MA: DaCapo, 1995)

2. Hillary Clinton, *It Takes a Village* (New York: Simon and Schuster, 1996).

3. William Gormley, *Everybody's Children: Child Care as a Public Problem* (Washington, DC: Brookings Institution, 1995).

4. A 1999 Department of Health and Human Services report documented substantial variations in state generosity. Cohen, *Championing Child Care,* 236.

5. Quoted in Melissa Healy, "Child Care to Get Brief Spotlight at a Crucial Time," *Los Angeles Times,* October 23, 1997, 1.

6. Jane Waldfogel, *What Children Need* (Cambridge, MA: Harvard University Press, 2006), 45–62. "Children tend to do worse [in measures of health, cognitive development, and social and emotional well-being] if their mothers work full-time in the first year of life" (61). But see Margaret Burchinal and Alison Clarke-Stewart, "Maternal Employment and Child Cognitive Outcomes: The Importance of an Analytic Approach," unpublished manuscript, University of California, Irvine, 2006.

   On maternal employment, see Lois Hoffman and Lisa Youngblade, eds., *Mothers at Work: Effects on Children's Well-Being* (New York: Cambridge University Press, 1999); Eugene Smolensky and Jennifer Gootman, eds., *Working Families and Growing Kids: Caring for Children and Adolescents* (Washington, DC: National Academies Press, 2003).

   California is the only state that offers up to six weeks' paid parental leave. The 1993 federal Family and Medical Leave Act enables parents to take unpaid leave, but 40 percent of all parents, those who work for companies with fewer than fifty employees, are not covered. National Partnership for Women and Families, *Expecting Better: A State-by-State Analysis of Paternal Leave Programs* (Washington, DC: National Partnership for Women and Families, 2005), *http://72.14.253.104/ search?q=cache:XY6wRGeutKQJ: www.nationalpartnership.org/default .aspx%3Ftabname%3Dlibrary%26fileid%3D224+parental+leave+califor nia&hl=en&gl=us&ct=clnk&cd=2.*

7. "The Kaiser Child Service Centers: An Interview with Lois Meek Stolz," in James Hymes, Jr., et al., eds., *Living History Interviews, Book Two: Care of the Children of Working Mothers* (Carmel, CA: Hacienda Press, 1979), 28. The discussion of the Kaiser centers is drawn from this account and from "Child Service Centers, 1943–1945, Final Report," December 1, 1945, p. 2 (unpublished), in Lois Stolz Papers, MS C 414, History of Medicine Division, National Library of Medicine, Bethesda, MD. See, generally, *www.nlm.nih.gov/hmd/manuscripts/ead/stolz.html.*

8. Quoted in Sonya Michel, *Children's Interests/Mothers' Rights: The Shaping of America's Child Care Policy* (New Haven, CT: Yale University Press, 1999), 143; this is a superb political history of child care. Alison Clarke-Stewart and Virginia Allhusen, *What We Know about Childcare* (Cambridge, MA: Harvard University Press, 2005), offers a valuable overview of the child care literature.

9. "Nurseries Solve Big Problem for Mothers in Kaiser Shipyards," *New York Times,* November 17, 1944, 16.

10. Hymes et al., *Living History Interviews,* 44.

11. James L. Hymes, Jr., *Teaching the Child under Six* (Columbus, OH: Charles E. Merrill, 1968), chap. 1.

12. "Child Service Centers, 1943–1945, Final Report," 2.

13. Oregon Shipbuilding Corporation, "Child Service Centers: An Experiment in Services for Employees," unpublished manuscript (no date), on file in History of Medicine Division, National Library of Medicine, Bethesda, MD.

14. Hymes et al., *Living History Interviews*, 55.

15. See, e.g., Jeanne Brooks-Gunn et al., "Depending on the Kindness of Strangers: Current National Data Initiatives and Developmental Research," *Child Development* 71, no. 2 (2000): 257–268; David Blau, *The Child Care Problem: An Economic Analysis* (New York: Russell Sage Foundation, 2001). Surveys show that child care support more than pays for itself. See, e.g., Leon C. Litchfield et al., "Increasing the Visibility of the Invisible Workforce: Model Programs and Policies for Hourly and Lower Wage Employees," Boston College Center for Work and Family, 2004. But aside from some Fortune 500 corporations or those on *Working Mother* magazine's list of "best places to work," few firms provide such support.

16. Because of budget constraints, Head Start has never served more than 60 percent of eligible children. Clarke-Stewart and Allhusen, *What We Know about Childcare*, 34.

17. Lois Meek Stolz, "The Nursery Comes to the Shipyard," *New York Times Sunday Magazine*, November 7, 1943, 20.

18. Perry Preschool's David Weikart confronted such doubts when he proposed his early education program for poor three- and four-year-old children; see Chapter 2.

19. For discussion of the research conducted by the University of Iowa Child Welfare Research Station in the 1930s, see Chapter 4.

20. The welfare-to-work requirement was initiated by President John Kennedy. See Ron Haskins, "Child Development and Child-Care Policy: Modest Impacts," in David Pillemer and Sheldon White, eds., *Developmental Psychology and Social Change: Research, History and Policy* (New York: Cambridge University Press, 2005), 140–170; quotation on 147. Child care encompasses all nonparental care from birth to adolescence, including after-school and summer programs, not just the care of infants and toddlers. The amorphousness of child care, as contrasted with preschool, a school-day (or half-day) program to educate three- and four-year-olds, adds another layer of complication to the issue.

21. This history has been recounted many times. See, e.g., Michel, *Children's Interests/Mothers' Rights;* Cohen, *Championing Child Care;* Gilbert Steiner,

The Children's Cause (Washington, DC: Brookings Institution Press, 1976).

22. *Congressional Record*, Daily Edition, December 10, 1971, pp. S 21129–21130. The veto message included a number of other objections to the bill, including the cost of the legislation and its administrative unwieldiness.

23. See, generally, Clarke-Stewart and Allhusen, *What We Know about Childcare*; Waldfogel, *What Children Need*.

In 2003 the National Research Council and the Institute of Medicine, which had earlier published the influential book *From Neurons to Neighborhoods* summarizing the research in brain science, released a similarly trenchant volume, Eugene Smolensky and Jennifer Appleton Gootman, eds., *Working Families and Growing Kids* (Washington, DC: National Academies Press, 2003), but it had considerably less impact.

24. Joan Lombardi, *Time to Care: Redesigning Child Care* (Philadelphia: Temple University Press, 2003), 46–48.

25. Ralph E. Smith, *The Subtle Revolution: Women at Work* (Washington, DC: Urban Institute, 1979). Ellen Goodman, "The End of Motherhood as We Knew It," *Boston Globe*, September 17, 1995, 39.

26. Jonathan Alter, "Making Child Care Macho," *Newsweek*, November 3, 1997, 70.

27. Lombardi, *Time to Care*, 48.

28. Haskins, "Child Development and Child-Care Policy," 168.

29. Smolensky and Gootman, *Working Families and Growing Kids*, 50. Louise Stoney, *Looking into New Mirrors: Lessons for Early Childhood Finance and System-Building* (Boston: Horizons Initiative, 1998); Karen Schulman, *The High Cost of Child Care Puts Quality Care Out of Reach for Many Families* (Washington, DC: Children's Defense Fund, 2000).

30. Harriet Presser, *Working in a 24/7 Economy* (New York: Russell Sage Foundation, 2003).

31. Eleanor Galinsky et al., *The Study of Children in Family Child Care and Relative Care* (New York: Families and Work Institute, 1994).

32. Mary Dublin Keyserling, *Windows on Day Care* (New York: National Council on Jewish Women, 1972); Galinsky et al., *The Study of Children in Family Child Care and Relative Care*.

33. Blau, *The Child Care Problem*, 29; Melissa Healy, "Child Care to Get Brief Spotlight at a Crucial Time," *Los Angeles Times*, October 23, 1997, 1.

In August 2006 the Institute of Industrial Relations at Berkeley released a report on the qualifications of those working in licensed child care centers and homes in California. "Wages are low [about $10 an hour for the highest paid assistants]; turnover is 26 percent a year

[less than the national average, which is more than 30 percent] . . .
Given the documented relation between staffing stability and program
quality, the persistence of high turnover in California's early childhood
education workforce is of serious concern." Center for the Study of
Child Care Employment, *California Early Care and Education Workforce
Study* (Berkeley: Institute of Industrial Relations, University of California at Berkeley, 2006), 10. See also Suzanne Helburn, ed., *Cost, Quality
and Child Outcomes in Child Care Centers* (Denver: Center for Research
in Economic and Social Policy, University of Colorado, 1995). See, generally, Stephen Herzenberg et al., *Losing Ground in Early Childhood
Education: Declining Workforce Qualifications in an Expanding Industry,
1979–2004* (Washington, DC: Economic Policy Institute, 2004).

34. Lombardi, *Time to Care.*

35. Deborah Lowe Vandell and Barbara Wolfe, "Child Care Quality: Does
It Matter and Does It Need to Be Improved?" report prepared for
the U.S. Department of Health and Human Services, 2000, available
at *http://aspe.hhs.gov/hsp/ccquality00/index.htm;* Jack Shonkoff and
Deborah Phillips, *From Neurons to Neighborhoods: The Science of Early
Childhood Development* (Washington, DC: National Academy Press,
2000), 315–317; Waldfogel, *What Children Need,* 11–126; J. Arnett,
"Caregivers in Day-Care Centers: Does Training Matter?" *Journal
of Applied Developmental Psychology* 10, no. 3 (1989): 541–552; Marcy
Whitebook et al., *Who Cares? Child Care Teachers and the Quality of Care
in America: Final Report,* National Child Care Staffing Study (Oakland,
CA: Child Care Employee Project, 1989); Robert Pianta, ed., *Beyond
the Parent: The Role of Other Adults in Children's Lives* (San Francisco:
Jossey-Bass, 1992); Marcy Whitebook and Laura Sakai, "Turnover Begets Turnover: An Examination of Job and Occupational Instability
among Child Care Center Staff," *Early Childhood Research Quarterly* 18,
no. 3 (2004): 273–293. Helburn et al., *Cost, Quality and Child Outcomes
in Child Care Centers.*

36. See, e.g., Blau, *The Child Care Problem;* Lombardi, *Time to Care;* Ed-
ward Zigler and Matia Finn-Stevenson, *Schools of the Twenty-First
Century: Linking Child Care and Education* (Boulder, CO: Westview,
1999); W. Steven Barnett, "New Wine in Old Bottles: Increasing
Coherence in Early Childhood Care and Education Policy," *Early
Childhood Research Quarterly* 8, no. 4 (1993): 519–558; James Walker,
"Funding Child Rearing: Child Allowance and Parental Leave," *The
Future of Children* 6, no. 2 (1996): 122–136; Sharon Kagan and Nancy
Cohen, eds., *Reinventing Early Care and Education: A Vision for a Qual-
ity System* (San Francisco: Jossey-Bass, 1996); Suzanne Helburn and

Barbara Bergmann, *America's Child Care Problem: The Way Out* (New York: Palgrave, 2002). Haskins, "Child Development and Child-Care Policy," focuses on what's politically achievable rather than what's ideal, and proposes incremental rather than wholesale changes in the existing system.

37. Albert Kahn and Sheila Kamerman, *Child Care: Facing the Hard Choices* (Dover, MA: Auburn House, 1987).

38. The Abecedarian Project, a model program, had in fact enrolled children from infancy, but because many of them remained in the program through kindergarten, its results were construed as bolstering the argument for preschool; see Chapter 2.

6. Jump-Starting a Movement

1. The research and writing of this book were supported by grants from the Pew Charitable Trusts and the Packard Foundation. Since both foundations have played an important role in structuring and underwriting the preschool movement, any account that didn't describe their part would be incomplete. But the fact that I am writing about my benefactors unavoidably raises red flags. In this chapter, as in the rest of the book, I have tried for balance, neither pulling punches nor throwing haymakers. Ultimately it's up to the reader to decide whether I have succeeded.

2. Quoted in Mark Schmitt, "Kids Aren't Us," *American Prospect*, June 29, 2004.

3. National Commission on Children, *Beyond Rhetoric: A New Agenda for Children and Families*, 1991, www.eric.ed.gov/sitemap/html_0900000b8004d9b3.html.

4. Carnegie Task Force on Meeting the Needs of Young Children, *Starting Points*, 1995, http://www.carnegie.org/startingpoints/index.html.

5. Bruce Schimmel, "Thanks and No Thanks," *Philadelphia City Paper*, November 24–December 1, 2005, http://www.ushistory.org/presidentshouse/news/cp112405.htm.

6. For some years, the Foundation for Child Development (FCD) and the Ford Foundation funded studies of how children learn. FCD has supported initiatives to influence the policy conversation, but its budget is only about 10 percent of Pew's. In recent years it has focused on efforts to link preschool with early elementary education. See Gene Maeroff, *Building Blocks: Making Children Successful in the Early Years of School* (New York: Palgrave Macmillan, 2006).

7. Helen Blank, a senior staffer at the Children's Defense Fund for many years and one of the most respected children's advocates in Washington,

wrote a memo for the National Association for the Education of Young Children in 1983 that laid out a strategy for making prekindergarten a priority issue. Back then, however, no one was listening.

8. The environmental movement depends so heavily on Pew's support that Beth Daley of the National Committee for Responsive Philanthropy jokingly told the *National Journal,* "We should have a Pew liberation front committed to getting environmental organizations off the Pew dole." Quoted in Martin Wooster, "Too Good to Be True," *Wall Street Journal* (April 1, 2005).

9. See., e.g., Peter D. Hart Research Associates, *Voters' Attitudes toward Pre-K, October 2005 Survey,* a research study commissioned by Pre-K Now. The polls that Pre-K Now has commissioned are proprietary and were provided to the author.

10. Luntz, Maslansky Strategic Research, *Research Findings: An Overview,* December 8, 2005, report commissioned by the Center for Community Solutions and Ohio Early Care and Education Campaign.

11. Thomas Frank, *What's the Matter with Kansas?* (New York: Henry Holt, 2004).

12. The Joyce Foundation has also supported preschool policy initiatives. In 2003 it committed $6 million to promote universal access to pre-K in several Midwestern states.

13. The account of the preschool movement in California is fleshed out in Chapter 7.

14. The Packard Foundation commissioned the Rand Corporation to assess the economic impact of universal, high-quality preschool in California. Its estimate—a $2.62 return for every dollar invested—is in line with what similar studies from other states have shown. Rand Corporation, *The Costs and Benefits of Universal Preschool in California* (Santa Monica, CA: Rand, 2005).

15. See, generally, Chris Argyris and Donald Schon, *Organizational Learning II* (Reading, MA: Addison-Wesley 1996).

16. Darcy Olsen, "Assessing Proposals for Preschool and Kindergarten: Essential Information for Parents, Taxpayers, and Policymakers," *http:// www.goldwaterinstitute.org/article.php/542.html.*

17. Art Rolnick and Darcy Olsen, "Early Childhood Education: A Conversation," *www.americanexperiment.org/uploaded/files/aeq2005 springrolnickolsen.pdf.*

18. Matt Bai, "The Framing Wars," *New York Times Magazine,* July 9, 2005.

19. Frank Luntz, "The Fourteen Words Never to Use" (2005), quoted in *www.pbs.org/NOW/transcript 330_full.html.* Berkeley linguist George

Lakoff, who is widely credited as being the intellectual godfather of framing, offers a more detailed example of the subconscious nature of the process by which frames get absorbed, as well as the hidden process by which they can be manufactured and altered. "If you have something like 'revolt,' that implies a population that is being ruled unfairly, or assumes it is being ruled unfairly, and that they are throwing off their rulers, which would be considered a good thing. That's a frame," he says. But manipulate the language, "add the word 'voter' in front of 're-volt,' and you get a metaphorical meaning saying that the voters are the oppressed people, the governor is the oppressive ruler, that they have ousted him and this is a good thing and all things are good now. All of that comes up when you see a headline like 'voter revolt'—something that most people read and never notice." See Bonnie Azab Powell, "Framing the Issues: UC Berkeley Professor George Lakoff Tells How Conservatives Use Language to Dominate Politics," Berkeley News-Center, October 27, 2003, *http://www.berkeley.edu/news/media/releases/2003/10/27_lakoff.shtml.*

20. See George Lakoff, *Don't Think of an Elephant: Know Your Values and Frame the Debate—The Essential Guide for Progressives* (White River Junction, VT: Chelsea Green, 2004).

21. Lori Dorfman, *Framing the Economic Benefits of Investments in Early Childhood Development* (Berkeley: Media Studies Group, n.d.), *http://www.gcyf.org/library/library_show.htm?doc_id=365368.*

22. Aber adds that, "as always, Progressives lack synergies of scale. Everyone does one survey a year and pays the entire cost. But there's no powerful force to bring people together, sharing the costs of research and polling. Pew and Packard have bought into the super-frame of proprietary information, working for a client. That's the business model, the opposite of a scientific community." Reading the results of polls on preschool conducted in numerous states, each asking slightly different questions, with little aggregation of the results, confirms Aber's point that, in this field, less really would be more.

23. The Pew and Packard foundations have modified their philosophical preference for preschool for all children in light of on-the-ground realities, which sometimes make an incremental approach like selective universalism more feasible in the short term. See Chapter 7.

24. I am indebted to Lawrence Aber for developing this argument.

7. The Politics of the Un-Dramatic

1. In recent State of the State or budget addresses, a number of governors have cited research evidence of the benefits of preschool education

to support pre-K initiatives. Governor Timothy Kaine of Virginia, who made pre-K a major issue in his successful 2005 campaign, urged expansion of pre-K and other early childhood initiatives in 2006, commenting that "research demonstrates that children with access to prekindergarten have greater success in school, and throughout life, and require fewer social services, special education, or criminal justice intervention." Governor Rod R. Blagojevich of Illinois pointed to specific achievement and economic outcomes when announcing his Preschool for All initiative in 2006: "Countless studies demonstrate the benefits of early learning in preschool. Students who begin reading at age three or four do better throughout their academic careers. Students who attend preschool are 20 percent more likely to graduate high school, 41 percent less likely to need special education, and 42 percent less likely to be arrested for committing a violent crime. Studies also show that for every dollar spent on early childhood education, society saves at least seven dollars through decreased reliance on social services." Similar scientific evidence, particularly the results of the High/Scope Perry Preschool study, also encouraged Governor Michael Rounds of South Dakota to include state funding for preschool education for four-year-olds as part of his 2010 Education Initiative in 2006. In calling for increased funding to serve 3,000 more children in high-quality preschool programs, Governor Linda Lingle of Hawaii stated, "Study after study has shown that early childhood education is a key to success later in life." Similarly, Governor Kathleen Blanco of Louisiana called on the legislature to provide an additional $20 million to expand that state's LA-4 pre-K program: "Study after study shows that reaching and teaching children at an early age equals success in school and later in life." *Securing Access to Preschool Education* (Newark, NJ: Starting at Three, 2006), *http:// www.startingat3.org/research/index.html.*

2. A good argument could be made for looking at other states, among them Arkansas, which the National Institute for Early Education Research ranks as number one in terms of the quality of its preschools; New Jersey, where preschool in poor school districts came about because of a court order; West Virginia, which has put in place a program that guarantees to provide preschool for every child within a decade; Georgia, the pioneering state, which enrolls the country's highest percentage of its children in pre-K classes; and New York, where 1996 universal preschool legislation wasn't implemented (as of 2006). Some of those histories have been recounted elsewhere, while others await their bard (or political scientist).

3. The nickname comes from a historical event: when the federal govern-

ment authorized settlers to stake claims in 1889, some had jumped the gun, coming *sooner* to the new territory.

4. Maureen Dowd, "The Red Zone," *New York Times*, November 4, 2004, *http://www.nytimes.com/2004/11/04/opinion/04dowd*.

5. "Children's Defense Fund Action Council Scorecard Ranks Lawmakers on How Well They Protect Children," May 2005, *www.commondreams.org/news2005/0323–01.htm*.

6. "Oklahoma Social Indicator Survey," Bureau of Social Research, Oklahoma State University, 2004. (Nearly three-fourths of those surveyed favored government helping all children needing child care, regardless of their families' wealth.)

7. Head Start runs some of the pre-K classes in Oklahoma; if the Head Start is located in a public school, those teachers receive K–12 teachers' pay, but if the Head Start program is separate, its salaries are lower. The state is, over time, eliminating that difference and equalizing the degree requirements.

8. Sandy Garrett, *Investing in Oklahoma 2005: The Progress in Educational Reform*, *www.sde.sate.ok.us* (2006).

9. The Tulsa study is discussed at length in Chapter 2.

10. Only Florida, Oklahoma, and Georgia make pre-K available to all four-year-olds. West Virginia and New York have plans on the books to do so; *http://www.preknow.org/policy/factsheets/snapshot.cfm*.

11. Carl Hiassen, *Paradise Screwed* (New York: G. P. Putnam's, 2001).

12. Bill Kaczor, "Florida Lags in No Child Left Behind," *Naples News*, August 20, 2006.

13. See *Bush v. Holmes*, 767 So. 2d 668 (2006).

14. James Q. Wilson, *The Politics of Regulation* (New York: Basic Books, 1980).

15. Jim Hampton, "How Florida's Voters Enacted UPK When Their Legislature Wouldn't," 2004, *http://www.teachmorelovemore.org/UPK_Report.asp*.

16. Ibid.

17. Editorial, "Florida Pre-K Program Rates an Incomplete," *St. Petersburg Times*, July 31, 2006.

18. Susan Pareigis, "State's Pre-K Program Exceeds Goal," *Tampa Tribune*, October 20, 2005.

19. Steve Barnett, "What Kind of Pre-K House Hath Florida Built?" *Hernando (FL) Today*, August 25, 2006.

20. The Palm Beach material is taken from Sonja Isger, "Faith-Based Pre-K Programs Thrive with State Money," *Palm Beach Post*, March 5, 2006.

21. David Lawrence, Keynote Address, First National Conference on the

Law and Politics of Universal Preschool, Loyola Law Center, Loyola University, October 13, 2006, *www.luc.edu/law/academies/special/center/children/law_policy_preschool.shtml.*

22. James Ryan, "A Constitutional Right to Preschool," *California Law Review* 94, no. 1 (2006): 49.

23. In an exchange on the floor of the Texas Senate that stunned the lawmakers into momentary silence, one senator was moved to ask a colleague who was hurling verbal Molotov cocktails at public education, "Is there really a heart beating underneath that buttoned-down shirt?"

24. See *http://www.statesman.com/opinion/content/editorial/05/5cheerleader_edit.html.*

25. See, e.g., Kevin Hula, *Lobbying Together* (Washington, DC: Georgetown University Press, 1999); Michael Heaney, "Brokering Health Policy: Coalitions, Parties, and Influence Group Influence," *Journal of Health Politics, Policy and Law* 31, no. 5 (2006).

26. Jamie Story, "Universal Pre-K? A Losing Proposition," Texas Public Policy Foundation, July 19, 2006.

27. Lori Taylor et al., "A Cost-Benefit Analysis of Universally Accessible Pre-Kindergarten Education in Texas," Bush School of Government, Texas A&M University, May 2006.

28. Eugene Bardach, *Getting Agencies to Work Together* (Washington, DC: Brookings Institution Press, 2004).

29. In 2006 the program's advocates were able to add a new category of children to the rolls of state pre-K; see Chapter 9.

30. Peter Schrag, *Paradise Lost: California's Experience, America's Future* (Berkeley: University of California Press, 1999).

31. Chapter 4 details Reiner's interest in neuroscientific research and involvement with children's policy.

32. Tim Cavanagh, "Meathead Start," *Reason* Online, August 22, 2002, *http://www.reason.com/hod/tc082202.shtml.*

33. "Hot Topic: Proposition 82: Universal Preschool," Institute of Governmental Studies, University of California, Berkeley, July 14, 2006, *http://www.igs.berkeley.edu/library/htUniversalPreschool.html.*

34. Lynn Karoly and James Bigelow, *The Economics of Investing in Universal Preschool Education in California* (Santa Monica, CA: Rand, 2005).

35. Dan Morain, "TV Ads Put Focus on Reiner; Some Ask Whether the Tax-Funded Spots Helped Tout the Producer's June Preschool Initiative," *Los Angeles Times*, February 20, 2006.

36. Editorial, "Accountability for Beginners," *Los Angeles Times*, February 21, 2006.

37. Dana Hull, "Voters Reject Prop. 82," *San Jose Mercury News*, June 7,

2006, *http://www.mercurynews.com/mld/mercurynews/news/local/states/california/the_valley/14759361.htm.*

38. California Primary Election, Official Voter Information Guide, "Text of Proposed Law: Proposition 82," August 3, 2006, *http://voterguide.ss.ca.gov/props/prop82/prop82_text_proposed_laws.htm.*

39. Editorial, "Times Endorsements; For the Primary Ballot," *Los Angeles Times,* June 4, 2006.

40. Ibid.

41. Philip Matier and Andrew Ross, "Teachers' Union Questions Staging of 'No on 82' Ads," *San Francisco Chronicle,* May 21, 2006.

42. See, e.g., Bruce Fuller, "The Preschool 'Spin'; Claims That Prop. 82 Could Lift Enrollments and Help All Children Don't Hold Up," *Los Angeles Times,* April 4, 2006; "No Toddler Left Behind?" *Sacramento Bee,* national edition, May 7, 2006, E1. Fuller subsequently published a book that elaborates his views; see Bruce Fuller, *Standardized Childhood: The Political and Cultural Struggle over Early Education* (Palo Alto: Stanford University Press, 2007).

From the department of full disclosure: I participated in the ongoing public discussion of Proposition 82, as what might best be described as a critical friend of the measure. In December 2005, I wrote an op-ed in the *Los Angeles Times* summarizing the studies on the effects of preschool; David Kirp, "Universal Preschool's Big Payoff," *Los Angeles Times,* December 7, 2005. In March 2006 I was asked by the Packard Foundation to organize a conference of preschool experts for the California media. Because of the foundation's legal status, discussion of the ballot measure was explicitly off-limits. In May 2006 I debated Bruce Fuller on several occasions and coauthored an opinion piece, with the dean of the Stanford School of Education, that supported the ballot measure. See David Kirp and Deborah Stipek, "Preschool Is a Smart Investment," *San Francisco Chronicle,* June 1, 2006, *http://www.sfgate.com/cgi-bin/article.cgi?file=/chronicle/archive/2006/06/01/EDGDOIJM8F1.DTL.* I was interviewed by members of the editorial boards of the *San Francisco Chronicle* and the *Sacramento Bee* as they were deciding what position to take on the ballot measure, and was later asked by KQED radio, a public station in San Francisco, to comment on the election results. While I would have favored a simpler measure that simply committed California to developing a high-quality universal preschool program, and I publicly criticized many of the details of Proposition 82, I supported it because I saw it as far preferable to the status quo in the state. I leave it to the readers to decide whether my involvement has prejudiced my judgment of the campaign.

43. Carrie Sturrock, "Preschool Study Finds Bright Side, Dark Side; It

Helps Language, Math—Can Hurt Social Development," *San Francisco Chronicle*, November 1, 2005.

44. Michael Boskin, "Off and Running: Quit Taxing the Rich to Fund Your Pet Projects," *Los Angeles Times*, May 28, 2006.

45. David Brooks, "Good Intentions, Bad Policy." *New York Times*, June 4, 2006.

46. Arnold Schwarzenegger, "Transcript of Governor Arnold Schwarzenegger's Remarks at Herman Leimbach Elementary School, Tuesday, June 13, 2006, *http://www.governor.ca.gov/state/govsite/gov_htmldisplay.jsp?sCat Title=Speeches&sFilePath=/govsite/selected_speeches/20060613_Herman _Leimbach.html&sTitle=2006&iOID=79242*.

47. The proposal also called for a one-time expenditure of $50 million for new preschools and teacher training.

48. The Democratic gubernatorial candidates carried both states in the 2006 election.

49. Quoted in "Budget 2004," *Financial Mail*, *http://free.financialmail.co.za/ budget2004/index.html*.

50. David Tyack, *The One Best System: A History of American Urban Education* (Cambridge, MA: Harvard University Press, 1972).

51. Pragmatically, a public-private system is often a necessity, since the already-overcrowded public schools don't have the space to house classes for three- and four-year-olds.

52. Ryan, "A Constitutional Right to Preschool."

53. See *www.governor.ca.gov/state/govsite/gov_htmldisplay.jsp?sCatTitle= Speeches&sFilePath=/govsite/selected_speeches/ 20060613_Herman_Leimbach.html&sTitle=2006&iOID=79242*.

8. English Lessons

1. A study contrasting the effects on later school performance of attending an *école maternelle* starting at age two versus age three finds remarkable differences. Based on measures of cognitive and language skills as well as behavioral measures, all children benefited; children from the least advantaged families benefited the most. No "fadeout effect" was recorded. The test-score gains actually increased over time. See E. D. Hirsch, Jr., "Equity Effects of Early Schooling in France," *www .coreknowledge.org/CK/Preschool/frenchequity.htm*. At the time the study was undertaken, it was assumed that the powerful benefits of starting at age three were already established. M. Dutoit, "L'enfant et l'école: Aspects synthétiques due suivi d'un échantillon de vingt mille élèves des écoles," *Education et Formations* 16, no. 1 (1988): 3–13, cited in Hirsch, ibid.

2. See, e.g., *Ready to Learn: The French System of Early Education and*

Care Offers Lessons for the United States (New York: French American Foundation, 1999). John Merrow's documentary film, *The Promise of Preschool* (2002), *www.pbs.org/merrow/preschool/index.html*, vividly contrasts the French and American experiences. Sheldon Danziger and Jane Waldfogel, eds., *Securing the Future: Investing in Children from Birth to Adulthood* (New York: Russell Sage Foundation, 2000), provides insightful comparative analysis. Harold Wilensky, *Rich Democracies: Political Economy, Public Policy, and Performance* (Berkeley: University of California Press, 2003), is a detailed and illuminating account of the structural differences among postindustrial democracies. See also Peter Evans, Dietrich Rueschemeyer, and Theda Skocpol, eds., *Bringing the State Back In* (New York: Cambridge University Press, 1985).

3. John Hills, "The Blair Government: An Extra One Percent for Child Poverty in the United Kingdom," in Isabel Sawhill, ed., *One Percent for the Kids* (Washington, DC: Brookings Institution, 2003).

4. Steven Tales, "Can New Labor Dance the Clinton?" *American Prospect*, April 1, 1997.

5. Jared Bernstein and Mark Greenberg, "A Plan to End Child Poverty," *Washington Post*, April 3, 2006. See, generally, Michael Tomasky, "Party in Search of a Notion," *American Prospect*, May 3, 2006.

6. See John Hills and Kitty Stewart, eds., *A More Equal Society* (Bristol, UK: Policy Press, 2004); Anthony Seldon and Dennis Kavanagh, eds., *The Blair Effect 2001–2005* (Cambridge: Cambridge University Press 2005).

7. Polly Toynbee and David Walker, *Did Things Get Better?* (London: Penguin, 2001), 10.

8. *Guardian*, March 17, 2000.

9. Mike Brewer and Paul Gregg, *Eradicating Child Poverty in Britain: Welfare Reform and Children since 1997* (London: Institute for Fiscal Studies, 2001).

10. "Introduction," in Hills and Stewart, *A More Equal Society*.

11. See *http://www.the-weekly.net/display_archive.asp?c=294*, March 24, 2006.

12. HM Treasury, *Tackling Child Poverty* (London: HM Treasury, 2001), iii.

13. See David Card and Alan Krueger, *Myth and Measurement: The New Economics of the Minimum Wage* (Princeton, NJ: Princeton University Press, 1995).

14. Surprisingly few families—15 percent of eligible couples, 24 percent of single parents—have taken advantage of the program. National Audit Office, *Early Years* (London: The Stationery Office, 2004).

15. Rupert Jones, "Nest-Egg Scheme Hatched," *Guardian*, April 10, 2003.

16. Poverty is defined, for these purposes, as 60 percent of the national me-

dian income. This makes "ending child poverty" a moving—and almost impossible to reach—target. "Aspiration" would be a better description.

17. Polly Toynbee, "Our Children Deserve the Best, So We Must Be Prepared to Pay Up," *Guardian*, April 7, 2006.

18. See *www.chester.ac.uk/cphr/resources/new_steps.pdf.*

19. Polly Toynbee, "Labour's Best Achievement Hangs in the Balance, But They Do Nothing," *Guardian*, June 30, 2006; compare *www.number-10.gov.uk/output/page10158.asp* (October 5, 2006).

20. National Evaluation of Sure Start, *The Impact of Sure Start Local Programmes on Child Development and Family Functioning: A Report on Child Preliminary Findings* (London: Institute for the Study of Children, Families and Social Issues, Birkbeck College, 2005); National Audit Office, *Value for Money: Sure Start Children's Centres, http://www.nao.org.uk/publications/nao_reports/06–07/0607104es.htmhttp://www.surestart.gov.uk/research/evaluations/ness/latestreports/* (December 2006).

21. This almost happened to Head Start after the Westinghouse Learning Corporation released it unflattering study of Head Start in 1969. The Westinghouse study is discussed in Chapter 2.

22. Department for Work and Pensions, Benefit Expenditure Tables, Departmental Report 2003, *www.dwp.gov.uk/publications/dwp/2003/dwpreport/pdfs/chapter6.pdf.*

23. The economics of running a private center are difficult: each year about half as many centers close as new centers are opened. Kathy Sylva and Gillian Pugh, "Transforming the Early Years in England," *Oxford Review of Education* 31, no. 1 (March 2005): 18.

24. Department for Education and Skills, "Every Child Matters," *www.everychildmatters.gov.uk/_files/F9E3F941DC8D4580539EE4C743E9371D.pdf.*

25. Organization for Economic Cooperation and Development, *Education at a Glance* (OECD Publishing, Centre for Educational Research and Innovation, 2005).

26. See *education.guardian.co.uk/schools/story/0,,1775622,00.html* (June 2006); *www.number10.gov.uk/output/Page10158.asp* (October 2006).

27. Sylva and Pugh, "Transforming the Early Years in England," 13.

28. Ibid.

29. Carol Aubrey, "Implementing the Foundation Stage in Reception Classes," *British Educational Research Journal* 20, no. 5 (2004).

30. The Effective Provision of Pre-School Education Project, "Effective Preschool Education," *www.ioe.ac.uk/cdl/eppe.*

31. *Equality of Educational Opportunity Study* (Washington, DC: U.S. Department of Health, Education, and Welfare, 1996) is the landmark

American study on this issue. Whether preschool should be universal or targeted is discussed in Chapter 3.

32. Heckman's work is discussed in Chapter 3.

33. Office for Standards in Education, *Early Years: The National Picture* (London: Ofsted Publications Centre, 2003).

34. Toynbee, "Our Children Deserve the Best, So We Must Be Prepared to Pay Up."

35. Karen Gold, "Sure Start, Sure Finish," *Guardian*, November 21, 2006, *http://education.guardian.co.uk/earlyyears/story/0,,1952808,00.html.*

9. Kids-First Politics

1. While North Carolina prides itself on being the most politically modern state in the South, its progressivism is relative. Even as the state was electing Jim Hunt, it sent Jesse Helms, a longtime opponent of civil rights, to the U.S. Senate for five terms, and Lauch Faircloth, the state's less well known senator, described Helms as a liberal by comparison to himself.

2. In 1993 Hunt put a full-day kindergarten program in place across the state.

3. Since the inception of Smart Start, Wachovia has contributed more than $7 million for child care facilities, health awareness efforts, and outreach to Spanish-speaking families.

4. The Smart Start Web site includes links to budgetary material as well as evaluations of the program; *http://www.ncsmartstart.org/.*

5. The best study of co-optation in politics remains Philip Selznick, *TVA and the Grass Roots: A Study in the Sociology of Formal Organization* (Berkeley: University of California Press, 1949).

6. Office of the State Auditor, *Performance Audit of the North Carolina Partnership for Children, Inc. and the Smart Start Program* (Raleigh, NC: Office of the State Auditor, April 2003).

7. Abecedarian is discussed in Chapter 2.

8. Because of the cost of this requirement, it is being phased in over time; some for-profit preschools have received temporary waivers.

9. Rob Christensen, "Ex-Governor Still a Force of Nature Four Years Later," *Raleigh News and Observer*, November 27, 2005.

10. Billy Lee Brammer, *The Gay Place* (New York: Crest, 1964).

11. The basis for that canard was that Edwards had voted for a bill expanding home rule for the District of Columbia, where gay couples are able to adopt children.

12. Wohlgemuth had a long track record of antagonism toward children's health insurance. During the 1999 Texas legislative session she "ob-

jected to a resolution that Houston Democrat Garnett Coleman had placed on the local and consent calendar. The resolution simply noted that there are 1.5 million children without health insurance in Texas and urged that funding be made available to help them get insurance. Wohlgemuth . . . went ballistic . . . '[W]e cannot assume that children are poor just because they do not have health insurance. Their parents might be making $10,000 a year. Or they might be making $1 million a year. It is still our right in this country not to have health insurance.'" Louis DuBose, "Who Gets Eaten and Who Gets to Eat," *Texas Observer* (1999), *http://www.bushfiles.com/bushfiles/eaten.html.*

13. Edwards isn't the first candidate for national office to use the "anti-child" card effectively, pollster Geoff Garin points out. In the 1998 New York state senate race between Charles Schumer and Alfonse D'Amato, one of Schumer's most effective commercials pointed out that D'Amato had voted to cut the school lunch program. "Pick on someone your own size" was the text. And years earlier William Patman had won a seat in Congress by attacking his opponent for voting against child immunization.

14. "Wohlgemuth Loss a Rejection of Mean Tactics," *Dallas Morning News,* November 4, 2004.

15. Cindy Culp, "Averitt Files Bill to Restore CHIP Cuts," *Waco Tribune-Herald,* November 9, 2004.

16. "Vote Kids: Making Children a Political Priority" (Washington, DC: Vote Kids, 2004); "Texas: A Case Study" (Washington, DC: Vote Kids, 2004). See *www.votekids.org.*

17. After Texas's Seventeenth Congressional District, the 2005 Virginia governor's race was the next step for Petit. But political contributions have been hard to come by ("If I had a dime for everyone who told me I should go to George Soros, I wouldn't need a millionaire," he sighs) and so in that race Petit could only gather data and provide information, not promote a candidate. However, he was encouraged by what he learned from polling there. Virginia voters said that kids' issues should be on the top of the state lawmakers' agenda; that they were more important than the economy and jobs, more important in 2005 than in previous years. Every Child Matters Education Fund, *Winning New Public Investments for Children* (Washington, DC: Every Child Matters Education Fund, 2005); Michael Petit, *Direct Involvement in Elections: A Winning Strategy to Build Support for New Investments in Children* (Washington, DC: Every Child Matters Education Fund, n.d.), *www.everychildmatters.org.*

18. Rick Santorum, *It Takes a Family: Conservatism and the Common Good* (Wilmington, DE: Intercollegiate Studies Institute, 2005). On the

book's cover is a Renaissance painting that depicts the infant Jesus in Mary's arms.

19. See *http://www.votekids.org/site/PageServer.pagename.vk_2006election .html.*

20. See *www.partnershipforsuccess.org.*

21. Jagadeesh Gokhale, "The Public Finance Value of Today's Children (and Future Generations)," Working Paper No. 1, Invest in Kids Working Group, May 2003, *www.ced.org/docs/report/report_ivk_gokhale10 _2003.pdf.*

22. An organization called Generations United brings together lobbying groups that represent seniors and children, in hopes of developing common strategies. Although the interests of the two generations differ (and children's advocates justifiably view themselves as shortchanged), in certain cases, like the Florida constitutional amendment guaranteeing high-quality preschool, seniors have supported children's issues. See *www.gu.org.*

23. *Official Proceedings of the White House Conference on Child Health and Protection* (Washington, DC: United States Daily Publishing Corporation, 1930).

24. See Chapter 7 for a discussion of the earlier expansion of the Texas prekindergarten program.

ACKNOWLEDGMENTS

IF YOU'VE made it this far, you might be curious to know how this book came into being. Serendipity played a large part in the process.

In the fall of 2003, while taking a hike on the beach at Point Reyes National Seashore, Doug Jutte, a pediatrician who had recently reentered academe, enthused about the long-term effects of preschool. "Don't those effects fade out?" I asked, recalling the conventional wisdom of years back; but Doug was talking about the Perry Preschool study, about which I knew nothing. That story was a revelation to me—a long-term investigation of the life-changing impact of an exemplary prekindergarten. Because I wanted to learn more about Perry, I made my way to Ypsilanti, Michigan, where the experiment had taken place and home to the High/Scope Educational Research Foundation, which has carried on the research. There, Larry Schweinhart, president of the foundation, spent many hours answering my questions, and also gave me entrée to a number of the participants in the study. Van Loggins, the indispensable link between the researchers and the participants since the 1970s, tutored me on Ypsilanti and accompanied me to the interviews. That trip generated an article in the *New York Times Magazine* about the implications of the Perry project. Alex Star, who edited the *Times* piece as well as a subsequent article on the nature-versus-nurture debate, sharpened my analysis and my prose.

More serendipity: even as I was writing the Perry Preschool article, *The American Prospect* asked me to craft a piece on state preschool initiatives. What I learned about the programs in Georgia and Oklahoma made me want to know more about the issue, and that curiosity propelled me to write this book.

Like Blanche DuBois in *A Streetcar Named Desire*, I've always depended on the kindness of strangers—friends as well—and for this project the list of thank-yous is a long one.

A Berkeley "bridging" grant for faculty who are taking up a new line of research, as well as a grant from the Center for Child and Youth Policy at Berkeley, got me started. When I approached Libby Doggett, the executive director of Pre-K Now, about my interest in writing a book, she immediately embraced the idea. Libby has a Rolodex that rivals the Manhattan phone book and a remarkable capacity for grace under pressure. In the past few years she has answered countless factual queries and introduced me to some of the most talented people in the field. Support from the Pew Charitable Trusts enabled me to recruit students to work with me, to take the time to read across an array of disciplines—boning up on everything from politics to program evaluation, economics to brain science—as well as to travel across the country, visiting preschools and conducting scores of interviews. The Pew grant, as well as a grant from the David and Lucile Packard Foundation, made it possible for me to turn my voluminous field notes into a book. Sara Watson and Sue Urahn at Pew, and Lois Salisbury at Packard, have been the very models of the modern foundation officer, helpful to a fault. Their detailed comments saved me from making factual errors; and they appreciated that, while their foundations were underwriting the book, they could have no hand in determining its contents.

I spent many hours crouching in nurseries and preschool classrooms during my travels. Preschools and child care centers are hectic places where minutes are precious, and I appreciate the time that the teachers, administrators, parents, and children spent with me. In particular, Laurence Hadjas and Barbara Tchaou in Chicago, and Nell Barnes in Raleigh, have forgotten more about early education than I'll ever know, and I'm grateful that they shared some of their knowledge with me.

In Chicago I visited Ray School Pre-Kindergarten, the Head Start classrooms at McCutcheon Elementary School and Jordan Elementary School, the University of Chicago Laboratory Schools, Bridgeport Catholic Academy, the Von Humboldt and Hansberry Child-Parent Centers, the Chicago Commons Association New City Day Care Center, the Teddy Bear Day Care Centers, and the Chinese-American Service League Child Development Center.

In Los Angeles, I visited the YWCM Union Pacific Children's Center, the Edison State Preschool in Redondo Beach, and Domino's Nursery Center in Lynwood.

In the greater Miami area, I visited the South Miami Lutheran Early Childhood Center, the REM Learning Center, the Early Childhood Center at the YWCA of Greater Miami, Little Disciples Child Care Center, Our Little Ones Child Care Center, the Temple Beth Shira Early Childhood Center, and La Petite Academy.

In Tulsa, I visited the McClure Early Learning Center, the Disney Early Learning Center, the Bunch Early Childhood Development Center, and the YWCA Early Learning Center.

While in the Raleigh, North Carolina, area, I visited Learning Together, the Infant/Toddler Center of the First Baptist Church, and Building Blocks Child Care Development Center in Clayton.

For more than thirty years I've had the privilege of teaching at

the University of California at Berkeley. That's also serendipi-
tous—when I graduated from law school, I had no intention
of becoming a professor—and the Goldman School of Public
Policy is the best place in the world at which I could have wound
up. The students with whom I've worked are amazingly smart;
they combine a willingness to root around in data with a passion
for ideas. Several chapters are collaborations in the fullest sense:
my special thanks to coauthors Rachel Best (PhD candidate, Department of Sociology), Deborah Kong (MPP 2007, Goldman
School of Public Policy), and Jeff Wolf (PhD candidate, Department of History). Other Berkeley students worked on chunks
of the project. Goldman School students Cynthia Czerwin (MPP
2006) and George Willcoxon (MPP 2006) tracked down scholarly and media accounts of preschool policy and politics in
Florida and Georgia, enabling me to meet the hurry-up demands
of magazine editors. Trisha McMahon (MPP 2006) explored the
intricacies of the Children's Health Insurance Program. Heather
Barondess (MPP 2007) looked closely at North Carolina's Smart
Start program and Britain's Sure Start program. Tony Xu (BA
2006) delved into the Web sites of conservative think tanks.
Andrew Ramroth (BA 2006) combed the archives for historical
background material, and demonstrated his intellectual versatility
reviewing molecular genetics research. Liz Saroki (BA 2007) became a jack-of-all-fields, locating stray references in out-of-the-
way places. Albert Fang (BA 2007) worked on the project for two
and a half years, drafting insightful memos on topics that ran the
gamut from California preschool politics to political theory. As I
was preparing the final draft of the manuscript, my assistant,
Rebecca Boles, managed superbly to extract order from chaos.
Google merits a mention: the search engine par excellence was
indispensable, instantly connecting me to everything from ob-

scure medical journals to fifty year-old facsimiles of the *New York Times Magazine*. While we have come to take Google for granted, this virtual research assistant saved me hundreds of hours.

Thirty years ago, Donna Leff, a professor at the Medill School of Journalism at Northwestern University, was a student of mine at Berkeley. We have been close friends ever since, and we became even better friends while collaborating on the Chicago chapter. My good friend Doug Jutte, who introduced me to the world of preschool research, helped me understand the intricacies of brain science.

My interview notes run some seven hundred single-spaced typed pages. I'm thankful for the willingness of world-renowned scholars to spend hours at a clip giving me an education. Their names are scattered across the pages of the book. In addition to those who read chunks of the manuscript, I want particularly to thank Barbara Bowman, Tom Boyce, Greg Duncan, Jim Heckman, Tom Lewis, Mary Ann Mason, Jane Mauldon, Neil Gilbert, Steven Sugarman, Jill Duerr Berrick, Sue Bredekamp, Art Rolnick, Jeanne Brooks-Gunn, Gary Henry, Bill Dickens, Alison Gopnik, Bill Gormley, Susan Landry, Art Reynolds, Deborah Stipek, Sheila Kamerman, Vivian Paley, Tom O'Connor, David Reiss, Michael Rutter, Jack Shonkoff, and Belle Sawhill.

Over the years I've turned to reporters for material that never makes into the newspaper. Especially helpful were Sonja Isger, Marilyn Brown, and Pia Lopez.

Others who know this territory inside out became sounding boards. Jason Sabo in Texas; Karen Ponder and Sue Russell in North Carolina; Steven Dow in Oklahoma; Karen Hill-Scott, Maryann O'Sullivan, Catherine Atkin, Susanna Cooper, Graciela Italiano-Thomas, Dave Gordon, and Ben Austin in California; Helen Blank, Joan Lombardi, Mike Petit, and Rob Dugger in

Washington, D.C.; Maria Whelan, Sessy Nyman, and Jerry Stermer in Illinois: these are among the most effective policy analysts and advocates I've encountered in all my research. If they could be cloned, early education would be much higher on the national priorities list. Without the passion of Rob Reiner in California and David Lawrence in Florida, prekindergarten would not be such a major item on those states' agendas. Without the commitment of George Kaiser in Oklahoma, Harriet Meyer in Chicago, and Susan Buffett in Nebraska, the exemplary Educare model would not have such national significance. When it comes to fighting for what children need, Jim Hunt, the governor of North Carolina for sixteen years, truly is, as the *Raleigh Observer* described him, a "force of nature."

Larry Aber, Steve Barnett, Clive Belfield, Marilyn Brown, Alison Clarke-Stewart, Dick Clifford, Libby Doggett, Naomi Eisenstadt, Ron Haskins, Hank Levin, John Love, Sam Meisels, Chuck Nelson, Cheryl Polk, Jason Sabo, Ross Thompson, and Eric Turkheimer scrutinized chapters of the book. Each of them saved me from making rookie mistakes and pushed me to do the hard work of rethinking. Although he was scrambling to complete his own book, my Berkeley colleague and intellectual partner in crime Robert Reich read the entire manuscript. Better than anyone I know, Bob can frame the biggest policy dilemmas of the day, and his comments helped situate my writing in a broader policy perspective.

Rhea Wilson, who had an office down at the hall from me during my stint as an editorial writer at the *Sacramento Bee* in the 1980s, has been a great friend ever since. She's also the best editor with whom I've ever worked. When Rhea should have been writing her novel, she gave the manuscript a close reading. She has the uncanny ability to make explicit my implicit line of reasoning, and from my draft she extracted a framework that enabled me to shape my sometimes baggy prose.

I had the chance to talk through some of the material in the book at a lecture at the Center for Child and Family Policy at Duke; my thanks to Ken Dodge and Noah Pickus for making that possible. I have also discussed my ideas with a number of old friends and faculty colleagues in the Berkeley Forum on the Family.

From the time I started working on this book through his critique of the manuscript, Ed Zigler has been unstinting with his time and unflagging in his enthusiasm. That has mattered a great deal to me, for I'm a novice in territory that Ed knows as well as anyone. Over many decades, he has been a dedicated public servant and a passionate teacher whose thinking has influenced several generations of scholars and practitioners. To call him prolific is indulging in understatement: at last count he'd written thirty-two books and over six hundred articles. He is both a mentor and a mensch.

Carol Mann has been an exemplary agent, handling the delicate business of negotiating a contract with skill and grace. Elizabeth Knoll at Harvard University Press, who also edited my previous book, *Shakespeare, Einstein, and the Bottom Line: The Marketing of Higher Education,* has been a critical enthusiast and an enthusiastic critic—just what an author needs. Paul Adams knows the marketing world very well, and has used that knowledge to great advantage. Julie Hagen, the copy editor, caught infelicities and clarified confusing points.

Portions of the book are adapted from "You're Doing Fine, Oklahoma!" *American Prospect,* November 2, 2004; "Life *Waay* after Head Start," *New York Times Magazine,* November 22, 2004; "All My Children," Education Section, *New York Times,* July 31, 2005; "Before School," *Nation,* November 21, 2005; "Preschool *Cum Laude*" (with Donna Leff), *Chicago Tribune Magazine,* July 16, 2006; and "After the Bell Curve," *New York Times Magazine,* July 23, 2006.

INDEX